Constructivist Learning Environments
Case Studies in Instructional Design

Constructivist Learning Environments

Case Studies in Instructional Design

Brent G. Wilson
University of Colorado at Denver
EDITOR

FOREWORD
David N. Perkins
Harvard University

**Educational Technology Publications
Englewood Cliffs, New Jersey 07632**

Library of Congress Cataloging-in-Publication Data

Constructivist learning environments : case studies in instructional
　　design / Brent G. Wilson, editor ; foreword by David N. Perkins.
　　　p. cm.
　　Includes bibliographical references and indexes.
　　ISBN 0-87778-290-3
　　　1. Instructional systems--Design--Case studies. 2. Constructivism
(Education)--Case studies. 3. Classroom environment--Case studies.
I. Wilson, Brent G. (Brent Gale)
LB1028.38.C66 1996
371. 3'078 --dc20　　　　　　　　　　　　　　　　　95-30145
　　　　　　　　　　　　　　　　　　　　　　　　　CIP

Copyright © 1996 by Educational Technology Publications, Inc., Englewood Cliffs, New Jersey 07632. All rights reserved. No part of this book may be reproduced or transmitted, in any form or by any means, electronic or mechanical, including photocopying, recording, or by any information storage and retrieval system, without permission in writing from the Publisher.

Printed in the United States of America.

Library of Congress Catalog Card Number:
95-30145.

International Standard Book Number:
0-87778-290-3.

First Printing: January, 1996

Foreword

Minds in the 'Hood

David N. Perkins

Suppose you were asked to name something that you had learned really well. What would you mention? Perhaps you would say high school biology or 19th century American history or whatever your favorite subject was. But let me propose a very different example: your own childhood neighborhood. Think about it: You learned where things were—the park with swings two blocks away, the shop on the corner, the gas station opposite. You learned how to get to them all and from each one to another. You learned what every one offered: swinging, sodas, talk about cars. You learned who hung out where and what they did and how to hang out with some of them yourself. To put a phrase to the whole enterprise, you knew your way around your neighborhood.

From the standpoint of the present volume, what's interesting here is that your neighborhood was what most school subject matters are not: an environment. It had the dimensions of an environment—length and breadth, places and parts, nonliving and living, simplicity and complexity, constancy and change. You could move through it and learn your way around it bit by bit. Getting started wasn't hard, but you were never done. There was always more.

In his introduction to this volume, Brent Wilson aptly points out that the idea of a learning environment evokes the notions of place and space, room to move and explore, and generous access. Just like your neighborhood. Wilson also suggests that among the many ways we think of knowledge, the notion of a learning environment resonates best with a vision of knowledge as meaning constructed by interaction with one's environment.

Perhaps we can get even more precise about the kind of knowledge in question. What conception of knowledge goes best with an environmental conception of learning? Here's one way to think about it. There is a tradition in philosophy that looks to our everyday language for insight into the character of knowledge.

For example, we say "I know that such-and-such" and "I know how to do such-and-such." Oxford philosopher Gilbert Ryle (1949) underscored the distinction between knowing that and knowing how. A view of knowledge fixated only on knowing that—knowing facts or more broadly propositions—simply lacks compass. John Anderson (1983) and other cognitive scientists make a somewhat, although not entirely, similar distinction in contrasting propositional and procedural knowledge.

Harvard philosopher Israel Scheffler (1965), building on Ryle's work, emphasizes how many areas of know-how forbid perfect mastery. No matter how good a chess player or writer you are, you can always aspire to advance. Vernon Howard (1982), writing about how singers and other artists are taught, draws further senses of knowing from everyday discourse. For example, he notes how teachers of singers often strive to get their students to hit a high note or muster some other effect once—because then they will *know what it is to* do that. When we know what it is to do something, even if we have only done it once, that helps us strive to do it again.

So can we find a phrase about knowing that especially evokes what we learn from an environment? In fact, one was already mentioned: *knowing your way around.* A common expression usually unreflectively used, knowing your way around subtly underscores what knowledge is generally like in rich multidimensional situations. And not just physical neighborhoods. We can sensibly speak of knowing your way around the stock market, playing baseball, and any discipline, for instance, physics or English literature. To really know any of these domains requires a kind of flexible orientation to what things and places they contain, what resources they afford, and how to get jobs done (see Perkins, 1995, Chapter 10).

The notion of knowing your way around amplifies the dimensions of our conceptions of knowing. A sparse notion of knowledge that includes only knowing that and knowing how is not enough for most kinds of learning we aspire to. To be sure, knowing your way around anything from your neighborhood to quantum physics and beyond certainly calls for knowing that and knowing how. But it depends on much more as well—having a sense of orientation, recognizing problems and opportunities, perceiving how things work together, possessing a feel for the texture and structure of the domain. It encompasses not just explicit but tacit knowledge, not just focal awareness but peripheral awareness, not just a sense of what's there but what's interesting and valuable, as urged by Michael Polanyi (1958). Better than knowing that, knowing how, or like names for knowledge, knowing your way around resonates with the notion of a learning environment.

Regrettably, a spacious conception of knowledge like knowing your way around seems too large to fit inside most textbooks and classrooms. Instead, we usually find implicit a circumscribed conception of knowledge that foregrounds knowing that and the more pedestrian side of knowing how. Students learn the facts about an area and certain basic procedures, and that's about it. They usually have little real chance to learn their way around a discipline and do not even come close to knowing their way around. If they learn their way around anything, it is the academic games many schools play. As Brent Wilson emphasizes, referring to my own analysis of learning environments in his

Foreword

introduction to this volume, most school settings tend to offer a minimalist rather than a rich environment for learning.

Of course, your childhood neighborhood also falls short of a learning environment in the sense of the present volume. Although a rich environment where much learning occurs, a neighborhood is not learner-friendly. It is not especially tuned to support and sustain learning. A real neighborhood can be downright dangerous, as in director John Singleton's film *Boyz N The Hood*. Even if the neighborhood is safe, only because we live there so long and have so much practical motivation to learn our way around do we make out all right. In contrast, the pedagogical notion of a learning environment looks to settings that calculatedly support and stimulate the learner, making ideas accessible, avenues apparent, mysteries inviting, problems approachable. The many contributors to this volume are to be applauded for their diverse but committed approaches to this venture, because in well-crafted learning environments if anywhere we would expect to find the multidimensional learning implied by the phrase knowing your way around.

With all that, it's worth remembering that the circumstances of learning can be quirky indeed. What turns out to be a good learning environment for whom may surprise us now and then. For instance, ask me to name something I learned very well, and, if I did not say my neighborhood, I might say Euclidean geometry in high school.

Euclidean geometry does not appear on most people's lists of school's greatest hits. But it was on mine. I was a pretty good student in general, but, like few other subject matters I have studied, I really knew my way around those definitions, axioms, and theorems, and what to do with them.

In those days I thought nothing of it, but today I have to ask what it was about this ordinary school subject and its teaching that helped me not just to play the school game but to learn my way around geometry. And answers come to mind. For one, our class had an energetic and lucid teacher by the name of Theodore Emery, who carried everyone along with a nice balance of humor and discipline. For another, Mr. Emery offered some elbow room, a critical feature of a learning environment. Because I and another student were especially interested, he encouraged us to work ahead in the textbook. For a third, he issued a challenge. There was one particularly complex problem late in the book that no student over the years had ever solved. Anyone who did, he swore, would get an automatic A. This was a sly promise, since anyone who understood enough geometry to solve it would likely deserve an A in any case—a point that Mr. Emery admitted with a grin. Finally, the other student was another candidate for the gold ring of this never-solved problem. Would she make it and I not? Unthinkable.

Our format for homework was the classic two-column proof, a staid tradition that for me worked wonders. Writing all those proofs, I found it a nuisance to keep looking up the wording of theorems, axioms, and definitions in the text, so I memorized them all. This rote exercise produced an unexpected spinoff: a heady fluency in thinking with the concepts.

I did solve the killer problem (so did the other student). But more important, I felt that I really knew my way around Euclidean geometry. To put it another way, I had constructed what Noel Entwistle and Ference Marton (in press) call a "knowledge object," a mental representation (not necessarily visual) of a subject area that allows both panoramic overviews and flexible access to the details of any part. One of the most important long-term consequences of this was that I *knew what it was* to know my way around a subject matter. The experience became a yardstick for me, something to measure degrees of understanding with.

I was lucky in my teacher. For me, and many others I think, he created a learning environment within a traditional context. So I not only learned geometry but learned something about learning. Now imagine that we could bring to almost everyone the kinds of well-wrought constructivist-oriented technologically-supported learning environments discussed in this volume. They might give many students a chance not just to know their way around something academic, but to *know what it is* to know their way around something academic. When you know what this is, you are in a better position to function as a learner. You are more oriented to the enterprise of learning. Knowing what it is to know your way around is a compass for minds in any 'hood.

References

Anderson, J. R. (1983). *The architecture of cognition.* Cambridge, MA: Harvard University Press.

Entwistle, N. J., & Marton, F. (in press). Knowledge objects: Understandings constituted through intensive academic study. *British Journal of Educational Psychology.*

Howard, V. A. (1982). *Artistry: The work of artists.* Indianapolis: Hackett Publishing Company.

Perkins, D. N. (1995). *Outsmarting IQ: The emerging science of learnable intelligence.* New York: The Free Press.

Polanyi, M. (1958). *Personal knowledge: Toward a post-critical philosophy.* Chicago: The University of Chicago Press.

Ryle, G. (1949). *The concept of mind.* London: Hutchinson House.

Scheffler, I. (1965). *Conditions of knowledge: An introduction to epistemology and education.* Glenview, IL: Scott, Foresman and Company.

David N. Perkins is Co-director of Project Zero, Associate of the Educational Technology Center, and Senior Research Associate, all at the Harvard Graduate School of Education.

Table of Contents

Foreword: Minds in the 'Hood
David N. Perkins v

1. Introduction: What Is a Constructivist Learning Environment?
   Brent G. Wilson 3

Part One: Computer-Based Microworlds

2. Seven Goals for the Design of Constructivist Learning Environments
   Peter C. Honebein 11

3. An Interpretation Construction Approach to Constructivist Design
   John B. Black and Robert O. McClintock 25

4. Tutoring for Transfer of Technical Competence
   Sherrie P. Gott, Alan Lesgold, and Ronald S. Kane 33

5. Case-based Teaching and Constructivism: Carpenters and Tools
   Christopher K. Riesbeck 49

Part Two: Classroom-Based Learning Environments

6. Rich Environments for Active Learning
   in the Higher Education Classroom
   Joanna C. Dunlap and R. Scott Grabinger 65

7. Developing Statistical Reasoning Through Simulation Gaming
   in Middle School: The Case of 'The Vitamin Wars'
   Helena P. Osana, Sharon Derry, and Joel R. Levin 83

8. From Constructivism to Constructionism: Learning *with*
   Hypermedia/Multimedia Rather Than *from* It
   David H. Jonassen, Jamie M. Myers, and Ann Margaret McKillop 93

9. Epistemic Fluency and Constructivist Learning Environments
   Donald Morrison and Allan Collins 107

10. Implementing Jasper Immersion: A Case of Conceptual Change
    Michael F. Young, Bonnie K. Nastasi, and Lynette Braunhardt 121

11. Problem Based Learning: An Instructional Model and
    Its Constructivist Framework
    John R. Savery and Thomas M. Duffy 135

Part Three: Open, Virtual Learning Environments

12. Constructivism in the Collaboratory
    Daniel C. Edelson, Roy D. Pea, and Louis Gomez 151

13. The Evolution of Constructivist Learning Environments:
    Immersion in Distributed, Virtual Worlds
    Chris Dede 165

Part Four: Reflections on the Effectiveness of Constructivist Learning Environments

14. Mapping More Authentic Multimedia Learning Environments
    Brockenbrough S. Allen, Robin T. Chiero, and Robert P. Hoffman 179

15. Alternative Assessment for Constructivist Learning Environments
    Thomas C. Reeves and James R. Okey 191

16. Instructional Design and Development of Learning Communities:
    An Invitation to a Dialogue
    *Xiaodong Lin, John D. Bransford, Cindy E. Hmelo, Ronald J. Kantor,
    Daniel T. Hickey, Teresa Secules, Anthony J. Petrosino, Susan R. Goldman,
    and The Cognition and Technology Group at Vanderbilt* 203

A Constructivist Sampler
*May Lowry, Victoria L. Wood, R. Scott Grabinger, Robert W. Davis,
Maggie Trigg, Richard Morse, and Karen M. Myers* 221

Author Index 233

Subject Index 239

Constructivist Learning Environments

Case Studies in Instructional Design

1

Introduction

What Is a Constructivist Learning Environment?

Brent G. Wilson

My purpose in this Introduction is to clarify what we mean by constructivist learning environments and to explain why the idea is worthy of study.

Consider the different assumptions underlying common metaphors for instruction:
— *Time and place* definitions suggest that instruction is what goes on in classrooms during 50-minute intervals.
— The *product delivery* metaphor suggests an information-processing and transmission model of instruction.
— *Systems and process* definitions of instruction tend to emphasize the steps or stages, inputs and outputs, interlocking mechanisms, and control of flow.

The constructivism movement in instructional design has shown the correspondence between our underlying views of knowledge and how we think about instruction. Table 1.1 briefly summarizes how different philosophical conceptions can influence our views about instruction.

The table suggests that viewing instruction as a learning environment is related to a meaning-construction view of knowledge. A learning environment is a place where people can draw upon resources to make sense out of things and construct meaningful solutions to problems. Adding "constructivist" to the front end of the term is a way of emphasizing the importance of meaningful, authentic activities that help the learner to construct understandings and develop skills relevant to solving problems.

IF YOU THINK OF **KNOWLEDGE** AS...	THEN YOU MAY TEND TO THINK OF **INSTRUCTION** AS...
• a quantity or packet of content waiting to be transmitted	• a **product** to be delivered by a vehicle.
• a cognitive state as reflected in a person's schemas and procedural skills	• a set of **instructional strategies** aimed at changing an individual's schemas.
• a person's meanings constructed by interaction with one's environment	• a learner drawing on tools and resources within a rich **environment**.
• enculturation or adoption of a group's ways of seeing and acting	• participation in a **community**'s everyday activities.

Table 1.1. How our views of knowledge influence our views of instruction.

The Idea of a Learning Environment

Thinking of instruction as an environment gives emphasis to the "place" or "space" where learning occurs. At a minimum, a learning environment contains:
— the learner;
— a "setting" or "space" wherein the learner acts, using tools and devices, collecting and interpreting information, interacting perhaps with others, etc.

This metaphor holds considerable potential because instructional designers like to think that effective instruction requires a degree of student initiative and choice. An environment wherein students are given "room" to explore, and determine goals and learning activities seems an attractive concept. Students who are given generous access to *information resources*—books, print and video materials, etc.—and *tools*—word-processing programs, e-mail, search tools, etc.—are likely to learn something if they are also given proper support and guidance. Under this conception, learning is fostered and supported, but not controlled or dictated in any strict fashion. For this reason, we tend to hear less about "instructional" environments and more about "learning" environments—instruction connoting more control and directiveness, being replaced by the more flexible idea of learning. A learning environment, then, is a place where learning is fostered and supported.

Difficulties remain, however, with the idea of a learning environment. For one thing, learning environments seem intrinsically fuzzy and ill-defined. That is, an environment that is good for learning cannot be fully prepackaged and defined. If students are involved in choosing learning activities and controlling pace and direction, a level of uncertainty and uncontrolledness comes into play. This places the teacher or instructional designer in a condition of continuing tentativeness and guardedness. Despite much care and attention, the system will often appear chaotic to outside observers and even participants. Instructional design theorists would maintain, however, that the complex nature of learning–environments interactions is no excuse for careful planning and design to the extent possible. Teachers must remain vigilant to ensure that an environment includes proper support and guidance, and rich resources and tools. The job of instructional-design theory is to articulate a set of principles or conceptual models to aid teachers and designers in creating supportive, nurturing learning environments where students are successful in attaining learning goals.

Another problem lies in the individualist connotation of "environment." The metaphor of person-in-environment, at least in psychology, tends to isolate individuals and treat other people as objects within the environment to be used or manipulated. The picture comes to mind of a nerdy "surfer" of the Internet, exploring all kinds of resources, yet remaining reluctant to relate to a true peer group of learners—electronic or otherwise.

The idea of "learning communities" may be more appropriate in this regard. Communities of learners work together on projects and learning agendas, supporting and learning from one another, as well as from their environment. Thus, in an effective learning environment, an individual's tool-using and information-using activities need to be complemented by the powerful resources presented by other people and by the surrounding culture. In our use of the term, constructivist learning environments are places where groups of learners learn to use tools of their culture—including language and the rules for engaging in dialogue and knowledge generation (*cf.* Morrison & Collins, this volume).

In summary, a number of metaphors may be appropriate for thinking about instruction, depending on the situation. Process, product, and systems metaphors of instruction continue to dominate the field. At the same time, the idea of learning environments is appealing because it reflects values of the constructivist movement in instructional design. One definition of a constructivist learning environment then would be:

> **a place where learners may work together and support each other
> as they use a variety of tools and information resources
> in their guided pursuit of learning goals and problem-solving activities.**

This definition can serve as a launching point for this book, but it has no universal acceptance among the authors contributing to the volume. Different definitions and views of constructivist learning environments are presented by the various authors, depending on their focus and the nature of their projects.

"Parts" and "Kinds" Analysis

A thing can be analyzed into its constituent "parts" and into its various subcategories or "kinds" (Reigeluth & Stein, 1983). In this section, we analyze key components of a typical learning environment, then present a simple typology suitable for our purposes.

Perkins (1991) suggests that all learning environments, including traditional classrooms, include the following key components or functions:

— *Information banks.* Information banks are sources or repositories of information. Examples would include textbooks, teachers, encyclopedias, videotapes, videodiscs, etc.

— *Symbol pads.* These are surfaces for the construction and manipulation of symbols and language. Examples include student notebooks, index cards, word processors, drawing programs, and database programs.

— *Phenomenaria.* Perkins defines phenomenaria as "areas" for presenting, observing, and manipulating phenomena (aquariums, *SimCity*, physics microworlds, etc.) Of course, *SimCity* is a simulation of real-world cities, and not the thing itself. The key idea is that aspects of the world are brought and made available to student inspection and exploration. To my understanding, phenomenaria are roughly parallel to instructional simulations. I like Perkins's term because it emphasizes the instructional nature of the simulation (contrasted to non-instructional simulations intended for scientific or technical purposes).

— *Construction kits.* These are similar to phenomenaria, except they are less tied to natural phenomena. Construction kits are packaged collections of content components for assembly and manipulation. They may have no clear counterpart in the "real" world. Examples include Legos, learning logs, math-manipulation software such as the *Geometric Supposer*, or authoring tools such as *HyperStudio*.

— *Task managers.* In any learning environment, a function of control and supervision exists. Task managers are those elements of the environment that set tasks, and provide guidance, feedback, and changes in direction. Task management is often assumed by the teacher, but a variety of tools and documentation supports this role. Task managers may include assignments within textbooks, grading programs, assessment devices, devices for conveying rules and expectations, and computer-based instruction programs. Within constructivist learning environments, the student becomes a co-task manager along with the teacher.

With these identified components, Perkins distinguishes between "minimalist" and "rich" learning environments:

— *Minimalist* learning environments emphasize information banks, symbol pads, and task managers. A traditional classroom would be a lean learning environment with relatively few tools for manipulating and observing content, making exploration and problem solving difficult.

— *Richer* environments contain more construction kits and phenomenaria, and place more control of the environment in the hands of the learners themselves. Students are typically engaged in multiple activities in pursuit of multiple learning goals, with the teacher serving the role of coach and facilitator. Rich learning environments could more easily be called "constructivist" learning environments, whereas normal classrooms may be thought of as "traditional" learning environments.

Perkins also notes differences in the amount of guidance or direct instruction found in learning environments. Varying degrees of guidance pose different instructional challenges for the learning environment. As the teacher relinquishes control over content, pacing, and specific activities, students need corresponding increases in decision and performance support. Poorly planned learning environments are vulnerable to failure due to lack of support, leaving students feeling stranded and faced with unreasonable performance expectations. This problem is complicated by the fact that learners differ dramatically in their need for support. Managing the support and advisement function within learning environments is one of the challenges addressed repeatedly by the chapters in this volume.

I have grouped the chapters in this volume into the three categories of learning environments presented below. In truth, most of the projects reported in the book fit more than one category. The simple typology is not definitive, but instead is designed to elucidate differences in emphasis among different learning environments.

- *Computer microworlds.* Students "enter" a self-contained computer-based environment to learn. These microworlds may be supported by a larger classroom environment, but may also stand alone. Examples in this section include the *Sherlock* project reported by Gott, Lesgold, and Kane, and the case-based teaching programs reported by Riesbeck. The chapters by Honebein and by Black and McClintock also address issues related to the design of computer microworlds. Their chapters are also helpful in presenting sets of principles to guide the design of constructivist learning environments.
- *Classroom-based learning environments.* In many settings, the classroom is thought of as the primary learning environment. Various technologies may function as tools to support classroom learning activities. Examples of classroom-based environments include Harel's research on teaching fractions via student-generated computer lessons (Harel & Papert, 1990) and Vanderbilt's anchored instruction modules taught in regular classrooms. Dunlap and Grabinger begin the section with a description of their model of REALs (Rich Environments for Active Learning). They take particular care to define their terms and articulate a set of principles for guiding instructional design. Additional contributors in this section include chapters by Osana, Derry, and Levin on middle-school 'Vitamin Wars'; Morrison and Collins on knowledge-generating cultural forms they call "epistemic games"; the Young, Nastasi, and Braunhardt field report on the use of the *Jasper* math modules in 5th grade classrooms; and Savery and Duffy on problem-based learning in medical schools and other settings. Jonassen, Myers, and McKillop's chapter on hypermedia projects as learning activities is included here because of its emphasis on hypermedia as a learning tool rather than a self-contained microworld.

— *Open, virtual environments.* Some computer-based learning environments are relatively open systems, allowing interactions and encounters with other participants, resources, and representations. These "virtual" environments are contrasted with the more closed, self-contained microworld environments presented in the first section of the book. Students interact primarily with the computer in a microworld; in a virtual environment, they interact primarily with other networked participants, and with widely disseminated information tools. Open, virtual environments have tremendous potential for learning, but they carry their own set of design challenges and concerns. Edelson, Pea, and Gomez present one model of such environments—the CoVis project (Learning Through Collaborative Visualization)—and Dede presents a vision of the potential for such environments as technology and design models continue to evolve.

The *final section* of the book addresses general issues of design and assessment. Allen, Chiero, and Hoffman reflect on methods for conceptualizing and designing multimedia learning environments that depart from traditional ID models. Reeves and Okey discuss approaches to assessment appropriate for constructivist learning environments. Lin and colleagues from the Cognition and Technology Group at Vanderbilt conclude by arguing for an approach to the design of learning environments that draws on both the instructional-design and cognitive-psychology traditions.

In closing, I would like to thank the contributors to the volume for their insights and willingness to report their work to a larger audience. Collectively, the chapters presented herein constitute a considerable advancement of our understanding. In future works, I hope to see a continued conversation addressing specific methods for designing constructivist learning environments.

References

Harel, I., & Papert, S. (1990). Software design as a learning environment. *Interactive Learning Environments, 1*(1), 1–32.

Morrison, D., & Collins, A. (this volume). Epistemic fluency and constructivist learning environments.

Perkins, D. N. (1991, May). Technology meets constructivism: Do they make a marriage? *Educational Technology, 31*(5), 18–23.

Reigeluth, C. M., & Stein, R. (1983). Elaboration theory. In C. M. Reigeluth (Ed.), *Instructional-design theories and models: An overview of their current status.* Hillsdale, NJ: Lawrence Erlbaum Associates.

Brent G. Wilson is associate professor of information and learning technologies at the University of Colorado at Denver. His research interests include instructional design theory and assessing the impact of technology in learning organizations.

Part One

Computer-Based Microworlds

2

Seven Goals for the Design of Constructivist Learning Environments

Peter C. Honebein

Introduction

Designers of constructivist learning environments live by seven pedagogical goals (Cunningham, Duffy, & Knuth, 1993; Knuth & Cunningham, 1993):

1. **Provide experience with the knowledge construction process.** Students take primary responsibility for determining the topics or subtopics in a domain they pursue, the methods of how to learn, and the strategies or methods for solving problems. The role of the teacher is to facilitate this process.
2. **Provide experience in and appreciation for multiple perspectives.** Problems in the real world rarely have one correct approach or one correct solution. There are typically multiple ways to think about and solve problems. Students must engage in activities that enable them to evaluate alternative solutions to problems as a means of testing and enriching their understanding.
3. **Embed learning in realistic and relevant contexts.** Most learning occurs in the context of school whereby educators remove the noise of real life from the learning activity. For instance, word problems in math textbooks rarely relate to the types of problems found in real life. The result is the reduced ability of the students to transfer what they learn in school to everyday life. To overcome this problem, curriculum designers must attempt to maintain the authentic context of the

learning task. Educators must ground problems within the noise and complexity that surrounds them outside the classroom. Students must learn to impose order on the complexity and noise as well as solve the core problem.
4. **Encourage ownership and voice in the learning process.** This illustrates the student-centeredness of constructivist learning. Rather than the teacher determining what students will learn, students play a strong role in identifying their issues and directions, as well as their goals and objectives. In this framework, the teacher acts as a consultant who helps students frame their learning objectives.
5. **Embed learning in social experience.** Intellectual development is significantly influenced through social interactions. Thus, learning should reflect collaboration between both teachers and students, and students and students.
6. **Encourage the use of multiple modes of representation.** Oral and written communication are the two most common forms of transmitting knowledge in educational settings. However, learning with only these forms of communication limits how students see the world. Curricula should adopt additional media, such as video, computer, photographs, and sound, to provide richer experiences.
7. **Encourage self-awareness of the knowledge construction process.** A key outcome of constructivist learning is knowing how we know. It is the students' ability to explain why or how they solved a problem in a certain way; to analyze their construction of knowledge and processes. Cunningham *et al.* (1993) call this "reflexivity," an extension of metacognitive and reflective activities.

This article discusses how to put these goals into practice by examining two constructivist learning environments, the Lab Design Project (LDP) (Honebein, Chen, & Brescia, 1992; Honebein, Duffy, & Fishman, 1993), and the SOCRATES curriculum (*S*tudent-*O*riented *C*urriculum: *R*eflection *a*nd *T*echnology as *E*ducational *S*trategies) (Honebein, 1994). In Wilson's (1996) scheme for classifying constructivist learning environments, in Chapter 1, the LDP reflects a virtual environment, while the SOCRATES curriculum reflects a classroom environment. I first describe each of the learning environments, then follow with an analysis explaining the construction of these environments in light of the pedagogical goals noted above.

Lab Design Project

The Lab Design Project (LDP) is a hypermedia system that simulates a biotechnology building. The purpose of the LDP is to provide a learning environment in which learners can:
- practice their sociological research skills;
- better understand the social, architectural, and scientific forces driving the design process for new biotechnology research centers; and
- better understand how lab design shapes scientific practice.

The LDP contains almost all the data to which a researcher has access at the actual building. These include documents from the construction of the building, interviews with inhabitants of the building, and observations of various labs and spaces in the form of photographs. The task of the learner is to pose research questions, such as, "What is the social impact of having researchers' desks in the labs instead of outside the labs?" The learner then seeks answers to those questions by exploring the simulation and its accompanying database.

The learner starts his or her exploration of the building with a diagram showing the outside of the building (Figure 2.1). The learner clicks on the floor he or she wants to view, and a schematic of that floor appears on screen (Figure 2.2). The learner clicks on the lab he or she wants to view, and a schematic of the lab appears on screen (Figure 2.3). To view a particular area of the lab, the learner clicks on that area. Once in the lab (Figure 2.4), the learner clicks on buttons to view color photographs showing the equipment, experiments, and details of the lab. The text field at the bottom left of Figure 2.4 explains the equipment shown in the photograph.

Besides exploring the labs, the learner can review transcribed interviews with inhabitants of the building (Figure 2.5), or any one of 4000 pages of documents (Figure 2.6). These documents include memoranda between architects, builders, and administrators, building plans, letters of authorization, and sketched

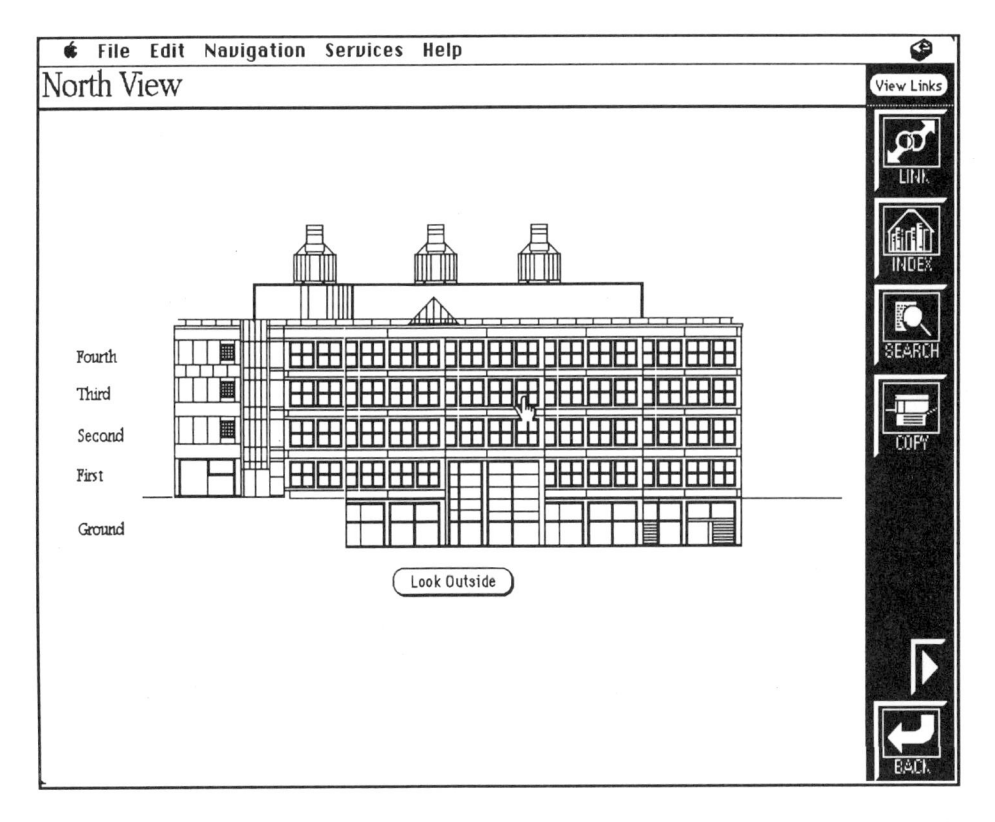

Figure 2.1. *Building View.* Here the learner can click on any floor to go to a floorplan graphic of that floor. In this example, the learner is clicking on the third floor.

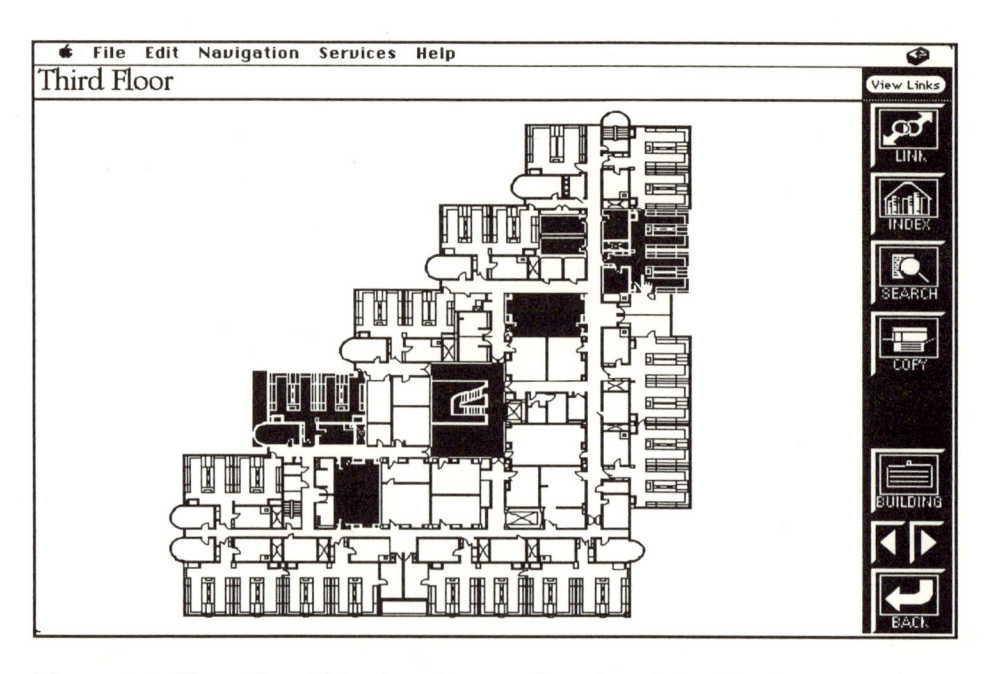

Figure 2.2. *Floor View.* This view shows a floorplan of the third floor. The rooms which are highlighted can be clicked on to zoom into a closer view of that room. In this example, the learner is clicking on Lab 321.

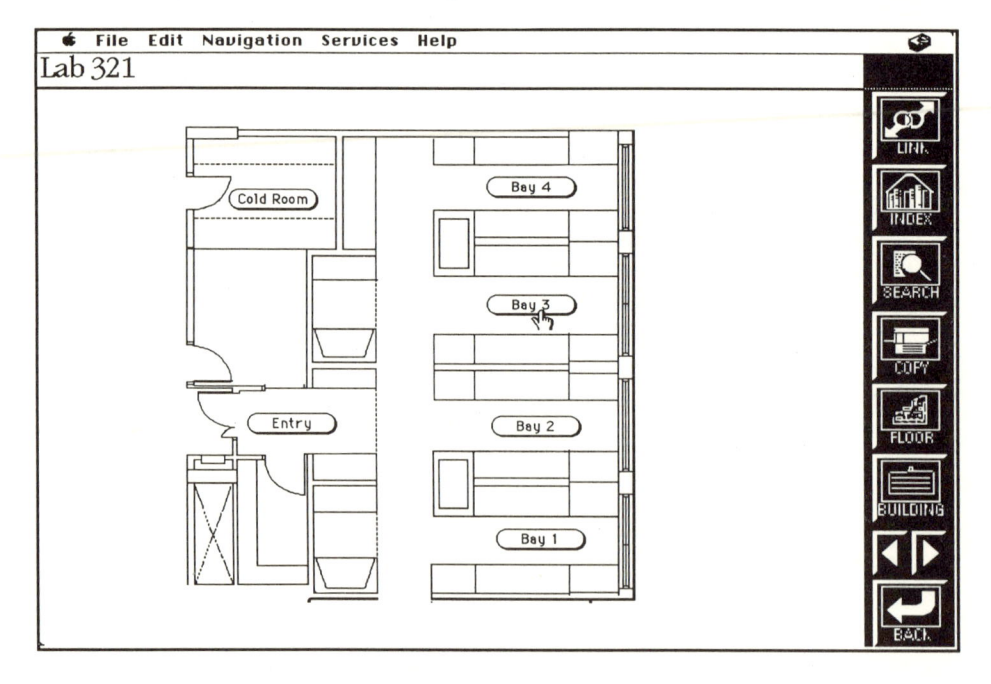

Figure 2.3. *Lab (or Room) View.* This view is a closeup of the floorplan for the laboratory. The buttons allow the learner to zoom into each one of the bays for greater detail. The learner is about to zoom into Bay 3.

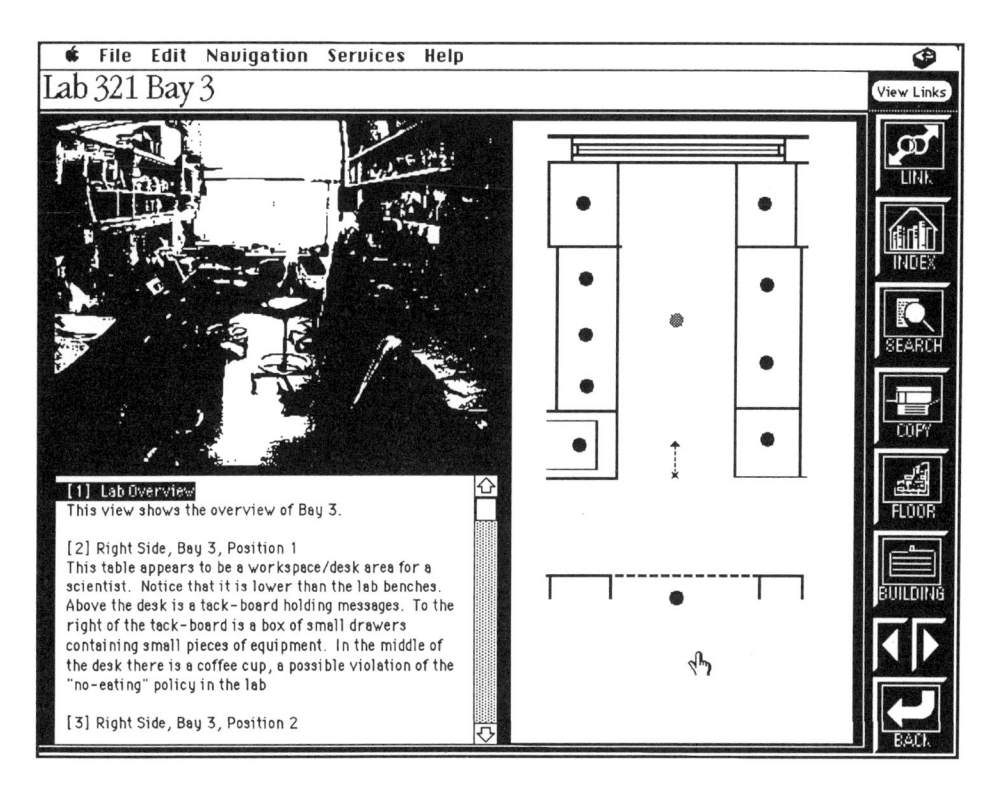

Seven Goals for the Design of Constructivist Learning Environments 15

Figure 2.4. *Photograph View.* In this view, the learner is presented with a color photograph of the bay, text describing the bay, and a schematic of the bay. By clicking on the black circles in the schematic, the learner can "walk around" the bay, viewing color photographs from of a variety of perspectives. Notice the X shows the location and the arrow points the direction of the camera when the photograph was taken.

schematics. The learner accesses these interviews and documents through an index, or through a search tool that can find documents based on text and keyword queries.

Another feature of the LDP is linking. Learners complete weekly assignments by linking photographs and documents (each called nodes) that illustrate the research questions, and writing an explanation why the link is important. For example, the learner finds a photograph in a lab showing a desk at the lab bench. The learner also finds an interview with a researcher explaining that desks in the lab are a bad idea because one cannot eat food in the lab; thus, the researcher cannot eat at his desk. The learner links the photograph and the interview, and writes an annotation explaining how the two pieces of data help answer her research question. All links are public: other learners can read and follow any links created by their peers. The LDP faculty reviews each learners' links weekly, and provides comments directly to each learner through an electronic mail system built into the LDP.

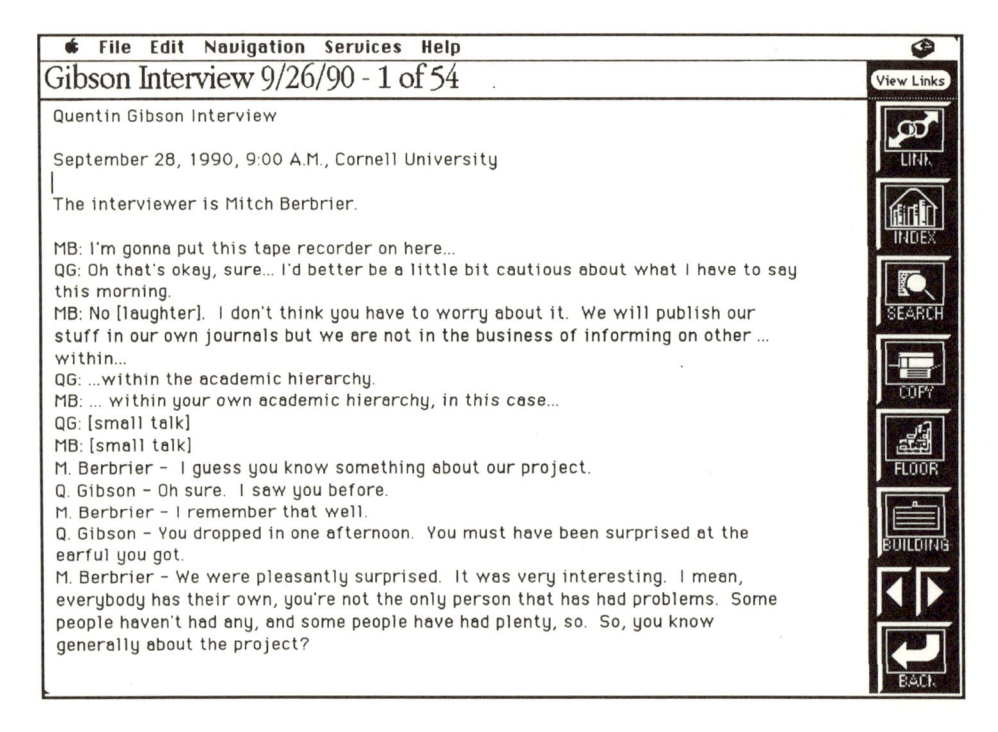

Figure 2.5. Example of an interview.

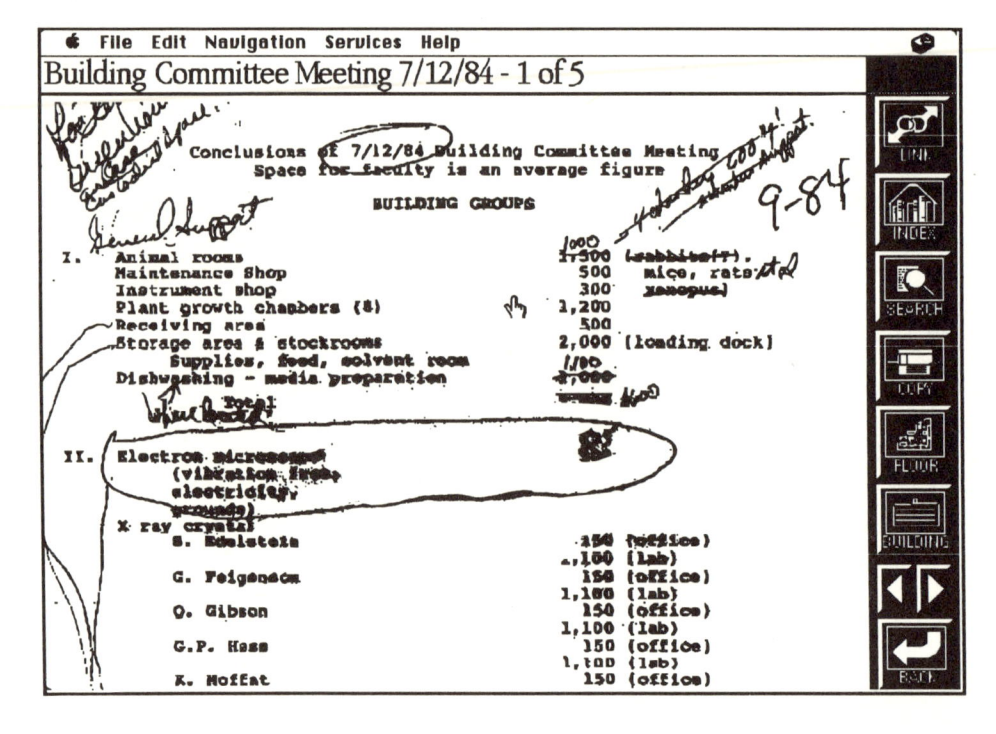

Figure 2.6. Example of a document card (containing hard-written notations).

SOCRATES Curriculum

The SOCRATES curriculum is a week-long workshop. Its purpose is to teach second-year medical students how to care for and manage patients with diabetes mellitus.

The curriculum requires approximately nine hours of class work, eight hours of work outside the class in independent or group study, and three hours of assessment. Classes are scheduled Monday, Wednesday, and Friday. Independent and group study are expected on Tuesday and Thursday. Learner assessment, consisting of a short essay examination, a clinical examination, and evaluation questionnaires, is on Saturday.

There are three primary learning activities in the workshop:
- **DiaSim**, a computer-based simulation of diabetes patients;
- **Patient Case Analysis and Plan**, an activity where students analyze a patient's chart and formulate a plan for an office visit; and
- **Stump the Specialist**, an activity where students create patient cases and observe how diabetes experts handle the cases.

DiaSim

The learners' task in the DiaSim activity is to manage the care of a person with diabetes. To do this, learners use a computer software program called *DiaSim* (Eli Lilly, 1988). DiaSim presents learners with a patient who has a problem with his or her blood glucose level. Learners make modifications to the patient's medication, diet, and exercise to optimize the patient's blood glucose profile. Learners see the results of their decisions by viewing a graph depicting the patient's blood glucose levels over a period of two days.

After learners complete their solutions, the preceptor leads a debriefing session. Each group presents and explains its solution. The preceptor and other learners may ask questions of the presenting group. The objective of this debriefing is to show students the different types of solutions to the problems and the rationale behind each of the solutions.

Patient Case Analysis and Plan

The learners' task in the Patient Case Analysis and Plan (PCAP) activity is to analyze a patient's chart and log book, then formulate a plan for an office visit with the patient. This activity is one that task analysts identified during clinic observations and that expert physicians described in interviews.

The preceptor assigns two patient cases in the workshop. One case is assigned on Monday and discussed in class Wednesday. The other is assigned Wednesday and discussed in class Friday. For each case, learners get a worksheet, an actual patient's chart and, if available, the patient's records of home glucose monitoring. Then, working independently and in groups, learners analyze the chart and formulate their plan. The preceptor encourages learners to use any materials or resources to help them with their analysis and plan.

In the next class session, each group presents its analysis and plan. The preceptor and the other groups have the opportunity to question the group and have the group further explain its conclusions. After each group presents its analysis and plan, the preceptor shows a video of an actual physician-patient examination featuring the patient in the chart.

While watching the video, the preceptor or learners may stop the video to discuss items of interest. The preceptor may also supplement the discussion by showing video interviews with the patient, the examining physician, or another expert physician. In these interviews, the interviewees provide analysis and critique of the examination.

Stump the Specialist

The learners' task in the Stump the Specialist (STS) activity is to use DiaSim to create a diabetes patient they believe is difficult to care for. During the last hour of the last class, an expert physician comes to class and attempts to solve the learners' cases using DiaSim.

To create a problem case, learners work in their groups to write a one-page narrative describing the patient's history. Groups then use the custom patient feature of DiaSim to define the patient's physical characteristics, type of diabetes, insulin therapy, diet, and exercise. Along with creating the patient's problems, the groups must also solve the patient's case by creating a regimen that optimizes the patient's blood glucose level.

In class, the expert selects a group's case. The expert then "thinks out loud" (Schoenfeld, 1985) during the analysis of the case and the attempted solutions. The expert enters solutions (changes to the patient's insulin, diet, or exercise) into DiaSim (which is projected so all students can see), then checks the results by showing the simulation graph. The expert repeats this process until he or she solves the case or is "stumped." A short debriefing session follows the expert's solution. During this debriefing, the expert can explain strategies in more detail, learners can ask specific questions, and the group whose case the expert used can present its solution.

Analysis of LDP and SOCRATES

The seven pedagogical goals stated at the beginning of this chapter offer a framework for the design of constructivist learning environments. Designers who use these goals as the theories behind their practice are well on their way to creating learning environments that are "constructivist." However, it is important to note that these goals provide just the framework; the designer's interpretation of the goals and subsequent translation into learning activities is the real art in the design of constructivist learning environments. In this next section, I want to share with you the thinking and rationalization that took place to put constructivist *theory into practice* for these two exemplars.

Experience with the Knowledge Construction Process

Self-directed learning is at the heart of the knowledge construction process. To achieve this goal, designers need to conceive learning activities that provide learners a level of autonomy in the learning process. The instructor should guide learners to pursue topics that interest or are relevant to *the learner* and encourage learners to experiment with various methods of solving problems.

In the LDP, the research questions serve this function. Each learner is responsible for formulating research questions. Since the questions are relevant to a learner's own interests, there is a high level of self-direction. In addition, the research questions influenced how the learner interacts with the LDP environment, from the selection of data to the construction of links.

The design strategy for the SOCRATES curriculum is similar. In the DiaSim and PCAP activities, it is each learner's responsibility to generate questions about the case, then seek answers to those questions. The questions reflect each learner's interest in the case and drive his or her search for the appropriate knowledge they need. For example, the patient's psycho-social problems interest some learners, while the patient's insulin therapy interests other learners. Regardless of the question, each learner pursues knowledge in a context that reflects what he or she feels is important about the case.

Experience in and Appreciation for Multiple Perspectives

It is helpful for the designer to adopt the premises that there are many right ways to solve problems and that there are many right answers to questions. Given these premises, the need for curricula that celebrate alternative ways of thinking and knowing becomes clear: learners experience alternative models on which they can base their own practice.

The LDP supports multiple perspectives in several ways. Through public links, learners can examine other learners' problem-solving processes. By following another learner's links and reading the link annotations, the learner sees an alternative way to conduct research. Weekly class meetings provide learners with the opportunity to discuss their research activities with their colleagues.

The nature of the SOCRATES learning activities also contributes to the learners' exploration of multiple perspectives. In the DiaSim activity, members in individual groups examine each other's perspectives on diabetes care while coming up with solutions to the patient's problem. Additionally, each group shares its solution with the other groups during the debriefing. The result is several solutions to the problem, each with a different strategy. In the Patient Case activity, group work and class debriefings facilitate the exploration of alternative perspectives, as does the patient-physician videotape and accompanying video interviews with physician, patient, and commenting physician.

Realistic and Relevant Activity

The creation of realistic and relevant activities requires a detailed understanding of the culture for which the learner is being prepared. Thus, in the cases of both the LDP and SOCRATES, the designer conducted task and cultural analyses to understand the practice of sociological researchers and the practice of physicians who care for persons with diabetes, respectively. From these analyses, the designer came to understand the nature of the problems in the culture, how problems were solved by experts, the knowledge and skill needed to be an effective practitioner, the sources of knowledge and skill (i.e., books), and the criteria for assessing successful performance.

The authentic activity in the LDP is sociological research. The task of the learner is to investigate the building as a sociologist would. Sociologists begin their research by exploring. They enter an environment and observe, looking for commonalties, oddities, and differences among elements of that environment. Their goal during this exploration is to develop a research question, such as, "Why is this the same as this?" or "Why does this occur here, but not there?" Sociologists then look for data that help them answer the questions they pose. All of these activities are possible with the LDP.

Similarly, the authentic activity for the SOCRATES curriculum is "playing doctor." In the DiaSim activity, the task of the learner is to care for a simulated patient, making "prescriptions" to the patient's insulin, diet, and exercise to bring the patient's blood glucose level under control. In the PCAP activity, learners play doctor in a richer authentic environment: learners receive an actual patient chart and must plan a visit with the patient. With the patient chart, learners must deal with such common problems as incomplete documents, illegible handwriting, and an overabundance of complex data. In this context, learners must learn to accommodate the everyday complexities of the job with the core knowledge and skill they need to solve the patient's problem.

Many people misunderstand the true nature of authentic activities. People ask, "How are simulations 'authentic' when by their very nature they are not authentic at all? They're still a simulation." The aim of an authentic activity is not just to simulate or replicate the physical environment, calling it "authentic." Rather, the aim is to design an environment in which learners use their minds and bodies as they would if they were practitioners in a domain. It is the purpose of the learning environment, whether it be simulation, actual practice, or independent study, to stimulate learners so that their thinking is related to actual practice (e.g., see Keegan, 1995). In the LDP, the simulation of the building is merely a vehicle to engage learners in the higher-level cognitive skills of observation, analysis, and synthesis—the skills of an expert sociologist. In the SOCRATES curriculum, the use of actual patient charts stimulate learners to not only develop their analytical and scientific skills, but their skills to decipher poor handwriting—all necessary for them to be proficient physicians.

How does a designer choose what parts of the learning environment are real, simulated, or fake? By examining the forces that surround the problem. For the LDP, it was too expensive to fly students to the actual building. Additionally, 20 graduate students roaming around the building would no doubt disrupt the environment and annoy the building's inhabitants. For the SOCRATES curriculum, it just didn't make sense to have second year medical students go at it with real patients.

Ownership and Voice in the Learning Process

Ownership and voice are closely tied to the goal of experience with the knowledge construction process, in that learning is student-centered rather than teacher-centered. A key indicator that a learning environment is student-centered is the role of the instructor. Typical roles for instructors in constructivist learning environments are facilitator, mentor, coach, or consultant. Designers must carefully consider the role of the instructor in their learning environment designs.

The primary role of the LDP instructor is mentor. As a mentor, the task of the instructor is to review the learners' work and provide feedback. Feedback typically consists of a critique of the quality of the work, alternative ways of thinking about the learners' research questions, and suggestions of where the learners might find additional data to support their hypotheses. In the LDP, it is the instructor's review of the learners' links and annotations that forms the mentoring relationship.

Since the activities in the SOCRATES curriculum are group-based, the instructor's primary role is that of facilitator. In this role, the instructor is responsible for encouraging groups to discuss their solutions to problems and facilitating the interaction between group members and groups themselves. The instructor draws out competing perspectives from the groups, leads the groups in analyzing those perspectives, and helps the learners synthesize the main points of the discussion.

Learning in the Social Experience

Learning in the social experience—or collaboration—is related to the previously discussed goal of experiencing multiple perspectives. Through collaborative activities, the designer lays the foundations for the sharing of multiple perspectives, as well as the social interactions learners undertake in their roles of practitioners: teamwork, leadership, negotiation, and cooperation.

There is little or no face-to-face collaboration in the LDP. Rather, the public links and annotations that learners create mediate the collaboration. Learners exploring the LDP view the links and annotations of peers. In addition, learners can bring in yet another perspective by adding comments to existing links and annotations.

Collaboration in the SOCRATES curriculum is extensive. In every learning activity, learners work with other group members to accomplish tasks. During debriefings, collaboration includes all groups and the instructor. All collaboration is face-to-face.

The LDP and SOCRATES curricula facilitate the analysis of two extremes of collaboration: independent and face-to-face. Since collaboration is computer mediated in the LDP, learners are freed from the burden of arranging group meetings and relying on others to accomplish tasks. The collaboration takes the form of colleagues helping each other. Collaboration in SOCRATES, on the other hand, requires more effort on the part of the learners. They are not individuals solving a task; rather, they are a team whose combined effort is needed for successful accomplishment. Is one type of collaboration better than the other? I do not have data the shows it is or isn't. All I have is anecdotal evidence that shows students are satisfied with both collaborative experiences, and that both types of collaboration designs appear to work in the contexts for which they were designed.

Multiple Modes of Representation

Multiple modes of representation is yet another facet of the goal of experiencing multiple perspectives. Different media represent knowledge in different ways, illustrated by the truism, "A picture is worth a thousand words." By combining several types of media in a learning environment, the designer allows learners to see the world in different lights, so that their understanding of facts, concepts, procedures, and principles is rich and multi-faceted.

The LDP delivers an environment composed of many media types. A combination of photographs, graphics, text, animation, and realia (real things) form the content domain for the environment, and contributes to various representations of knowledge. For instance, the learner might find an architectural document showing a drawing of a lab. To compare the architectural document to the actual lab, the learner can navigate to that lab to see a photograph of the lab. Yet another perspective finds the learner reviewing a text interview with the scientist who works in the lab, in which the scientist describes the layout and equipment in the lab. Each medium provides the learner with a different picture of the same thing.

Computer simulation, videos, books, patient charts, and written communication are the primary media in the SOCRATES curriculum. As in the LDP, the media provide different representations. For example, the patient charts (which are text) provide one picture of the patient, while the physician-patient video and the patient interview video provide an alternative picture of the patient. The richness of both the textual representation and the video representation provides learners with valuable insights on understanding the problems and needs associated with the patient.

The selection of the media mix should relate in some way to the authentic nature of the task. Ask yourself these questions: What media are available to practitioners as they go about doing their job? How do they use the media to accomplish tasks? The answers to these questions should provide a good list of media options. For the LDP, the media reflect what expert sociologists look at during their research.

Next, think about how to acquire the media, or substitute one medium with another if the first is unavailable. The SOCRATES curriculum, for example, substituted videotapes of physician-patient examinations for the real thing, since observing actual examinations was not possible.

Self-Awareness of the Knowledge Construction Process

In constructivist learning environments, *how* a learner knows is more valuable than *what* a learner knows. Self-awareness is very similar to many of our grade school experiences, when math teachers made us "show our work," allowing the teachers to examine how we solved problems. Thus, the designer must create learning activities that encourage or require learners to show their work, explain why their solutions are valuable, or defend their positions. Collins, Brown, and Newman (1989), in their cognitive apprenticeship model, refer to these explanations as articulation.

The annotations learners write when they create links in the LDP are the method used to examine learners' thinking processes. In the annotations, learners restate their research question, then explain how the two nodes provide an answer to the question. When the instructor reviews a learner's links and annotations, the instructor gets a sense of how the learner is navigating through the database and how the learner is constructing evidence to answer the research question. The links and annotations make the learners' problem-solving process explicit, enabling the instructor to provide the learner guidance in developing research skills.

Articulation in the SOCRATES curriculum is a very public activity that takes place during the group activities and the classroom debriefing. The instructor and the worksheets direct learners to explain their solutions. For example, why did the learner prescribe a certain regimen? How did the learner know a patient exhibited certain symptoms? In classroom debriefings, the instructor constantly asks, "Why?" in response to a learner's decision. For example, a learner might state that he or she increased the patient's lente insulin one unit at 7 AM. The instructor would ask why, and the learner would articulate the reason: The patient has a high blood glucose level from noon to 8 PM; thus, a long-acting insulin should reduce the glucose level during these hours.

Conclusion

The seven pedagogical goals of constructivism offer designers a solid framework on which to build learning environments. By designing learning activities that satisfy the goals, the designer makes an effort to put theory into practice. However, the pedagogical goals are only a framework. The designer must strive for creativity in translating these goals into actual activities.

Different types of learning environments obligate the designer to conceive of different instructional methods and strategies to bring the pedagogical goals alive. For instance, the LDP (a virtual environment) addresses the collaboration goal by building in a public system of links and annotations that are accessible by all learners. SOCRATES (a classroom environment) addresses the collaboration goal with face-to-face communication between individual group members and between groups and the instructor.

As you read the other project descriptions in this book, reflect on how the various elements of their design address the seven pedagogical goals. I am sure you will find other creative twists in how to put the theory into practice.

References

Collins, A., Brown, J. S., & Newman, S. E. (1989). Cognitive apprenticeship: Teaching the crafts of reading, writing, and mathematics. In L. B. Resnick (Ed.) *Knowing, learning, and instruction: Essays in honor of Robert Glaser* (pp. 453–494). Hillsdale, NJ: Lawrence Erlbaum Associates.

Cunningham, D., Duffy, T. M., & Knuth, R. (1993). Textbook of the future. In C. McKnight (Ed.), *Hypertext: A psychological perspective*. London: Ellis Horwood Publishing.

Eli Lilly, Inc. (1988). *DiaSim* [computer software]. Indianapolis, IN: Eli Lilly, Inc.

Honebein, P. C. (1994). *The effects of a problem-based learning curriculum for diabetes management and care in a large medical school*. Unpublished Doctoral Dissertation.

Honebein, P. C., Chen, P., & Brescia, W. (1992). Hypermedia and sociology: A simulation for developing research skills. *Liberal Arts Computing*, Winter, 9–15.

Honebein, P. C., Duffy, T. M., & Fishman, B. J. (1993). Constructivism and the design of learning environments: Context and authentic activities for learning. In T. Duffy, J. Lowyck, & D. Jonassen (Eds.), *Designing environments for constructivist learning* (pp. 87–108). Berlin: Springer-Verlag.

Keegan, M. (1995). *Scenario educational software: Design and development of discovery learning.* Englewood Cliffs, NJ: Educational Technology Publications.

Knuth, R. A., & Cunningham, D. J. (1993). Tools for constructivism. In T. Duffy, J. Lowyck, & D. Jonassen (Eds.), *Designing environments for constructivist learning* (pp. 163–187). Berlin: Springer-Verlag.

Schoenfeld, A. H. (1985). *Mathematical problem solving.* New York: Academic Press.

Wilson, B. (1996). Introduction to this volume.

Peter C. Honebein, Ph.D., is an instructional systems consultant based in the high desert above Reno, Nevada. You can communicate with him on the Internet: HeyHoner@aol.com.

Acknowledgments

Thanks to Tom Gieryn, principal investigator of the LDP and practicum leader, for providing the environment for innovative curriculum development. The LDP was funded by a grant from the Andrew Mellon Foundation.

Tom Duffy, David Marrero, and Stephanie Kraft were team members on the SOCRATES curriculum. The SOCRATES curriculum was supported by the Diabetes Research and Training Center at the Regenstief Institute, Indiana University School of Medicine, and a grant from the National Institutes for Health.

3

An Interpretation Construction Approach to Constructivist Design

John B. Black
Robert O. McClintock

Study is a key concept in making design more fruitful in education. We propose that what students are doing when they construct knowledge is studying. Specifically, we think that the term *study* captures better what should be going on during knowledge construction then does the term *learn*. Thus, in designing for knowledge construction we see ourselves as designing Study Support Environments (SSEs) instead of "instructional systems" or "learning environments." Creating SSEs allows us to create "a place for study in a world of instruction" (McClintock, 1971). The core of study is the hermeneutic activity of constructing interpretations. Hermeneutics as a field focused initially on interpretation of texts, but has broadened to interpretation in general (Gadamer, 1976; Palmer, 1969). From this perspective, the basis for cognition (and *being* in general) is interpretation based on background knowledge and beliefs (Heidegger, 1962; Winograd & Flores, 1986). Consistent with these philosophical arguments for the centrality of interpretation in cognition are the many research results from cognitive psychology showing that understanding involves making a large number of inferences (Black, 1984, 1985). Thus, the key consideration in designing a SSE is fostering the construction of interpretations based on observations and background contextual information.

Teachers College, Columbia University has been collaborating with the Dalton School (a K–12 independent school in New York City) on the Dalton Technology Plan. The general aim of this plan is to develop a digital knowledge-base and information infrastructure for all aspects of the K–12 educational experience, and to implement educational strategies designed to make use of this infrastructure, enhancing significantly an already excellent educational experience. In this chapter, we describe a framework for SSE design and describe its application to three specific SSEs created as part of the Dalton Technology Plan. After describing the SSEs we report evaluations that demonstrate their effectiveness.

Interpretation Construction (ICON) Design Model

1. **Observation:** Students make observations of authentic artifacts anchored in authentic situations.

2. **Interpretation Construction:** Students construct interpretations of observations and construct arguments for the validity of their interpretations.

3. **Contextualization:** Students access background and contextual materials of various sorts to aid interpretation and argumentation.

4. **Cognitive Apprenticeship:** Students serve as apprentices to teachers to master observation, interpretation and contextualization.

5. **Collaboration:** Students collaborate in observation, interpretation and contextualization.

6. **Multiple Interpretations:** Students gain cognitive flexibility by being exposed to multiple interpretations.

7. **Multiple Manifestations:** Students gain transferability by seeing multiple manifestations of the same interpretations.

Some of these constructive design principles are adaptations from proposals by others. For example, the Cognitive Apprenticeship principle comes from Collins, Brown, and Newman (1989), the Multiple Interpretations one from Spiro, Feltovich, Jacobson, and Coulson (1992), and the Collaboration one from Johnson, Johnson, Holubec, and Roy (1984). The Observation principle is a combination of recommendations by Brown, Collins, and Duguid (1989) and the Cognition and Technology Group at Vanderbilt (1990), but our focus on authentic artifacts is unique. Further, our emphasis on Interpretation Construction, Contextualization, and Multiple Manifestations is distinctive.

Three Example Study Support Environments (SSEs)

To illustrate the application of this design framework, we describe three SSE programs created for the Dalton Technology Plan. Specifically, we describe how these constructive design principles apply to the *Archaeotype* program used in 6th grade history, to the *Galileo* program used in 11th and 12th grade science (particularly for students not scientifically oriented), and the *Playbill* program used in 10th grade English at the Dalton School.

In the *Archaeotype* program, students study ancient Greek and Roman history by using observations of simulated archaeological digs to construct interpretations of the history of these sites, while drawing upon a wide variety of background information. The *Archaeotype* program (implemented in *SuperCard* on Apple Macintosh computers), which is the earliest and most fully-developed of the Dalton Technology Plan projects, presents the students with a graphic simulation of an archaeological site. Then the students study the history of the site through simulated digging up of artifacts, making various measurements of the artifacts in a simulated laboratory (**Observation**), and relating the objects to what is already known using a wide variety of reference materials (**Contextualization**). The students work cooperatively in groups (**Collaboration**), while the teacher models how to deal with such a site, then fades his or her involvement while coaching and supporting the students in their own study efforts (**Cognitive Apprenticeship**). The students develop ownership of their work by developing their own interpretations of the history of the site and mustering various kinds of evidence for their conclusions (**Interpretation Construction**). By arguing with the other students and studying related interpretations in the historical literature, they get a sense of other perspectives (**Multiple Interpretations**). By going through the process a number of times and bringing each contextual background to bear on a number of different artifacts, the students learn and understand the many ways that the general principles behind what they are doing become manifest (**Multiple Manifestations**).

In the *Galileo* program, students study astronomy and science in general by using observations of telescopic plates and a computer simulation of the sky to construct and test interpretations of astronomical phenomena. Students examine and make measurements on photographic plates from observatory telescopes and computer simulations of the sky (**Observation**), then relate these analyses to reference materials (**Contextualization**) containing what is known about astronomical objects (i.e., stars, planets, etc.). The teacher initially talks through how he or she would analyze and interpret examples of such astronomical data (**Cognitive Apprenticeship**). Then the students form groups to work on some data (**Collaboration**), while the teacher coaches and advises them as they proceed. The students develop their own hypotheses and test them against the astronomical data (**Interpretation Construction**). Students defend their hypotheses using their analyses and reference materials both within and between the groups, and such argumentation together with background readings exposes them to various ways to interpret the data (**Multiple Interpretations**). As they proceed through the course, the students see how basic principles of astronomy, physics and chemistry can be used to make sense of different sets of astronomical data (**Multiple Manifestations**).

In the *Playbill* program, students study Shakespearean drama and English literature in general by using the text of a play and two or more videos of performances of the play. *Playbill* provides the students with highly indexed access to the text of *Macbeth*, two videos of performances of *Macbeth* and written commentary on *Macbeth*. Using this multimedia indexing system (implemented in *SuperCard* on Apple Macintosh computers), students can read a portion of *Macbeth* (e.g., a scene) and then immediately jump to see one or two performances of what they have read (**Observation**). The students can also use this indexing system to jump to commentaries on the same portion of the play (**Contextualization**). Using portions of the play, the teacher models how to integrate reading the play, watching the performances, and reading the commentaries (**Cognitive Apprenticeship**). The students work together in groups (**Collaboration**) to develop their own interpretations of the play and how it should be performed (**Interpretation Construction**). Comparing their interpretations of the play with the other students, both within the same group and then in different groups, gives the students a sense of the many different reactions that people can have to a play like *Macbeth* (**Multiple Interpretations**). The multimedia indexing system also facilitates the students jumping around in the text and videos to see how the same entities (e.g., characters, themes, etc.) can be manifested in many different ways in the text and performances (**Multiple Manifestations**).

As these programs spanning history, science and literature show, while the basic material or data observed is widely different in different fields of study, our design framework is applicable to all. Another perspective on these programs is provided by the five facets of learning environments proposed by Perkins (1992). Specifically, Perkins proposed that one can analyze any learning environment, from traditional classroom settings to futuristic technology-based settings, according to how they implement the following five facets: information banks (traditionally encyclopedias and dictionaries), symbol pads (traditionally notebooks and blackboards), construction kits (traditionally TinkerToys and Legos), phenomenaria (traditionally aquariums and terrariums), and task managers (traditionally the teacher's scheduling of classroom activities). The *Archaeotype*, *Galileo*, and *Playbill* programs focus mainly on the information bank and phenomenaria facets. In particular, the archaeological site simulation, the sky simulation and telescopic plates, and the multimedia play text and video indexing system are all phenomenaria designed to give the students the basic observational information they need to do their interpretation construction. However, to make these interpretations intelligently and to defend them well, the students in all three of these programs also make extensive use of various kinds of information banks varying from background texts, to on-line databases, to individual experts (including teachers), to videodiscs (e.g., the *National Gallery* videodisc) and to museums (e.g., the *Metropolitan Museum of Art*). The symbol pads used are mostly standard word processing programs, although there has been some use of *HyperCard* as a more advanced form of symbol pad. There are no particular construction kits in the three programs we have covered here, and the task managers are a combination of the traditional teacher scheduling (for the overall class scheduling) and the time management within the student groups. Another interesting distinction that Perkins (1992) makes is between BIG (Beyond the Information Given) constructivism and WIG (Without the Information Given) constructivism. Our focus is on WIG constructivism, since we give the students the raw material for their observations, but they have to analyze this raw material, come up with interpretations, present the interpretations and defend them.

Evaluation of Study Support Environments

Since we believe that interpretation is central to cognition and learning, we evaluated whether the *Archaeotype* and *Galileo* SSE programs would increase students' interpretation skills. Specifically, we tested whether the students who had been through these programs could make observations and interpretations in a completely new area better than students who had not been through the programs. For these studies, we chose an area unlikely to be familiar to precollege students—namely, experimental psychology.

In the *Archaeotype* evaluation study, 6th grade students who had participated in the *Archaeotype* program and a comparable group of students that had not participated were each given a booklet describing four psychology experiments examining how people remember lists of words. The students had to examine the basic observations report on the results of the studies, find patterns in the results, devise explanations and argue for those explanations. They were also given some background readings in the psychology of memory. The reports the students wrote were then scored for how many they got of the 60 possible points they could have earned for recognizing the patterns in the data, representing the data in insightful ways, explaining the patterns of results, and arguing for the explanations. The students who had been through the *Archaeotype* program were able to get 42% of the possible points after four hours work, whereas the non-*Archaeotype* students were only able to get 32%. Most striking, almost all of this superiority was due to the *Archaeotype* students getting 45% of the possible points on the explanation and argumentation part of the scoring, while the non-*Archaeotype* students only got 26% on this portion (these two differences are highly significant statistically). Clearly, in addition to learning about archeology and ancient history, the *Archaeotype* students were acquiring a general ability to interpret and argue in new areas of study.

Similarly, the 11th and 12th grade students who had been through the *Galileo* program were compared to a comparable group on how well they could interpret and link three related cognitive psychology studies and their underlying principles. The students were given booklets containing descriptions of basic observations made in these three psychology studies together with various informational resources including relevant and irrelevant background material. The students were given three hours to perform the task and write a final report. As in the previous study, these reports were scored for the possible points that could be covered recognizing patterns in the data, representing the data insightfully, interpreting the data, and arguing for the interpretations. Here again the students who had been through the *Galileo* program were much better than students who had not—with the *Galileo* students getting 44% of the possible points whereas the non-*Galileo* students only got 32% (this difference is highly significant statistically). In fact, the *Galileo* students showed this superiority in all the areas we scored for—namely, pattern recognition, data representation, interpretation and argumentation. Clearly, the *Galileo* program, like the *Archaeotype* one, teaches students general interpretation skills in addition to specific content.

While we designed the evaluation studies as appropriate for what we were trying to accomplish with the SSEs, it is instructive to examine them in terms of the constructivist learning evaluation criteria proposed by Jonassen (1992). Our evaluations are goal-free, since we did not look for particular interpretations by students but merely how well formulated and argued their interpretations were. Our evaluations also met Jonassen's criteria of using authentic tasks (the students interpreted actual psychology experiments and results), involving knowledge construction (the students constructed the interpretations and argumentation), being context-driven (students were evaluated in the context of making sense of psychological observations), involving multiple perspectives (different interpretations were proposed and argued by different students) and involving socially constructed meaning (the students worked in groups to make sense out of the observations). However, Jonassen also proposed three criteria that our evaluations did not meet—namely, that the evaluations should be process oriented and multimodal (for simplicity we merely evaluated the end-product report of the students' deliberations), and that the goals of the evaluation should be set by the learners (we were looking for whether these programs fostered interpretation construction and argumentation skills). Our evaluation studies could probably be improved by including process data and multimodal products (although that would have made it much harder to conduct the studies), but we are unsure how letting the learners set the goals of the evaluation would apply to our situation.

Conclusions

We have proposed an approach to constructivist design (ICON) that makes interpretation construction of authentic artifacts in the context of rich background materials the central focus. We have shown how this approach can be applied to Study Support Environment programs in widely different fields of study—namely, history, science and literature. We have also shown that in addition to learning specific content, students using these programs acquire generalizable interpretation and argumentation skills. Thus, our constructivist design framework is useful both for guiding design and for producing valuable learning results.

References

Black, J. B. (1984). Understanding and remembering stories. In J. R. Anderson & S. M. Kosslyn (Eds.), *Tutorials in learning and memory*. New York: W. H. Freeman.

Black, J. B. (1985). An exposition on understanding expository text. In B. K. Britton & J. B. Black (Eds.), *Understanding expository text*. Hillsdale, NJ: Lawrence Erlbaum Associates.

Brown, J. S., Collins, A., & Duguid, P. (1989). Situated cognition and the culture of learning. *Educational Researcher, 18*(1), 32–42.

Cognition & Technology Group at Vanderbilt (1990). Anchored instruction and its relation to situated cognition. *Educational Researcher, 20*, 2–10.

Collins, A., Brown, J. S., & Newman, S. E. (1989). Cognitive apprenticeship: Teaching the crafts of reading, writing, and mathematics. In L. B. Resnick (Ed.), *Knowing, learning, and instruction: Essays in honor of Robert Glaser* (pp. 453–494). Hillsdale, NJ: Lawrence Erlbaum Associates.

Gadamer, H. (1976). *Philosophical hermeneutics* (translated and edited by D. Linge). Berkeley, CA: University of California Press.

Heidegger, M. (1962). *Being and time* (translated by J. Macquarrie & E. Robinson). New York: Harper and Row.

Johnson, D., Johnson, R., Holubec, E., & Roy, P. (1984). *Circles of learning*. Alexandria, VA: ASCD.

Jonassen, D. H. (1992). Evaluating constructivist learning. In T. M. Duffy & D. H. Jonassen (Eds.), *Constructivism and the technology of instruction: A conversation*. Hillsdale, NJ: Lawrence Erlbaum Associates. Originally in *Educational Technology*, 1991, *31*(9).

McClintock, R. (1971). Toward a place for study in a world of instruction. *Teachers College Record, 72*, 405–416.

Palmer, R. E. (1969). *Hermeneutics*. Evanston, IL: Northwestern University Press.

Perkins, D. N. (1992). Technology meets constructivism: Do they make a marriage? In T. M. Duffy & D. H. Jonassen (Eds.), *Constructivism and the technology of instruction: A conversation*. Hillsdale, NJ: Lawrence Erlbaum Associates. Originally in *Educational Technology*, 1991, *31*(5).

Spiro, R. J., Feltovich, P. J., Jacobson, M. J., & Coulson, R. L. (1992). Cognitive flexibility, constructivism, and hypertext: Random access instruction for advanced knowledge acquisition in ill-structured domains. In T. M. Duffy & D. H. Jonassen (Eds.), *Constructivism and the technology of instruction: A conversation*. Hillsdale, NJ: Lawrence Erlbaum Associates. Originally in *Educational Technology*, 1991, *31*(5).

Winograd, T., & Flores, F. (1986). *Understanding computers and cognition: A new foundation for design*. Norwood, NJ: Ablex.

John B. Black (Ph.D., Stanford U., 1979) is Professor of Computing and Education and Professor of Educational Psychology at Teachers College, Columbia University.

Robert O. McClintock (Ph.D., Columbia U., 1968) is Professor of Communication and Education and Professor of History and Education at Teachers College, Columbia University.

4

Tutoring for Transfer of Technical Competence

Sherrie P. Gott
Alan Lesgold
Ronald S. Kane

Coached Apprenticeship as a Form of Constructivist Training[1]

The constructivist movement has grown largely as a reaction to problems in education that come from excessive emphasis on algorithmic performance and rote memorization as the core processes of education. It has been noted that saying the words of a principle does not produce understanding of what those words mean. Also, as long ago as Whitehead (1929), it was observed that having learned something in school did not imply that one would use the acquired knowledge when it was relevant in real life. This fundamental problem, that schooling seemed too internally focused and did not prepare people for life outside the context of school performances, led to the constructivist viewpoint that students must construct their own knowledge and that education consists of providing appropriate learning situations that afford a student opportunities to develop personal knowledge that will be useful in later life.

At one extreme, the constructivist approach takes on an idealized humanistic character. Within this view, it is thought inappropriate for the teacher even to have explicit goals for learning. The student is to be free to develop his own mind, his own understanding, his own competence. The viewpoint we have taken is perhaps closer to the other extreme. We realize the need for the student

---

[1] The opinions expressed herein reflect the views of the authors and are not intended as official doctrine of the Armstrong Laboratory or the U. S. Air Force.

to build knowledge anchored in his/her own prior knowledge and understanding, but we see many situations in which a culture has specific learning goals for its novitiates and in which seeking instruction into that culture implies acceptance of at least a partial goal structure for learning.

Even in this more restrictive view, a constructivist approach is powerful and perhaps necessary. The knowledge a student will acquire must still be anchored in his/her experiences. The nouns and verbs in statements of principle must still have meaning for the student. At the same time, the learning environment must afford opportunities to reflect on how a particular community of practice talks about the world, how it represents the world, and how it determines how to act in the world. We have focused our attention on a particular community of practice, technicians who use and maintain specialized electronic equipment that itself is used to facilitate testing and repair of aircraft navigation equipment. Because this community is defined partly by its responsibilties to a larger community that includes pilots and tacticians who count on having working aircraft, effective practice is constrained partly by cultural responsibilties. It is also constrained by the need to be able to talk to other community members about the work of the community and especially the responsibility to be ready to take on new, but related sets of tasks. Below, we describe and evaluate an approach to training that pursues this particular variant of the constructivist theme.

For the last ten years, we have worked with a team of colleagues from the University of Pittsburgh Learning Research and Development Center and U. S. Air Force Armstrong Laboratory to develop an instructional approach we call intelligent coached apprenticeship[2] (Eggan & Lesgold, in press; Katz & Lesgold, 1991; Katz & Lesgold, in press; Katz, Lesgold, Eggan, & Gordin, in press; Gott, 1987, 1989; Gott, Hall, Pokorny, Dibble, & Glaser, 1992; Gott, Pokorny, Alley, Kane, & Dibble, in press; Hall, Gott, & Pokorny, in press; Kane, 1993; Lajoie & Lesgold, 1989; Lesgold, in press; Lesgold, Eggan, Katz, & Rao, 1992; Glaser, Lesgold, & Gott, 1986; Lesgold, Katz, Greenberg, Hughes, & Eggan, in press; Lesgold & Katz, 1992; Lesgold, Lajoie, Bunzo, & Eggan, 1992; Nichols, Pokorny, Jones, Gott, & Alley, in press; Pokorny & Gott, in press). This approach is based upon the opportunity to **experience** the most difficult aspects of cognitively-intense jobs in a simulated work environment where assistance, in the form of an intelligent computer-based coach, is always available and where there are opportunities to **reflect** on simulated work experiences. We have developed two generations of tutors for training a specialized electronics maintenance job in the

---

[2]Sherlock 2, the current embodiment of the ideas we discuss in this paper, has been a collaborative effort that has included Daniel Abeshouse, Marilyn Bunzo, Roberta Catizone, Dennis Collins, Richard Eastman, Gary Eggan, Mark Gallaway, Robert Glaser, Maria Gordin, Sherrie Gott, Linda Greenberg, Ellen Hall, Edward Hughes, Ron Kane, Sandra Katz, Dimitra Keffalonitou, David Kieras, Susanne Lajoie, Alan Lesgold, Robert Linn, Thomas McGinnis, Johanna Moore, Dan Peters, Bob Pokorny, Rudianto Prabowo, Govinda Rao, Rose Rosenfeld, Kurt Strobel, Gary Walker, and Arlene Weiner. Collins, Gallaway, Gott, Hall, Kane, Pokorny, Strobel, and Walker are U.S. Air Force uniformed or civilian employees; David Kieras is at the University of Michigan; Robert Linn is at the University of Colorado; the others are or were at the University of Pittsburgh.

U. S. Air Force, namely the F-15 manual avionics test station technician specialty (see Appendix I for an overview of the F-15 Manual Avionics Test Station job). The tutor focuses on the hardest part of the job, isolating failures in the test station itself. Both generations of the training system we have built, named Sherlock 1 and Sherlock 2, have worked remarkably well, in terms of success in fostering high levels of job expertise and, with Sherlock 2, promoting transfer to electronics troubleshooting tasks on novel equipment.

The primary activity within Sherlock is holistic work, at the highest levels of real-world difficulty, though often this requires coaching, which is available on demand. The approach has several distinguishing characteristics:
— Learning activity is centered in a simulated work environment.
— Learning activity is centered around problems that exemplify the hardest parts of the job for which one is being trained (problems defined in collaboration with master technicians on the job).

For each problem, two kinds of activities occur:
— The student solves the problem, requesting advice from the intelligent tutor/coach as necessary.
— The student reviews a record of her[3] problem-solving activity, receiving constructive critique from the coach.

Sherlock provides a simulation of the work environment for the F-15 avionics job, using a combination of video and computer graphic displays. Simulated controls can be operated with the computer mouse, and the displays change to reflect an underlying computer simulation of the devices being simulated. Since the fundamental activity of troubleshooting in this job is making tests with meters, this is provided realistically by having icons of meter probes that can be "attached" to video images of device test points.

To complement **coached learning by doing**, we have developed a collection of tools for post-performance reflection. One provides an intelligent replay of the trainee's actions. A trainee can "walk through" the actions he just performed while solving the problem. In addition, he can access information about what can in principle be known about the system, given the actions replayed so far (the work of troubleshooting is mostly the making of electrical measurements and then figuring out which possibilities are ruled out and which supported by the pattern of results). Also, he can ask what an expert might have done in place of any of his actions, get a critique of his actions, and have his actions evaluated by the system. In addition, extensive conceptual knowledge about the system's functions is available from intelligent hyper-graphic displays of an expert's circuit model schematic drawing. In these drawings, the boxes that stand for circuit components are all mouse-sensitive and can "tell about themselves." We have also built a tool for displaying an expert solution to the problem, again with extensive conceptual information available as appropriate to each step. Further, there is an option for side-by-side listing of an expert solution and the trainee's most recent effort.

---

[3]To enhance readability, we alternate between masculine and feminine pronouns rather than using more cumbersome forms. About 23% of the target population of the Sherlock system are women.

The tools we have built are motivated by substantial research on the reflective activities that might foster learning. For example, Chi and Van Lehn (1991) and Van Lehn, Jones, and Chi (1992) analyzed the activity of more and less effective learners in studying worked-out physics problems. They found that more effective learners showed a different pattern of study, paying more attention to the conditions under which various steps in the solution were taken, to the relations between actions and goals, to the consequences of actions, and to the underlying meanings for formalisms such as equations. Gott *et al.* (1992) made similar observations in a study where transfer of skill under naturalistic conditions was investigated. Bielaczyc, Pirolli, and Brown (1993, April; Pirolli & Bielaczyc, 1989) demonstrated that students could be taught a similar approach.

Working from the Chi, Bielaczyc, and Gott studies just cited, we can infer several possible roles for post-problem reflection. First, if the trainee reached impasses during her efforts and had to ask for help, then there is some learning work to be done. The trainee must figure out why the suggestions of the intelligent coach were useful and what rule(s) can be inferred. Second, problem solving experiences afford opportunities for tuning the generality of procedural knowledge and also for elaborating conceptual knowledge. This is especially the case where intuitive guessing was part of the solution process:

"I tried doing X because it seemed like it might work; why did I think it should work?"

In addition, problems can often be solved in non-optimal ways. When this happens, there is no impasse to cue the trainee that her knowledge needs further tuning. So, criticism may be a useful part of the reflection opportunity. Of special relevance are the trade-offs involved in testing hypotheses by swapping parts versus measuring electrical properties of the faulted system. Just as in football, part of what a coach can do is to point out possibilities for improvement that may not be evident to the trainee with respect to cost-benefit trade-offs in the selection of solution steps.

While this instructional approach differs radically from the approaches promoted by traditional instructional design schemes, it is equally dependent upon good task analysis. What is different is that the structure of learning tasks is more authentic, rooted in the needs of practice (or simulated practice) rather than being derived directly from task analysis structure (Gott, 1987; Hall, Gott, & Pokorny, in press).

One important component of our constructivist approach is the intelligent hyperdisplay. When Sherlock constructs a schematic diagram to help illustrate the advice it is providing, that diagram is organized to show expert understanding about the system with which the trainee is working (see Figure 4.1). The structure of the diagram reflects the expert representation of the circuitry involved in carrying out the function that failed, as revealed in a detailed cognitive task analysis. What is displayed is approximately what a trainee would want to know at that time, but every display component is "hot" and can be used as a portal to more detail or explanation. The part of the system on which the expert would be focusing at a given point in the problem solution process is allocated the most space in the diagram and presented in the most detail. All diagram components are "buttons" that can be pushed to expand their level of detail. Boxes in the diagram are color coded to indicate what is known

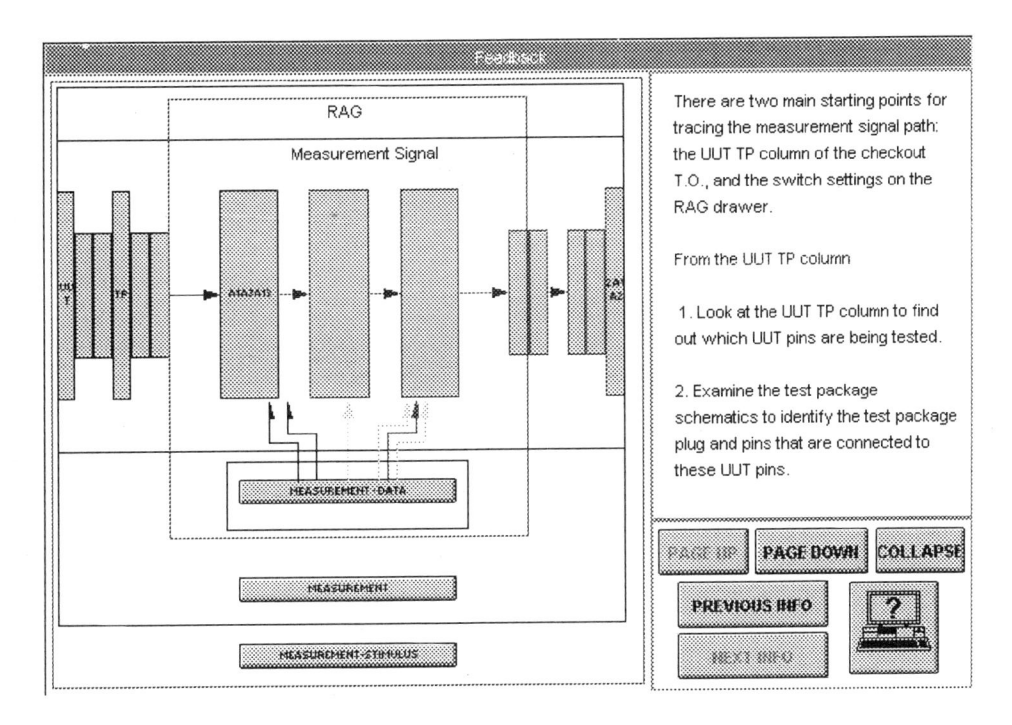

Figure 4.1. Equipment diagrams used in coaching.

about them, given the tests carried out so far. Circuit paths are color coded to indicate whether the electrical properties of those paths are known to be appropriate or inappropriate for the function that has failed. Sometimes during problem solving, information is deleted from the display before it is shown, so that the trainee doesn't substitute looking at labels in the displays for inferring what circuitry is involved in the functional failure being diagnosed.

Tutoring for Transfer

Our principal pedagogical goal in initiating the Sherlock project was to **accelerate** the development of complex, technical problem solving skills. Skill acceleration is a pressing need because in the real world, acquisition of avionics troubleshooting expertise can take 8 to 10 years. In Sherlock 2, this goal was accompanied by a second, equally important one, namely, to foster technical adaptiveness. Skill flexibility is vital in an era of rapid technological change. One focus in this article is on the transfer effectiveness of Sherlock 2.

Earlier work conducted by our research group in the area of transfer revealed some important findings about **intentional** transfer, or the undisguised requirement to transfer one's existing knowledge and skill to novel tasks (Gott et al., 1992). Those data revealed that mental models of devices exert strong influence on knowledge access, additional learning (knowledge extension), and subsequent diagnostic reasoning. In the domain of avionics troubleshooting, the primary content of transfer takes the form of abstract knowledge representations. Time and again, we observed good learners access their existing mental models of equipment structure and function and their schema of the troubleshooting task. They then used these models as flexible blueprints to guide their performance as they crafted solutions to new problems. Their prior models became interpretive structures, and when these models were inadequate, better learners flexibly used them as the basis for transposed and elaborated structures that could accommodate the novel situations. They were ready and willing to construct new knowledge that was grounded in their existing representational and functional competence.

By contrast, less able performers devised ways to avoid this adaptive learning experience. They displayed maladaptive behaviors as they oversimplified new problems and overgeneralized existing structures. As a result, their performance in the new domain appeared novice-like, without the benefit of abstract plans and adapted models. They were wedded to their old structures, unable to perceive that the functional variations in the devices in the novel domain were plausible extensions of their current understanding.

These findings in turn influenced instructional design decisions in Sherlock 2 in order to enhance the acquisition of **flexible** problem solving skills. They include the following: (a) high quality device models are fostered with liberal scaffolding in the form of illustrative **equipment diagrams** used in coaching and reflective followup; (b) **interactive video representations** of actual electronic devices dominate the learning environment (in constructivist terms, the video devices provide phenomenaria to be manipulated and otherwise exercised to build understanding); (c) in the tutor's coaching (or Information Banks) **general functional terms** are used to describe the electronic devices and tests, in addition to problem specific terminology; (d) general terminology is also be used to characterize the **goal structure** that typifies "the (generic) plan" for troubleshooting in this domain; (e) the **reasons** behind preferred goals and procedures are **made explicit** to reveal the expert's cost-benefit reasoning in evaluating alternative courses of action; and (f) **general troubleshooting principles** are emphasized during the post-problem reflective followup activities.

Purpose and Rationale for Tutor Evaluation Study

With these major instructional design decisions having been implemented, the goal of the Sherlock 2 evaluation study was to determine if an intelligent tutoring system that is informed by detailed cognitive models of expert, generalizable troubleshooting performances is effective in both accelerating skill acquisition and fostering adaptive expertise. A controlled experiment was conducted that involved 54 U. S. Air Force technicians at three geographically separated F15 flying wings. Apprentice technicians, who averaged 33 months' experience, were assigned to either the Experimental (Tutored) or Control (Untutored) group. Master technicians, who averaged 10 years and 4 months' experience, were tested to establish the upper levels of expertise in the domain.

It was hypothesized that the experimental group would demonstrate an accelerated rate of skill acquisition compared to the control group trainees in moving toward the level of performance displayed by advanced Master technicians. These expectations were predicated on the following premise: In a learning environment that provides direct but coached problem solving experiences and one in which cognitive skill components and processes have been precisely identified as instructional targets, the acquisition of complex skills (such as electronic troubleshooting) can be speeded up. The expected accelerated acquisition would be attributable to (a) better instructional content enabled by cognitive models that make the unobservable facets of troubleshooting knowable to learners, and (b) better methods where knowledge is tied to its uses in the world and learning is supported by direct manipulation experiences (phenomenaria), coaching, modeling, and other scaffolding embedded in the computer tutor.

It was further hypothesized that the experimental group would demonstrate adaptiveness in their newly acquired troubleshooting skills compared to the control group when tested on a novel equipment system. These expectations were predicated on several premises. First, a learning environment where extensive practice, supported by multi-level coaching, is available to trainees would afford potent **learning-by-doing** experiences. Knowledge constructed under those conditions would be assumed to be both robust and flexible. Secondly, all coaching and post-session reflective feedback would provide general as well as task specific explanations to inject elasticity into the system, procedural, and strategic knowledge components of troubleshooting skill.

To investigate the generality of troubleshooting skills acquired by subjects tutored on Sherlock 2, an avionics expert on our research team created a mythical equipment system called Frankenstation (Kane, 1993). Frankenstation is an automatic test station, not the type of manual station represented in Sherlock. Its primary uniqueness (vis-a-vis Sherlock) is that it is automated, meaning it is computer (not human) controlled. Therefore, Frankenstation technical data includes programming language notes, which would be one of many elements novel to the manual test station maintenance personnel who participated in the Sherlock evaluation study.

Results

Initial comparisons of the experimental and control groups on verbal and written troubleshooting proficiency tests and on other performance-related measures (aptitude and experience) revealed no statistically reliable differences **prior** to the intervention. This indicates that the groups are equivalent for purposes of this evaluation study.

Post Intervention Results

Experimental and Control Group Comparisons

As predicted, Sherlock posttest scores revealed large and statistically significant differences in favor of the experimental group over the controls. Pre to posttest changes are illustrated in Figure 4.2. The single holistic indicator of troubleshooting performance can be decomposed by an analysis of the components of troubleshooting known to be associated with expertise, per the cognitive task analysis. Such components include measuring to investigate the equipment rather than swapping equipment parts, systematicity in investigating circuitry versus random actions, and efficiency in targeting areas to investigate

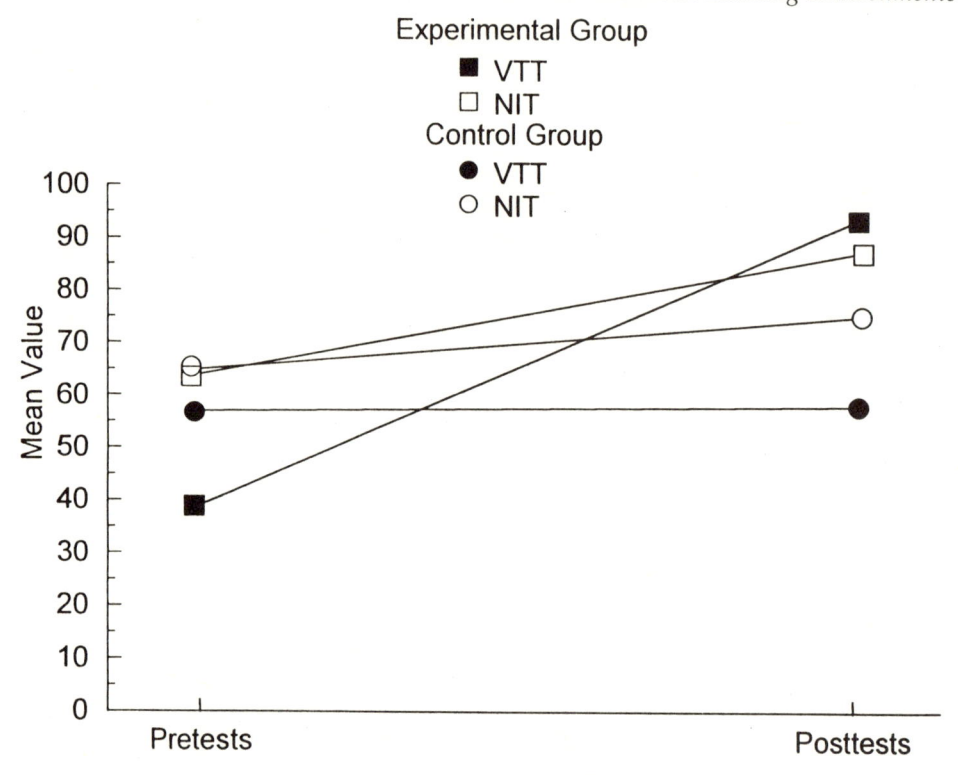

Figure 4.2. Pre to posttest changes: Sherlock 2 tests.

by optimizing the information value-to-cost ratio associated with each potential action. Results of this componential analysis are reported in Gott et al. (in press).

Also, as predicted, the Frankenstation posttest scores revealed large and statistically significant differences in favor of the experimental group over the controls. Performance differences across groups are illustrated in Figure 4.3.

The effect size for each of the posttest measures is shown in Table 4.1. As a basis for comparison, the average effect size for new science and math curriculum in U.S. schools is reported to be .3 sigma (Bloom, 1984).

Qualitative Analyses of Frankenstation Test Data

The single holistic indicator of Frankenstation troubleshooting performance can be decomposed into discrete components of troubleshooting skill that are embedded in the verbal protocols and known to be associated with expertise, per the cognitive task analysis data. A decomposition such as this provides more meaningful indicators about what Sherlock trainees actually learned and transferred to the Frankenstation tasks. The components include (a) thoroughly measuring suspect equipment components during troubleshooting rather than swapping equipment parts prematurely, (b) using automated diagnostic aids (such as system self-tests) in a targeted, efficient manner, (c) following a logical, efficient strategy in troubleshooting, and finally, (d) isolating the fault and thereby solving the problem within the time allowed.

FRANKENSTATION
Verbal Troubleshooting Posttests

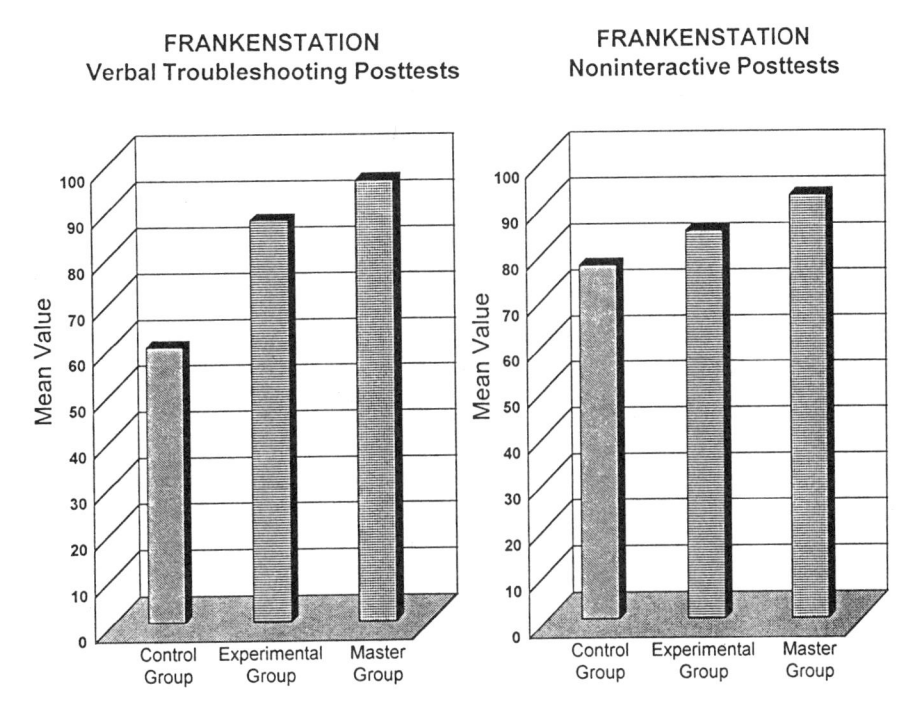

FRANKENSTATION
Noninteractive Posttests

Figure 4.3. Frankenstation test scores across groups.

Table 4.1. Effect size for posttest measures.

		Control			Experimental		Effect
Measure	N	M	SD	N	M	SD	Size
Verbal #1 (Sherlock)	23	59	37	18	95	5	1.27 SDS
Verbal #2 (Sherlock)	23	58	37	18	91	7	1.17 SDS
Written (Sherlock)	23	75	14	18	87	12	.87 SDS
Verbal (Frank'tn)	21	55	31	17	82	23	.96 SDS
Written (Frank'tn)	21	72	11	17	80	10	.76 SDS

Instances of swapping without testing clearly differentiated the untutored airmen (Control Group) from the Tutored and Master technicians. The Experimental group impressively outperformed the Control Group **and** the Masters in thoroughly testing the inputs and outputs of a faulty component prior to swapping it. While the three groups used the system self-test capability at the same relative frequency, the Control Group clearly differed in its manner of implementation. Of the 16 occasions when control subjects used self-tests, there were 11 times when they did so quite inefficiently. They chose to run the self-test from the beginning—until a fail was encountered—as opposed to selecting device-specific self-tests that targeted the test station devices that were being used in the failed test. Conversely, Master and Tutored airmen used the self tests efficiently because they could identify from the program listing and the test station schematics which test station devices were being utilized.

Also, instances of following the logical, most effective strategy in troubleshooting Frankenstation clearly favored the Tutored airmen, and the Tutored and Master subjects bettered the Controls in terms of isolating the faulty component in Frankenstation, i.e., solving the problem in the allotted time.

Discussion

A careful examination of the verbal troubleshooting "think aloud" protocols (from pre- and posttests) revealed more precisely what the tutored airmen had learned and generalized from Sherlock 2. First, their actions on the Frankenstation posttest showed they were looking for and locating devices in the novel equipment that served the same basic functionalities inherent to Sherlock. They identified the Frankenstation devices that performed the signal **generation, routing,** and **measurement** functions. In effect, the results suggest they learned and generalized an equipment schema for avionics test stations.

Secondly, they demonstrated a top-level plan or strategy that attached itself to the equipment schema. The plan established what areas of the equipment to target first, second, and so forth. Such a goal structure enabled them to proceed systematically to investigate an equipment system they had never seen before. Collectively, these findings replicate results from our earlier investigation of **intentional** transfer (Gott et al., 1992).

Although our study did not include conditions where instructional features were manipulated to gauge the power of individual instructional attributes, past research in the training of complex problem solving skills lend support to certain speculative explanations regarding Sherlock's effectiveness. The support centers around (a) cognitive models as input to instruction; (b) the sequencing of instructional events; (c) situated learning in a constructivist instructional environment; and (d) the sociology of the learning system.

Cognitive Models

Multicomponent cognitive models of troubleshooting performance derived from Master technicians provided the input to Sherlock. All content for the tutor came directly from expert performers in the domain. The performances targeted by the instruction were thus valid, complete, and precise. Too often, instruction involving complex skills focuses exclusively on one, or at best two, components of skill. For example, procedures, or problem solving operations, are often the focus of such instruction, but the procedures are too often presented instructionally as a **flat string** of actions or rules, not as hierarchical, goal-directed structures. Thus, they do not correspond to the internalized procedural representations of experts. Similarly, complex skill instruction can focus exclusively on device or system knowledge. But an emphasis on declarative knowledge usually translates into facts and formal laws being taught as "detached" pieces of information. The content is not tied to its conditions of use in the real world, that is, how and when it is useful in problem solving contexts. The Sherlock 2 instruction targeted the coordination of all components of troubleshooting skill, in a situated learning context.

Sequencing of Instructional Events

The acquisition of complex skills occurs incrementally, in successive approximations of mature practice; therefore, the sequencing of instructional events is critical since it must promote the maturation process. Our guiding principle regarding sequence was to **decompose** the targeted knowledge/skill base and **reorganize** it to fit learning. With most instruction, the reverse is true, that is, learning is expected to conform to the way knowledge is organized in some external curriculum (or system). The fit of knowledge to learning depends upon careful instructional sequencing so that the learner is always building on the foundation of prior knowledge. The cognitive task analysis findings gave us the skeleton for a learning trajectory to inform instructional sequencing. By contrasting the performances of novice, intermediate, and master technicians on problems of varying complexity (in the task analysis), it was possible to ascertain the relative learning difficulty of system components/functional areas, troubleshooting procedures, and strategic actions. Those findings in turn informed both the sequence of troubleshooting scenarios presented to students and the criterion performance levels to be met at each major stage along the learning trajectory.

Situated Learning

Following Dewey and in accord with the current constructivist movement (Perkins, 1991), the general principle of **learning by doing** is the touchstone of the Sherlock design. Students work on a graded series of authentic problems in an **extension** of their actual work environment. Working in Sherlock is like doing one's job in the real world—objects in the environment are acted upon to achieve certain goals. There are, however, several nontrivial bonuses in Sherlock that do not exist in the real world: learning does **not** depend on what equipment parts break and need to be fixed. Instruction can be sequenced in a more pedagogically viable manner. Secondly, **routine** task activities can be time-compressed so that valuable instructional time is devoted to the challenging part of the task, and finally, the Sherlock environment is forgiving; mistakes can be made without dire consequences—**plus**, expert coaching is always available. Even without extensive use of coaching, the student can explore and investigate the equipment as phenomenaria (Perkins, 1991) in the simulated environment as she attempts to make sense of the task and the equipment system.

In Sherlock 2, a **learning-by-reflection component** was introduced to enhance the learning-by-doing pedagogy. The value added for the student appears to come from several sources. First, the student's solution trace becomes a useful object of study, since the computer can represent the **process** of the solution and thereby externalize decisions for interpretation from a variety of perspectives. By treating each of his traces as useful objects of study, the student can come to view learning as an "incrementally staged process" that happens over time, not all at once (Collins, Brown, & Newman, 1989). Secondly, by having access to an exemplar solution from a Master (including the Master's normally tacit reasons for each action), the student can observe and even discover expert strategies and reasoning that subsequently can improve the trainee's own solution. Finally, after viewing a number of problem-specific traces, the student can derive abstractions from the patterns of actions and underlying reasons; for example, the top-level goal structure we observed tutored airmen transfer to the Frankenstation task.

Sociology of the Learning Environment

Above all else, instruction must be viewed as **relevant** to trainees; this is particularly true for an on-the-job training system like Sherlock. The training must serve their needs, profit them directly. "Drawing students into a culture of expert practice in cognitive domains involves teaching them to think like experts" (Collins, Brown, & Newman, 1989, p. 488). In effect, Sherlock seeks to do just that—draw students into a culture of expert practice, enable them to reach the mature levels of proficiency they observe being practiced by the Masters who are the acknowledged leaders in the shop.

On a daily basis during the lengthy field trials, we observed the tutored airmen make strides in becoming a part of the community of expert practice. They shared with us conversations they had with their Team Leaders when malfunction problems arose on the actual equipment that was covered in Sherlock. They sometimes consulted the acknowledged Masters in the shop (after a tutoring session) when they needed and wanted more elaboration about a Sherlock scenario than was available in the tutor. There were also occasions *during* tutoring sessions when trainees would want to get an opinion from one of the shop master technicians because they thought the tutor's interpretation or suggestion was too narrow or incomplete.

These observations provide one measure of Sherlock's effectiveness in socializing apprentices into the expert culture. They were learning to perform tasks that they recognized as having value in the shop—their culture. Moreover, the acquiring of skill and knowledge from Sherlock was enabling them to be more conversant with shop Masters about the domain. In short, their status in their culture was on the rise, and it is reasonable to attribute some of that ascendance to Sherlock.

Conclusion

What we have reported here are results from a culminating study in a body of empirical work that has spanned ten years. The instructional approach calls for detailed cognitive task analysis results to enable a learning environment where students construct understanding in authentic contexts, rooted in the needs of practice. Cognitive performance models provide detailed representations of expert task performance to use as the *targets of instruction*. In the details, the goals to which procedural knowledge applies and the strategic processes that are responsible for the organization, coherence, and general execution of the performance are clearly established. Knowledge is directly tied to its uses in the world, and tacit knowledge (including goals, strategies, and assumptions) is made explicit for teaching. Content is thereby richer, more precise, and surrounded by context that establishes conditions of use.

Better method has been achieved in Sherlock through a union of modern formulations of skill acquisition and traditional apprenticeship training techniques, such as modeling and coaching (Palincsar & Brown, 1984; Scardamalia & Bereiter, 1985; Schoenfeld, 1985). The common element in both is the notion of skill development as successive stages of increasingly mature performance. Hallmarks of apprenticeship training methods that are consistent with constructivist views include situated learning, external support or scaffolding in the instruction in the form of ideal modeling of the performance, hints, reminders, explanations, or even missing pieces of knowledge to assist the construction of understanding, and carefully sequenced learning activities that are both sensitive to changing student needs at different stages of skill acquisition and robust and diverse enough to foster integration and generalization of knowledge and skill (Collins, Brown, & Newman, 1989). Finally, to synthesize and reinforce the problem solving process, the solution steps are *reflected upon*, i.e., inspected, evaluated, and compared to examples of more advanced solutions at the end of each session. The Sherlock tutors were designed with these "better methods" driving the instructional blueprint.

References

Bielaczyc, K., Pirolli, P., & Brown, A. L. (1993, April). Strategy training in self-explanation and self-regulation strategies for learning computer programming. Report No. CSM-5. Berkeley, CA: University of California, School of Education.

Bloom, B. (1984). The 2 sigma problem: The search for methods of group instruction as effective as one-to-one tutoring. *Educational Researcher*, June/July.

Chi, M. T. H., & Van Lehn, K. (1991). The contents of physics self-explanations. *Journal of the Learning Sciences, 1*, 69–106.

Collins, A., Brown, J. S., & Newman, S. (1989). Cognitive apprenticeship: Teaching the crafts of reading, writing, and mathematics. In L. B. Resnick (Ed.), *Knowing, learning, and instruction: Essays in honor of Robert Glaser* (pp. 453–494). Hillsdale, NJ: Lawrence Erlbaum Associates.

Eggan, G., & Lesgold, A. (in press). Modelling requirements for intelligent training systems. In S. Dijkstra, H. P. M. Krammer, & J. J. G. van Merrienboer (Eds.), *Instructional-design models in computer-based learning environments*. Heidelberg: Springer-Verlag.

Glaser, R., Lesgold, A., & Gott, S. P. (1986). *Implications of cognitive psychology for measuring job performance*. Washington, DC: National Academy of Sciences Committee on the Performance of Military Personnel.

Gott, S. P. (1987). Assessing technical expertise in today's work environments. *Proceedings of the 1987 ETS Invitational Conference* (pp. 89–101). Princeton, NJ: Educational Testing Service.

Gott, S. P. (1989). Apprenticeship instruction for real-world cognitive tasks. In E. Z. Rothkopf (Ed.), *Review of research in education*. Vol. XV. Washington, DC: AERA.

Gott, S. P., Hall, E. P., Pokorny, R. A., Dibble, E., & Glaser, R. (1992). A naturalistic study of transfer: Adaptive expertise in technical domains. In D. K. Detterman & R. J. Sternberg (Eds.), *Transfer on trial: Intelligence, cognition, and instruction* (pp. 258–288). Norwood, NJ: Ablex Publishing Corp.

Gott, S. P., Pokorny, R. A., Alley, W. E., Kane, R. S., & Dibble, E. (in press). Development and evaluation of an intelligent tutoring system: *Sherlock 2—An avionics troubleshooting tutor*. AL/HR TR-95-XX. Brooks AFB TX.

Hall, E. P., Gott, S. P., & Pokorny, R. A. (in press). *A procedural guide to cognitive task analysis*. AL/HR TR-95-XX. Brooks AFB TX.

Kane, R. S. (1993). Frankenstation: Functional description and technical data. Unpublished manuscript.

Katz, S., & Lesgold, A. (1991). Modelling the student in Sherlock 2. In J. Kay & A. Quilici (Eds.), *Proceedings of the IJCAI-91 Workshop W.4: Agent modelling for intelligent interaction* (pp. 93–127). Sydney, Australia.

Katz, S., & Lesgold, A. (in press). The role of the tutor in computer-based collaborative learning situations. In S. Lajoie & S. Derry (Eds.), *Computers as cognitive tools*. Hillsdale, NJ: Lawrence Erlbaum Associates.

Katz, S., Lesgold, A., Eggan, G., & Gordin, M. (1992). Self-adjusting curriculum planning in Sherlock II. Lecture Notes in Computer Science. *Proceedings of the Fourth International Conference on Computers in Learning* (ICCAL '92). Berlin: Springer Verlag.

Katz, S., Lesgold, A., Eggan, G., & Gordin, M. (in press). Modelling the student in Sherlock 2. *Journal of Artificial Intelligence and Education* (Special issue on student modeling), Ed. J. A. Self. Association for the Advancement of Computing in Education (AACE).

Lajoie, S., & Lesgold, A. (1989). Apprenticeship training in the workplace: Computer coached practice environment as a new form of apprenticeship. *Machine-Mediated Learning, 3*, 7–28.

Lesgold, A. (in press). Assessment of intelligent training systems: Sherlock as an example. In E. Baker & H. O'Neil, Jr. (Eds.), *Technology assessment: Estimating the future*. Hillsdale, NJ: Lawrence Erlbaum Associates.

Lesgold, A., Eggan, G., Katz, S., & Rao, G. (1992). Possibilities for assessment using computer-based apprenticeship environments. In W. Regian & V. Shute (Eds.), *Cognitive approaches to automated instruction* (pp. 49–80). Hillsdale, NJ: Lawrence Erlbaum Associates.

Lesgold, A., Katz, S., Greenberg, L., Hughes, E., & Eggan, G. (in press). Extensions of intelligent tutoring paradigms to support collaborative learning. In S. Dijkstra, H. P. M. Krammer, & J. J. G. van Merrienboer (Eds.), *Instructional-design models in computer-based learning environments*. Heidelberg: Springer-Verlag.

Lesgold, A., & Katz, S. (1992). Models of cognition and educational technologies: Implications for medical training. In D. A. Evans & V. L. Patel (Eds.), *Advanced models of cognition for medical training and practice* (pp. 255–264). NATO ASI Series F, Vol. 97. Berlin: Springer-Verlag.

Lesgold, A. M., Lajoie, S. P., Bunzo, M., & Eggan, G. (1992). SHERLOCK: A coached practice environment for an electronics troubleshooting job. In J. Larkin & R. Chabay (Eds.), *Computer assisted instruction and intelligent tutoring systems: Shared issues and complementary approaches* (pp. 201–238). Hillsdale, NJ: Lawrence Erlbaum Associates.

Nichols, P., Pokorny, R., Jones, G., Gott, S. P., & Alley, W. E. (in press). *Evaluation of an avionics troubleshooting tutoring system*. AL/HR TR-94-XX. Brooks AFB TX.

Palincsar, A., & Brown, A. (1984). Reciprocal teaching of comprehension fostering and monitoring activities. *Cognition and Instruction, 1*(2), 117–175.

Perkins, D. N. (1991, May). Technology meets constructivims: Do they make a marriage? *Educational Technology, 31*(5), 18–23.

Pirolli, P., & Bielaczyc, K. (1989). Empirical analyses of self-explanation and transfer from learning to program. *Proceedings of the 11th annual conference of the Cognitive Science Society* (pp. 450–457). Hillsdale NJ: Lawrence Erlbaum Associates.

Pokorny, R. A., & Gott, S. P. (in press). *The evaluation of a real world instructional system: Using technical experts as raters.* AL HR TR-94-XX. Brooks AFB TX.

Scardamalia, M., & Bereiter, C. (1985). Fostering the development of self-regulation in children's knowledge processing. In S. F. Chipman, J. W. Segal, & R. Glaser (Eds.), *Thinking and learning skills: Research and open questions.* Hillsdale, NJ: Lawrence Erlbaum Associates.

Schoenfeld, A. H. (1985). *Mathematical problem solving.* New York: Academic Press.

VanLehn, K., Jones, R. M., & Chi, M. T. H. (1992). A model of the self-explanation effect. *Journal of the Learning Sciences, 2,* 1–59.

Whitehead, A. N. (1929). *The aims of education.* New York: Macmillan.

Appendix I: The F-15 Manual Avionics Test Station

A test station is a large switch, more or less like a telephone exchange. It also contains instruments for measuring electrical energy patterns, such as a digital multimeter and an oscilloscope, and devices for creating patterned energy inputs to the aircraft component being tested. Each test on a box from an aircraft (called a line-replaceable unit (LRU) or sometimes the unit under test (UUT)) involves applying patterned electrical energy to various inputs of the UUT and then connecting various of its outputs to a measurement device. A central section of the test station, called the relay assembly group (RAG) mediates the switching process. The technician sets various switches on the front of the test station to specify a particular test configuration, and then the RAG effects that configuration by energizing relays in giant switching trees. When all the relays are set properly, a signal circuit is created in which electrical inputs go from power supplies and signal generators on the test station, through an active connecting cable array (called the test package, TP), to the UUT, and outputs go from certain pins on the UUT's electrical interface through the switching array to a measurement device. On some test stations, a computer executes a series of tests of the UUT by directly controlling switching relays, but on the F-15 manual station, switching is effected via control settings on the test station's front panel.

When a test station fails, this failure is manifest in some function that the test station does not perform properly. A first requirement in the face of a possible failure is to be sure that the abnormal outcome is not due to a fault in the unit under test, the box from the aircraft. This is the most likely situation—after all the whole purpose of the test station is to reveal faults in aircraft components. Another possibility that must be ruled out is a failure of the test package, the component that connects the UUT to the test station. If both the UUT and the Test Package are operating normally, then the problem is in the test station itself.

The top-level diagnostic strategy would first attempt to isolate the problem into one of two main functional areas. Either the patterned energy inputs are not getting to the UUT, or its outputs are not getting to a measurement device successfully. A single test of the inputs of the test station to the UUT will reveal if the problem is on the signal input side or the output measurement side. The next step is to trace the signal through the pathway, ending with an identification of a component that receives good inputs but has faulty outputs. If this component is involved in the switching process, there are two ways it could be failing. Either it is broken itself, or it is receiving wrong control signals from the switches on the front panel of the test station. In this latter case, the control inputs to the component in question will be wrong, and attention should be turned to diagnosis of the path from control switches to the component now being addressed. On the other hand, if a component has good signal inputs, bad outputs, and good control inputs, then that component is a candidate for replacement.

This global strategy is really a combination of a weak or general method of space splitting, or "divide and conquer," with a specific model of the test station that provides an understanding of the meaningful units of the system that should be the focus of space splitting. The tactics for testing a particular subset of the test station, on the other hand, represent specific knowledge that can be generalized after appropriate experience and perhaps some expert suggestions.

Sherrie P. Gott is a Senior Research Psychologist at the Air Force Armstrong Laboratory, Brooks AFB, TX. Her research interests include the acquisition of complex problem-solving skills, applications of cognitive science to skill assessment and instruction, team learning and performance, and cognitive task analysis processes and methodologies. She recently directed a ten-year R&D effort for the Air Force that resulted in the development, evaluation, and implementation of intelligent tutors for aircraft maintainers who service the F15 aircraft.

Alan Lesgold conducts research on complex training skills and on applications of artificial intelligence to the design of computer-based learning and training systems. He is a professor in the Department of Psychology at the University of Pittsburgh and Associate Director of the Learning Research and Development Center (LRDC), where he leads a group addressing fundamental problems in schooling, and training people to be solid citizens and productive, flexible workers.

Master Sergeant **Ronald S. Kane** has sixteen years of experience in the United States Air Force, performing maintenance on the F15's Electronic Warfare (EW) systems. For the past four years, he has served as a subject matter expert and research associate with the Basic Job Skills (BJS) Research and Development program at the Armstrong Laboratory, Brooks AFB, TX. Prior to his assignment to Brooks, he served in Desert Storm. He became interested in the BJS program because it was the first electronics training system, to his knowledge, that focused on troubleshooting as a problem-solving skill, as opposed to emphasizing pure theory.

5

Case-based Teaching and Constructivism: Carpenters and Tools

Christopher K. Riesbeck

Introduction

The constructivist perspective on learning emphasizes the notion that knowledge is something that a student constructs, using his or her pre-existing knowledge. It is not something a teacher somehow tranfers into the student's head. Constructivism is not a particular model of learning, however. It does not describe a process or set of mechanisms by which this construction occurs. Hence, constructivism supports relatively weak claims for what learning environments should look like.

Case-based reasoning (CBR), on the other hand, is a well-developed model of reasoning and learning, quite compatible with constructivism, with specific claims about how knowledge is organized, acquired, and applied. Hence, CBR implies fairly specific principles for designing learning environments.

Our goal in this article is to describe (1) the case-based model of reasoning and learning, (2) the principles for learning environments that follow, (3) a class of learning environments, called Goal-based Scenarios, that embody these principles, and (4) the relationships between these principles and those that have been derived from purely constructivist approaches.

Case-based Reasoning

In essence, CBR means solving new problems by adapting old solutions, and interpreting new situations by comparing them to old situations. There are three basic processes: *retrieval*, *adaptation*, and *storage*. Given a new situation, the retrieval process finds a case in memory similar to it. A case is a description of some prior episode that *partially* matches the current situation. The adaptation process applies the information recorded in the old case to the new situation, taking into account the significant differences between the old and new situations. The storage process adds the new adapted case, along with any knowledge of how it performed, to memory for future use. Figure 5.1 is a sketch of a CBR system.

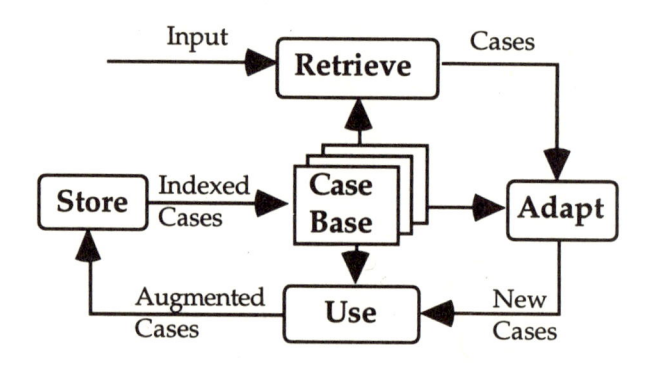

Figure 5.1. Basic CBR architecture.

Examples of CBR in everyday life include adapting recipes to include new ingredients, choosing a car by comparing it to cars you've owned before, designing a university building in the style of a British cathedral, and so on.

CBR is an alternative to the more traditional rule-based model of reasoning. Rules are traditionally smaller than cases, encoding one specific inference pattern, rather than an entire episodic chunk. Rules must be written as generally as possible, because there is no partial matching to ignore, no extraneous details. A rule either applies to a situation or it doesn't. A rule-based system constructs a new answer for each problem by combining the results of many rules. A CBR system, in contrast, retrieves a complete answer and modifies pieces of it to fit. Rule-based reasoning is similar to proving a theorem, while CBR is similar to reasoning by analogy, though the cases used are usually closer in content and structure than classical analogies, such as the analogy between an atom and the solar system.

Case-based Learning

The case-based model of reasoning implies that the most important things to learn are new cases and new ways to index cases. Learning cases means remembering what we've seen and done before, i.e., *learning by doing*. The problem, for both computers and people, is how to label the new cases appropriately so that they'll be retrieved later in relevant circumstances. This is called the *indexing* problem. If cases are labelled too specifically, they won't be remembered when similar situations arise. If they are labelled with irrelevant details, or too abstractly, they'll be remembered when inappropriate.

Case-based Teaching and Constructivism: Carpenters and Tools

Learning better ways to index cases means learning the underlying principles of what's important in a case. Our artificial intelligence research in building CBR systems has shown that *learning from failure* is an important means for learning new indices (Schank, 1986).

Let's follow an extended example of case-based reasoning and learning. Suppose I'm learning to program, and I come up with the following Pascal program for adding the numbers from 1 to 10:

```
program calcSum;
var i, sum: integer;
begin
sum := 0;
for i := 1 to 10 do sum = sum + i;
writeLn('The sum is ', sum)
end.
```

How should I index this example? If I index it as "how to add the numbers from 1 to 10," I won't recall it if I'm asked to *multiply* the numbers from 1 to 10. I won't even recall it if I'm asked to write a program to add the numbers from 1 to a *100!* On the other hand, if I index it as "a Pascal program," I will remember this program when it's not very helpful, e.g., when the problem is "print the largest of 5 numbers."

More reasonable indices focus on the goal ("collecting a sum") and the plan ("loop over a range of numbers"). Now the above code will be retrieved for problems such as "multiply the numbers from 1 to 20," which has a similar goal and plan. CBR research has shown that goals, plans, and their interactions are frequently good indices for cases (Hammond, 1989; Kolodner & Simpson, 1989; Riesbeck & Schank, 1989; Schank & Fano, 1992).

Now assume that I'm given the "multiply the numbers from 1 to 20" problem, I recall the above code, and I make the obvious changes to adapt it: I replace "sum" with "product," "+" with "*," and "10" with "20." This yields the following, with far less cognitive effort than the original program took:

```
program calcProduct;
var i, product: integer;
begin
product := 0;
for i := 1 to 20 do product = product * i;
writeLn('The product is ', product)
end.
```

Unfortunately, this leads to failure. When I run this code, it says that the product is 0. With a little work, I figure out that I'm multiplying 0 times 1 times 2 ...What I need to do is replace the "0" in the fourth line with a "1." Now it works.

What should I learn from this failure? At the least, I should learn that the type of operation involved (adding or multiplying) is an important feature for indexing and adapting examples of code. A tutor, watching what I do, would see this as a good opportunity to discuss the underlying concepts of additive and multiplicative identities. The post-failure explanation process is a critical period for learning new principles, as well as understanding better the principles implicit in previous cases (Ashley & Rissland, 1987; Schank, 1986).

Case-based Learning Environments

Primary Characteristics

CBR implies that what's important to learn are cases and the principles for indexing and adapting them. This implies the following design principles for learning environments:

- In order to learn cases, students need experiences. Hence, the learning environment should simulate a world in which they can have those experiences.
- In order to build a broad case base, students need more examples than they can possibly experience personally. Further, they need exposure to real cases, not just simulations. Hence, the learning environment should provide access to a case base of real-world experiences.
- In order to index cases with indices that promote recall and re-use, students need clear goals and plans. Hence, the learning environment should include clear roles and tasks for the student.
- In order to learn better indices, students need to fail sometimes. Hence, the learning environment should challenge students with hard problems.
- In order to construct those better indices, students need to construct good explanations of what went wrong. Hence, the learning environment must be very supportive of the explanation process.

Goal-based Scenarios

A *goal-based scenario* (GBS) is an architecture developed at the Institute for the Learning Sciences (ILS) for building case-based learning-by-doing courses (Schank et al., 1993). In a GBS, a student is given a role to play, e.g., owner of a trucking company or chief scientist at a nuclear research installation, and interesting problems to solve or goals to achieve. The role and problems should be of real interest to the student, e.g., feeding the world, getting rich, or flying a rocket to the moon, not artificial word problems, e.g., figuring out how much fence a mythical Farmer Brown needs.

The problem is solved by interacting with a simulated environment, e.g., an agricultural research lab, a command tent, or a hospital. The simulation includes graphical or video-based interactions with simulated agents.

When the student gets stuck or in trouble, a tutor, in video form, appears to offer advice, tell stories, and so on. The stories comes from a multimedia archive of texts and video interviews of experts in that domain, telling personal experiences similar to the student's simulated situation. These stories are also organized for browsing in a structure we call *ASK networks* (Ferguson et al., 1991).

In a GBS, the roles of tutor and expert are clearly separated. The experts are not teachers. They critique, suggest, comment, and so on, but their competence is in the subject material. They do not have curricula, pedagogical strategies, assessment methods, student models, and so on. That knowledge resides in the tutor module. Thus, while an expert may say "That bridge you've designed has a lot of problems," it is the tutor that says "Maybe this problem is too hard; let's try building an arch first." As a result, the expert's stories are re-usable in other pedagogical contexts, as are the tutor's teaching strategies.

Figure 5.2 summarizes the architecture of a GBS. Using Perkins' (1991) terminology, the construction kits and phenomenaria reside in the simulation module, the symbol pads in the interface, the information banks in the knowledge module, and the task manager in the teaching module. Most GBS's are designed as stand-alone virtual environments.

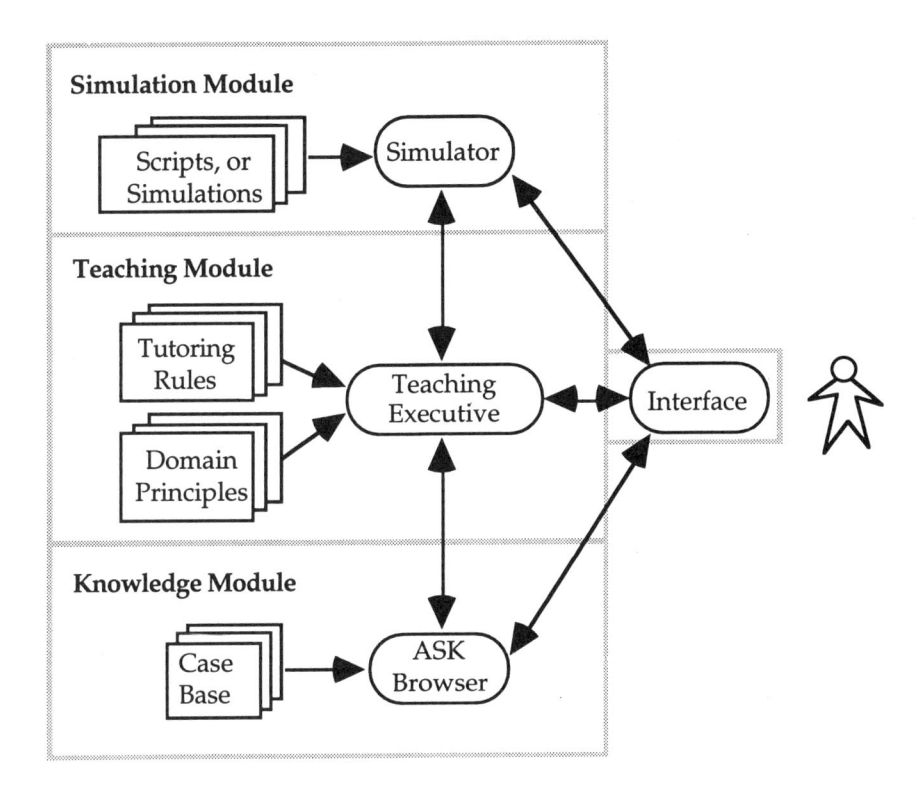

Figure 5.2. GBS architecture.

Types of Goal-based Scenarios

In our view, the goal of a course should be to learn skills, not facts. For example, we would not design a GBS to teach the Pythagorean formula, but we might design one where part of the student's job was to calculate distances, using that formula as one of several techniques. Similarly, when we have designed history GBS's, the goal has been to teach how to reason, explain, and predict from historical examples, e.g., in order to advise a decision maker such as the President, not to teach a particular set of historical facts.

There are two primary classes of skills students need to learn:
- process skills, e.g., being a bank teller, or flying a plane, where the focus is on learning one or more multi-step interrelated procedures. These are best taught with role-driven GBS's;

- outcome achievement skills, e.g., troubleshooting a diesel engine, or building a bridge, where the focus is on the result, and the techniques to achieve that result. These are best taught with outcome-driven GBS's.

Role-driven GBS's

In a role-driven GBS, there are right and wrong ways to do things, and the order in which they should be done is often important. Role playing in a GBS simulated situation reinforces the student's knowledge through rehearsal, repetition, and reflection. The specific GBS experiences motivate and exemplify the procedural principles. By letting students try different ways of doing things, they learn why things are done the way they are.

For example, Casper is an ILS-developed training system for customer service representatives (CSR's) (Kass, 1994). The CSR's work for a water utility and frequently have to deal with calls concerning water quality problems, e.g., water that has a funny color or smell. Many problems are not serious, but some are health-threatening. The goal of the CSR is to quickly determine what might be going on, and the goal of Casper is to teach procedures that quickly and accurately isolate possible causes. The tutor module in Casper watches for common problems, such as asking leading questions ("Is the water rust colored?"), making a diagnosis with too little evidence, failing to check important possibilities, getting stuck, and so on. When these happen, the tutor plays video clips of CSR's telling stories of what happened to them in similar situations, and uses a Socratic approach to guide the student along. A sample screen of Casper appears in Figure 5.3.

The heart of such a system is the richness and variety of the simulated interactions. These interactions are organized into *scripts* (Schank & Abelson, 1977). A script is a stereotypical sequence of events, often with branch points where events diverge, depending on what one of the actors in the script chooses to do.

The key to such courses is to have a large number of scripts, each with multiple branches, to encode the many things that can happen in the performance of some duty. For example, for someone to learn to be a bank teller, he or she needs to experience dealing with a wide variety of customers with a wide variety of requests.

Outcome-driven GBS's

In outcome-driven GBS's (Kass *et al.*, 1993–1994), the focus is on the result and the process by which it is achieved, not on procedures or scripts. There is rarely a single right next step, and there are usually many possible good answers.

The simulator lets the student try different actions and see what happens. The simulated environment responds, as the real world would, and, sometimes, the tutor appears to comment on what happened and answer questions about why it happened.

For example, Boss is an ILS-developed outcome-driven GBS for teaching management skills. One particular set of problems revolves around conflicts raised during employee evaluation. The student has to learn how to read evaluations, judge their fairness, critique the author of such evaluations in productive ways, deal with disagreements with those evaluations, and so on. As

Case-based Teaching and Constructivism: Carpenters and Tools 55

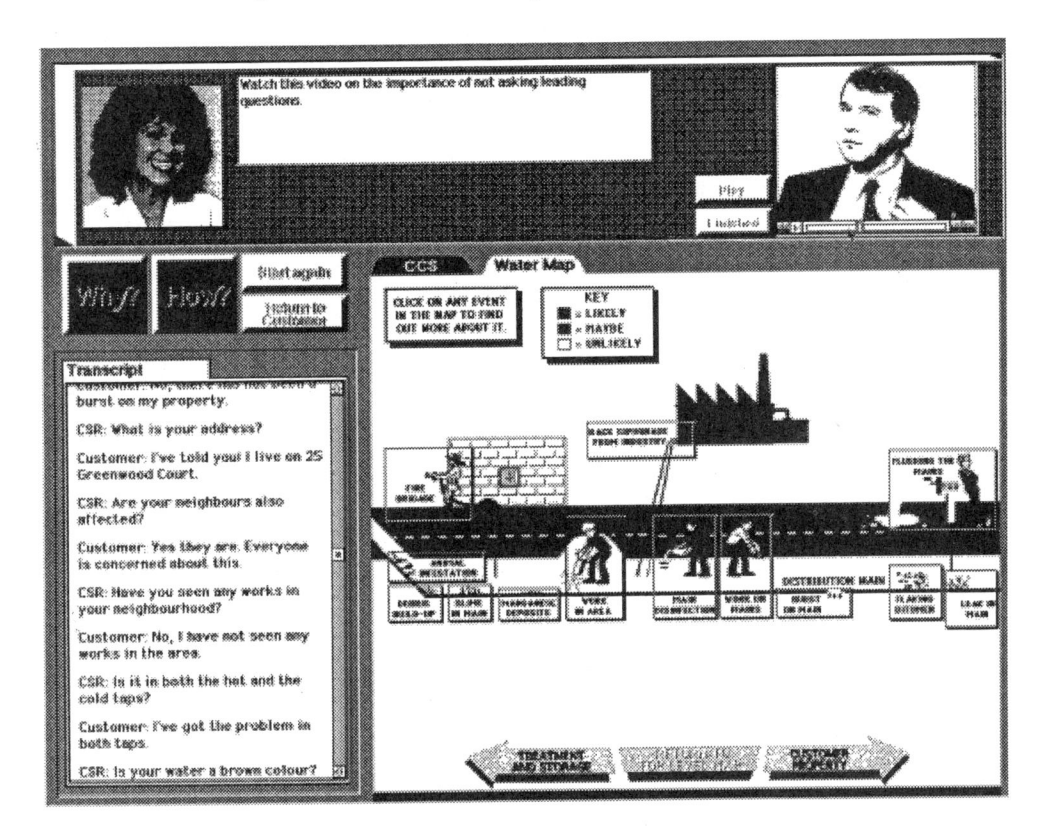

Figure 5.3. Sample screen from the Casper program.

in Casper, when the student gets stuck or makes a major mistake, video stories from experts are played by the tutor, illustrating important lessons to learn. A sample screen of Boss appears in Figure 5.4.

Instead of top-level scripts, outcome-driven simulations are built by specifying agents and objects (the tutor being one of the agents), their states and interrelationships, possible students actions, and how the states, relationships, and possible actions change for each action the student takes.

CBR and Constructivism, and Vice Versa

Representing Knowledge

CBR shows how constructivist principles can be embodied in a computational model, contrary to some views that the holistic nature of constructivism is incompatible with the analytic nature of computers, e.g., Jonassen (1991, p. 9). In particular, the CBR model fleshes out the constructivist notion that facts and concepts are not unitary items, but are distributed throughout memory. CBR's roots are in episodic memory (Schank, 1982). A concept like "hammer" is not a simple symbol, but an organizer of examples of hammer objects and of hammering. The latter is particularly important, because it is the examples of

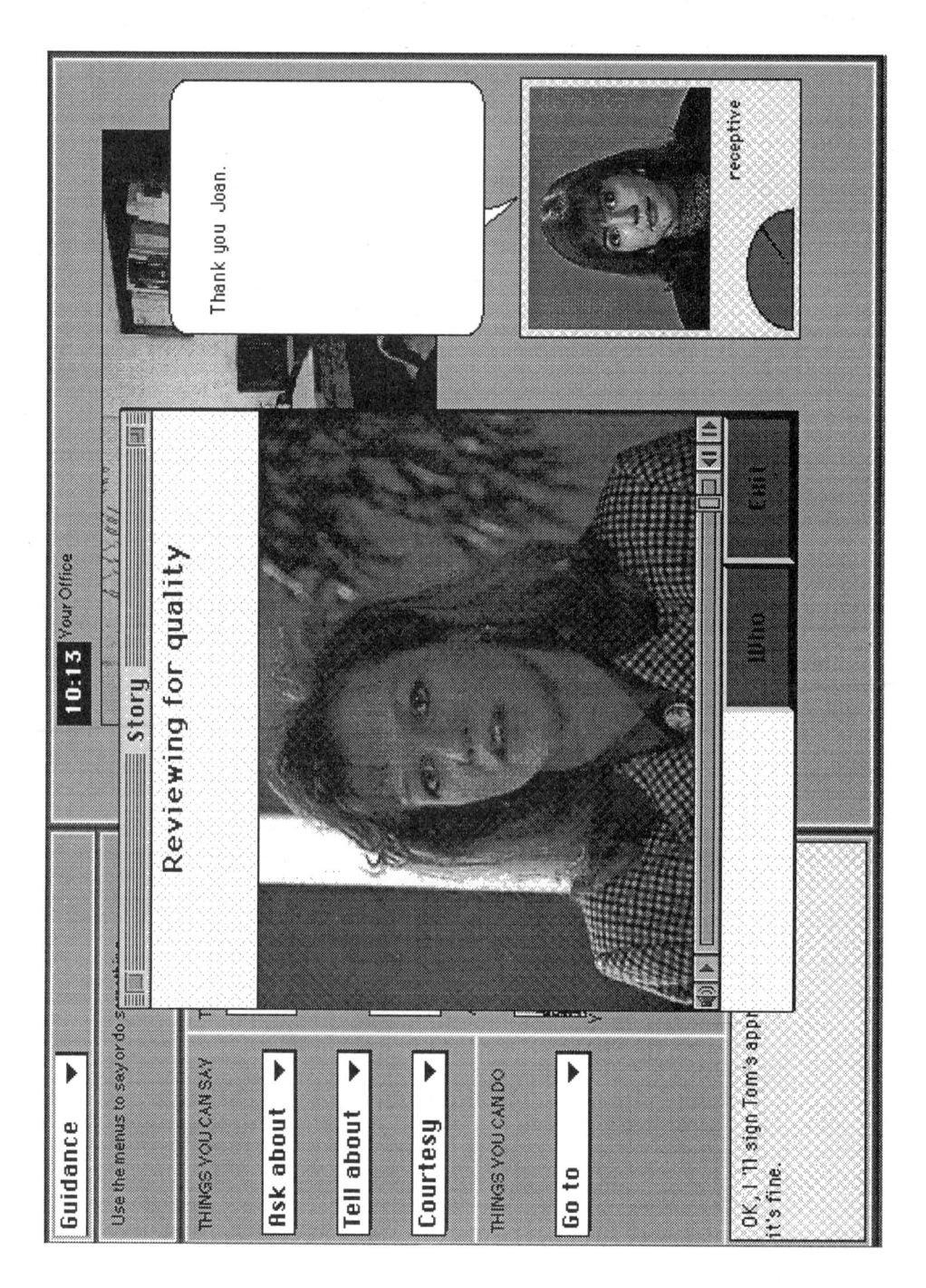

Figure 5.4. Sample screen from the Boss program.

hammering, not the examples of hammers, that allows someone to generalize "hammer" to rocks, baseball bats, and so on.

Constructivism in turn emphasizes a point about learning too often overlooked in discussions of case-based learning. It is quite common in CBR systems to talk about "adding new cases" or "initializing the case base," as if new cases are records in a database that can be simply added to the system. In fact, of course, except for some computer systems where programmers really can just ram data in, new cases have to be interpreted and integrated into memory just like everything else.

Constructing Knowledge

CBR implies a particular order to the construction of new knowledge. Particulars come before abstractions. Examples come before principles. This is because abstractions in CBR are used to organize, index, and adapt cases already in memory:

- Abstract categories subdivide sets of cases into more manageable subgroups.
- Abstract characterizations label cases for subsequent retrieval in relevant circumstances.
- Abstract models guide the adaptation process, identifying what is crucial and what can be changed or dropped when modifying a case.

Unless one of the above activities is occurring, generalization is—pun intended—an abstract exercise.

This view of abstractions, as organizers of existing experiences, rather than as universal categories under which future experiences will be placed, supports the common pedagogical principle of "do then reflect." It argues against both learning from lecture, where there is little opportunity for experience, and pure learning by doing, where there is no guidance in the formation of good abstractions.

"Deleting" Knowlege

CBR provides an answer to how knowledge can be "deleted." Much research in education and intelligent tutoring systems has focussed on the problem of identifying student misconceptions (Stevens et al., 1982), but, as noted in Smith et al. (1993–1994), there is an inherent conflict between constructivism and the notion that misconceptions can be replaced. Both constructivists and CBR researchers agree that knowledge is not something that can be deleted. Humans can't force themselves to stop remembering particular beliefs in certain situations.

Instead, in case-based learning, misconceptions are dealt with by putting the student in situations where those misconceptions cause failures and the failures have to be repaired. Tutoring helps the student extract the critical features of the situations to use as indices for the failure cases. When similar situations arise again, the student still recalls the misconceptions, but is also reminded of the failures. This lets the student consider whether to apply the old knowledge or not. If the old knowledge is consistently overridden by the new, eventually the retrieval of the new cases supersedes the old.

Direct Versus Indirect Instruction

Rieber (1992) argues that computer microworld systems, which would certainly include computer-based GBS's, can provide a compromise between direct instruction and the more undirected approach of constructivism. Rieber uses the example of teaching physics in the guise of training to be a space shuttle pilot. The student has a sense of control, because the sequences of activities fits naturally into a "career path." A curriculum designer, focussing on the presentation of physical principles, sees a traditional lesson plan.

Our argument is a little different. We don't see GBS's as occupying a middle ground on some scale of student control. The real issue is giving the student choices that matter to the student. For most students, it doesn't make sense to ask "Do you want to learn fractions or decimals first?" This is a blind choice. The student has no reason to care about either, much less which should be learned first. But it does make sense to ask "Do you want to be a space shuttle pilot, or run the shuttle transport business?" The latter question focusses on inherent student interests (Schank & Jona, 1991). No matter which answer they pick, we know they'll eventually have to learn some mathematics, but by letting them choose the task of greater interest, the relevance of what they'll have to learn will be clearer.

A choice between two options is still quite limiting. In our ideal school curriculum, there would be hundreds of GBS's, teaching the same basic skills in different guises. Students could be doctors, business tycoons, rocket scientists, engineers, explorers, environmentalists, and so on. All of these roles support scenarios that teach skills in reading, writing, mathematics, physics, social interaction, and so on.

Apprenticeship Versus Exploration

Exploratory environments, such as Logo (Papert, 1993), are sometimes viewed as embodying the constructivist ideal. In contrast, goal-based scenarios are more like apprenticeship situations (Stevens et al., 1982). The student gets to choose where to work, but, once on the job, the student is given very explicit goals. That is, the student picks whether to be a chemist or doctor or space shuttle pilot, but the system picks the initial goals to achieve.

Apprenticeship systems have obvious pedagogical advantages. The student encounters problems in a manageable order. The odds are higher that the student will get to more interesting places. The student can get some measure of progress and accomplishment. All of these are particularly important to beginners. As the student becomes more familiar with the territory, the system can "fade" (Collins et al., 1989) and let the student take over.

The apprenticeship approach also has practical advantages for case-based teaching systems. A case-based open-ended laboratory is simply not feasible in most subject areas, because (1) there are too many "uninteresting" places to get to, and (2) it's too hard to recognize the interesting places. The former is a standard problem with laboratory situations. The second is due to the current limitations of our computational models of intelligence. Recognizing the important features of something a student builds, when a student can do almost anything, is equivalent to the natural language understanding problem which remains an unsolved problem in AI.

Carpenters Versus Tool Kits

Related to the apprenticeship approach is the fact that case-based teaching emphasizes the presence of "experts." We believe that if you want to teach carpentry, you need carpenters. Tools alone are not enough. Tools give the student the power to build things, but do nothing to help evaluate what's been done, put it in perspective, or relate it to the real world

Experts provide such experience and perspective. Their stories have two important functions in a case-based system:

- Because the stories are about real experiences, they validate the simulated experiences of the student as relevant to real world activities.
- Because the stories are about analogous, but not identical situations, they encourage the student to abstract and generalize the simulated experiences.

We believe that both of these factors should increase transfer of knowledge learned in the simulation to real life.

Implementations

At the Institute for the Learning Sciences, we've implemented working prototypes of a number of computer-based GBS's. Three of them are:

- **Wetlands Manager:** The goal is teach biological and ecological principles. A student manages a wetlands area, trying to keep in balance the levels of water, vegetation, animal population, and human use. There are videos of wetlands in different states to show the student what their wetlands look like, and videos of wetlands managers talking about classic situations wetlands have fallen into.
- **FRA:** The goal is to teach business students the financial complexites of business. Students play the role of bank loan officers trying to decide whether to approve loans to various companies, based on various financial reports.
- **Sickle Cell Counselor:** Designed for the Museum of Science and Industry in Chicago, the goal is to teach the genetics underlying sickle cell disease. A student helps couples determine the likelihood of their children having the disease.

Summary

We've described the case-based model of reasoning and learning, which emphasizes the acquisition, organization, and application of episodic knowledge as the basis for human cognition. We've argued that this model implies that education should focus on teaching cases and case abstraction (indexing). We've presented an architecture for case-based courses, called goal-based scenarios, and briefly described some examples of GBS's in computer-based forms. Finally, we've contrasted this approach with constructivist methods. We've agreed that students do indeed construct their own knowledge, which is why learning by doing is so important. However, in order for the knowledge acquired to be recalled when relevant, it must be indexed properly. Good indexing is learned from failure, with a tutor guiding the explanation process, and experts providing the stories and the underlying principles of the subject matter.

Acknowledgments

This research was supported in part by the Defense Advanced Research Projects Agency, monitored by the Office of Naval Research under contracts N00014-91-J-4092 and N00014-90-J-4117. The Institute for the Learning Sciences was established in 1989 with the support of Andersen Consulting. The Institute receives additional support from its partners, Ameritech and North West Water.

References

Ashley, K. D., & Rissland, E. L. (1987). Compare and contrast: A test of expertise. *Proceedings of AAAI-87*, American Association for Artificial Intelligence, 273–278.

Collins, A., Brown, J. S., & Newman, S. E. (1989). Cognitive apprenticeship: Teaching the crafts of reading, writing, and mathematics. In L. B. Resnick (Ed.), *Knowing, learning, and instruction: Essays in honor of Robert Glaser* (pp. 453–494). Hillsdale, NJ: Lawrence Erlbaum Associates.

Ferguson, W., Bareiss, R., Osgood, R., & Birnbaum, L. (1991). ASK systems: An approach to story-based teaching. *Proceedings of the International Conference on the Learning Sciences* (pp. 158–164). Association for the Advancement of Computing in Education.

Hammond, K. J. (1989). *Case-based planning: Viewing planning as a memory task*. Boston: Academic Press.

Jonassen, D. H. (1991). Objectivism versus constructivism: Do we need a new philosophical paradigm? *Educational Technology Research and Development, 39*(3), 5–14.

Kass, A. (1994). *The Casper Project: Integrating simulation, case presentation, and Socratic tutoring to teach diagnostic problem-solving in complex domains*. The Institute for the Learning Sciences, Technical Report #51.

Kass, A., Burke, R., Blevis, E., & Williamson, M. (1993–1994). Constructing learning environments for complex social skills. *The Journal of the Learning Sciences, 3*(4), 387–427.

Kolodner, J. L., & Simpson, R. L. (1989). The MEDIATOR: A case study of an early case-based reasoner. *Cognitive Science, 13*(4), 507–549.

Papert, S. (1993). *The children's machine: Rethinking school in the age of the computer*. New York: Basic Books.

Perkins, D. N. (1991). Technology meets constructivism: Do they make a marriage? *Educational Technology, 31*(5), 18–23.

Rieber, L. P. (1992). Computer-based microworlds: A bridge between constructivism and direct instruction. *Educational Technology Research and Development, 40*(1), 93–106.

Riesbeck, C. K., & Schank, R. C. (1989). *Inside case-based reasoning*. Hillsdale, NJ: Lawrence Erlbaum Associates.

Schank, R. C. (1982). *Dynamic memory: A theory of learning in computers and people*. New York: Cambridge University Press.

Schank, R. C. (1986). *Explanation patterns: Understanding mechanically and creatively*. Hillsdale, NJ: Lawrence Erlbaum Associates.

Schank, R. C., & Abelson, R. (1977). *Scripts, plans, goals, and understanding*. Hillsdale, NJ: Lawrence Erlbaum Associates.

Schank, R. C., & Fano, A. (1992). *A thematic hierarchy for indexing stories in social domains*. The Institute for the Learning Sciences, Technical Report #29.

Schank, R. C., Fano, A., Jona, M. Y., & Bell, B. (1993). *The design of goal-based scenarios*. The Institute for the Learning Sciences, Technical Report #39.

Schank, R. C., & Jona, M. Y. (1991). Empowering the student: New perspectives on the design of teaching systems. *The Journal of the Learning Sciences, 1*(1), 7–35.

Smith, J. P. III, DiSessa, A. A., & Roschelle, J. (1993–1994). Misconception reconceived: A constructivist analysis of knowledge in transition. *The Journal of the Learning Sciences*, 3(2), 115–163.

Stevens, A., Collins, A., & Goldin, S. E. (1982). Misconceptions in students' understanding. In D. Sleeman & J. S. Brown (Eds.), *Intelligent tutoring systems* (pp. 13–24). Orlando, FL: Academic Press.

Christopher K. Riesbeck is with the Institute for the Learning Sciences, and the Department of Electrical Engineering and Computer Science at Northwestern University, Evanston, Illinois.

Part Two

Classroom-Based Learning Environments

6

Rich Environments for Active Learning in the Higher Education Classroom

Joanna C. Dunlap
R. Scott Grabinger

In today's complex and uncertain world, simply knowing how to use tools for gathering information is not enough to remain competitive. Industry specialists are reporting that people at every organizational level must be creative and flexible problem solvers—an ability based on knowledge construction skills and not simply information gathering skills (Lynton, 1989). Even members of the "blue collar" workforce are required to demonstrate an advanced level of problem solving skill in order to attain and retain employment. For example, employees working on computerized/robotic assembly lines need to be able to troubleshoot problems involving highly technical and advanced machinery. This requires the ability to flexibly use past experience and knowledge to address new problems. Employees working in customer service jobs must be able to diagnose a customer's problem and find information to solve that problem within a few minutes.

Consequently, learning to think critically and to analyze and synthesize information to solve technical, social, economic, political, and scientific problems are crucial for successful and fulfilling participation in a modern, competitive society. Changing circumstances and societal needs have strengthened the link between education—specifically, what happens in the higher education classroom—and the economy. However, according to Lynton (1989, p. 23), "At this time...education is far from fully contributing to the economic well-being of this country [United States]." It is difficult to give people the individual attention they need to develop critical thinking and problem solving skills in a typical higher education classroom setting. Yet, the responsibility for preparing people to be productive employees and members of society has fallen to higher education classroom educators (Lynton, 1989). In other words, educators have to consider how best to teach for transfer—to teach thinking skills that are transferable (Gagné, Briggs, & Wager, 1992), as opposed to specific skills for each situation which builds students' performance on a narrow range of school tasks (Perkins & Salomon, 1988).

Unfortunately, in spite of a great deal of research on transfer (for a review of research on transfer, see Butterfield & Nelson, 1989), there is still a considerable level of vagueness regarding how to teach for transfer (Perkins & Salomon, 1988). According to Butterfield (1988), successful transfer requires the acquisition of directly relevant knowledge, inferential reasoning and the monitoring and regulation of problem solving, and metacognitive skill. In typical higher education classroom environments, the emphasis of instruction is on the transfer of specific tasks, as opposed to providing instruction about skills leading to the ability to transfer (Winn, 1993).

To begin to address the issue of transfer in order to meet employer and societal needs, reasoning and problem solving skill development must be an integrated part of an interdisciplinary program of study in higher education classrooms (Lynton & Elman, 1987)—a program or environment that places students in situations where they can practice solving problems in a meaningful and constructive manner. One educational strategy that can be implemented in a higher education classroom in order to help bridge the gap between higher education and employment requirements is the use of rich environments for active learning (REALs). Providing an alternative approach to the typical lecture-based delivery of instruction found in many higher education classrooms, rich environments for active learning are comprehensive instructional systems that:

- encourage student responsibility and decision making and intentional learning in an atmosphere of collaboration among students and instructors;
- promote study and investigation within meaningful and information-rich contexts; and
- utilize participation in dynamic activities that promote high level thinking processes, including problem solving, experimentation, creativity, discussion, and examination of topics from multiple perspectives.

REALs encourage students to develop initiative and responsibility for their own learning within active and meaningful contexts.

This article presents an overview of rich environments for active learning by defining and describing critical features and strategies employed for effective use in higher education classroom settings. Descriptions of how REALs can be implemented in higher education classrooms are also provided.

What Are REALs?

Consistent with goals stated by educators attempting to restructure the way students learn (American Association for the Advancement of Science, 1989; National Council of Teachers of Mathematics, 1989; Resnick & Klopfer, 1989),

REALs are based on constructivist values including "collaboration, personal autonomy, generativity, reflectivity, active engagement, personal relevance, and pluralism" (Lebow, 1993, p. 5). Constructivist learning environments provide opportunities for learning activities in which students, instead of having knowledge "transferred" to them, are engaged in a continuous collaborative process of building and reshaping understanding as a natural consequence of their experience and interaction with the world (Goodman, 1984; Forman & Pufall, 1988; Fosnot, 1989). Advocating a holistic approach to education, constructivist learning environments reflect the assumption that the process of knowledge and understanding acquisition is "firmly embedded in the social and emotional context in which learning takes place" (Lebow, 1993, p. 6). These types of constructivist beliefs are strongly represented in the concepts of intentional learning (Scardamalia et al., 1989), authentic activity and situated cognition (Brown, Collins, & Duguid, 1989), and in such constructivist-based learning and instructional theories as cognitive flexibility theory (Spiro et al., 1991) and cognitive apprenticeship (Collins, Brown, & Newman, 1989).

A leader in the development of constructivist learning environments is the Cognition and Technology Group at Vanderbilt (CTGV). Through the Jasper Woodbury series of videodisc-based learning materials, environments for science and mathematical problem solving have been created based on three building blocks: generative learning, anchored instruction, and cooperative learning (CTGV, 1993). These three building blocks provide a helpful structure for describing the key characteristics of constructivist learning environments.

Generative Learning

An important requirement of constructivist learning environments is that learning must be generative. Generative learning, learning in which students are asked to deliberately take action to create meaning from what they are studying (Wittrock, 1974, 1978), requires students to "engage in argumentation and reflection as they try to use and then refine their existing knowledge as they attempt to make sense of alternate points of view" (CTGV, 1993, p. 16). This requires a shift in the traditional roles of students and instructors. Students become investigators, seekers, and problem solvers. Teachers become facilitators and guides, rather than presenters of knowledge. For example, students in an instructional technology teacher education class work with lesson plans and objectives and manipulate and change them to solve a new teaching problem rather than simply copying down information and memorizing it for an upcoming exam. They are, in essence, learning to apply these skills for the purpose of creating lessons. In other words, students learn how to *use* or *apply* the information in a variety of contexts; generative learning activities require students to take static information and *generate* fluid, flexible, usable knowledge.

Anchored Instruction

Anchored instruction occurs within a realistic context that is appealing and meaningful to students (Bransford et al., 1990). For example, students in an instructional design and development class work in teams with actual clients to develop instruction that will be delivered to another group of students. They must define the problem, identify resources, set priorities, and explore alternative solutions—the same skills and abilities that are required during realistic, outside-of-the-classroom problem solving and decision making activities. This is in direct contrast to the way students develop component skills and objectives in a more traditional classroom environment by working working with simplified, decontextualized problems using the same strategies and arriving at the same answers. Simply stated, it is the difference between providing meaningful learning activities and "I'm never going to use this" activities.

Cooperative Learning

Constructivists argue that cooperative learning and cooperative problem solving groups facilitate generative learning. Working in peer groups helps students refine their knowledge through argumentation, structured controversy, and reciprocal teaching. In addition, students are more willing to take on the additional risk required to tackle complex, ill-structured, authentic problems when they have the support of others in the cooperative group. Related, cooperative learning and cooperative problem solving groups also address students' need for scaffolding during unfamiliar learning and problem solving activities; in other words, with the support of others in the group, students are more likely to achieve goals they may not have been able to meet on their own.

Often, as soon as you mention cooperative groups in a higher education classroom, the response is, "Ahh...do we have to," or "Oh, no, not again." Unfortunately, many students have had negative experiences in cooperative groups because of unfair division of labor. However, we emphasize that true cooperative learning is not about division of labor. There are techniques for providing the appropriate amount of structure and scaffolding necessary for less-skilled groups to work together—equally, fairly, and in a way so that everyone gets something out of the experience. For generative learning to work, all students must be active learners, not only when they are working individually but also when they are working with others in a cooperative group. In order to use cooperative groups to support and enhance generative learning activities, instructors need to apply appropriate facilitating techniques to make sure all students are active learners.

REALs reflect current thinking in the area of constructivist learning environments. For example, in a recent article on constructivist values for instructional systems design, Lebow (1993) presents five key principles for designing constructivist learning environments:

1. Protect learners from potentially damaging instructional practices by promoting personal autonomy and learner control, supporting self-regulation, and making instruction personally relevant to the learner.
2. Create a context for learning that supports the development of personal autonomy as well as relatedness.
3. Provide learners with the reasons for learning within the learning activity.
4. Support self-regulation by promoting the development of the skills and attitudes that enable learners to take on increasing responsibility for their own learning.
5. Encourage intentional learning and examination of errors.

REALs fulfill the objectives of constructivist learning environments, as described by Lebow and others (see Honebein *et al.*, 1993; Kyle *et al.*, 1992; Presidential Task Force on Psychology in Education, 1993), by:
- extending students' responsibility and ownership (see also the chapter by Savery and Duffy in this book);
- promoting study, investigation, and problem-solving in authentic (i.e., reflecting the true complexity, ill-structuredness, and ever-changing nature of on-the-job, in-the-world problems and situations), meaningful, and satisfying contexts; and
- utilizing dynamic learning activities that promote higher-level operations (knowledge construction).

The following sections defines each of these three main design goals and describes how they can be realized in a higher education classroom.

1. Extending Students' Responsibility and Ownership

Picture a typical higher education classroom assignment such as worksheets, essays, papers, homework, problems, and so on. The assignment, developed by the instructor after considerable time and effort, provides students with the following information:
- what they will learn;
- how they will learn it, including the activities they have to do to complete the assignment;
- the questions that have to be answered;
- what classroom and/or library resources need to be used; and
- when the assignment is due.

In other words, everything the students have to do is mapped out for them in significant detail, leaving nothing left to speculation or the imagination. And, when the students have completed the assignment, the instructor assesses and evaluates them on how well they were able to follow the "rules" of the assignment. When considered in this light, we need to ask: who is, in fact, doing the major cognitive processing and learning on the assignments? Who should be doing all the work?

Usually, we think of the student as doing most of the work on assignments, and hopefully learning in the process. However, upon reflection, it is apparent that the instructor is doing most of the work, and most of the learning. When developing assignments for students, it is customary for instructors to set the goals, plan the objectives, select the strategies, ask the questions, and evaluate the work. The irony is that these tasks are all high level cognitive activities involving analysis, synthesis, evaluation, application, and assimilation. Aren't those the same kinds of activities that we want students to perform? Unfortunately, in many higher education classroom settings, students take less active roles, often simply receiving information and reacting to selected activities in instructor-determined ways; in other words, students engage in low-level rote or algorithmic activities that leave little room for higher level activities. In fact, students are usually not allowed to engage in these types of activities because instructors believe that they lack the skills needed to initiate and take on the responsibility for their own educational process. The following guidelines focus on strategies that instructional designers and instructors can use to make students more responsible for their own learning in a higher education setting.

1.1. Enable students to determine what they need to learn through questioning and goal setting.

Students should work to identify their knowledge and skill deficits and to develop strategies for meeting those deficits in the form of personal learning goals. Students should learn to compare what they know to what they do not know and ask questions to guide their quest for new knowledge. This is traditionally the role of the instructor. However, this does not absolve instructors from the responsibility of determining what is needed. Instead, it recognizes that the learner, too, must agree with what is needed in order to create a sense of ownership in the learning process.

One of the advantages of encouraging students to identify their own knowledge and skill deficits is that this treats knowledge lacks and mistakes in a positive way. Most instructional activities require students to display their knowledge; students are rewarded for showing knowledge gains and for hiding knowledge deficits. For example, an instructor may ask students to respond to a set of questions. If students provide the correct answers to the questions, then they have been "successful" and are rewarded with praise from the instructor and peer recognition. But, if a student does not know the correct answer, then his or her lack of knowledge emerges as a form of failure: the instructor may provide negative feedback (e.g., "No...that is incorrect.") and immediately call on another student to answer the question. As a consequence, the student may feel punished, embarrassed, or stupid. Instead, instructors need to place an equal emphasis on rewarding students for honest analysis and self-assessment in identifying what they do not know.

Another advantage of encouraging students to identify their own knowledge and skill deficits is that it is very difficult for one instructor in a higher education classroom to consistently assess what each student knows and doesn't know for each new concept covered. If instructors can help guide students in the identification of what they already know and what they need to learn, then students can assume more responsibility in addressing their learning needs during an instructional unit.

1.2. Enable students to manage their own learning activities.

After setting goals, students need to develop plans to achieve those goals. Ordinarily, selection of strategies, tactics, and resources falls within the province of the instructor. However, to become independent learners students must also learn to engage in those activities. A learning plan should describe priorities, instructional tactics, resources, deadlines, roles in collaborative learning situations, and proposed learning outcomes, including presentation and dissemination of new knowledge and skills, if applicable.

This is another place where the traditional roles of both instructors and students change radically. Remember, students are used to being "told" what to do (e.g., what to read, what to write, what to study, what to memorize); their involvement in the planning and development of learning activities is minimal. Teachers arrange the instructional events that occur during a semester or school year in order to achieve a specified set of predetermined objectives. Stated simply, instructors are used to being "obeyed" by students. The instructor assigns, the student does. It is a time honored role. However, a complex society demands members who are better able to act flexibly and to take initiative when facing a problem. Unfortunately, years of being told what to do by others does not foster the initiative or the ability to solve problems and to make decisions with any range of flexibility or innovation.

But, it isn't easy for students to learn to take the initiative. They cannot suddenly be "told" to start planning their own learning activities because it is a new role for which they have had little prior experience, practice, or training. (Teachers may also know many more learning options, including strategies and resources, than do students.) If left on their own, students may continue to choose the same learning strategies over and over again, even if they are inappropriate, ineffective, or inefficient. Teachers can provide students with options they have not considered or do not know about. Because of the difficulty involved in taking initiative in the learning process, students must be guided and supported by the instructor, slowly taking on more and more control within their zones of proximal development and at their own individual paces. Growth must be a progressive process beginning with small steps. Even in higher education this is true. Our own experiences in modifying classes to use these guidelines got off to a very shaky start because we assumed that adults in graduate school have these skills. That is not the case. Adults as well as children need a great deal of scaffolding to learn to be independent learners.

Students should be encouraged to write down their plans to serve as a reference during the learning activities. They can then use their plans to assess whether they have met their goals. Depending on the maturity and ability level of the students, instructors may provide varying levels of support, everywhere from no help to extensive lists of options (e.g., go to the library, interview expert, access on-line encyclopedias, conduct an experiment, etc.) for the students to use as thought stimulators. The teacher must help the students adopt the practice of reflecting on their experiences, plans, successes, and failures.

In order to manage their own learning activities, students also need to utilize basic project management skills. In a traditional operating mode, instructors tell the students how much time they have and when they must be finished. Everybody finishes at the same time. However, given different levels of complexity for problems being addressed or questions being researched, it is not realistic to expect everyone to finish at the same time. Students should be taught to estimate their own time requirements. Again, this can be done within a structure developed by the instructor. Perhaps a block of time can be assigned by the instructor or a terminal point. But, students should begin to get a concept of time and try to monitor how their learning progresses and how much time each step takes.

1.3. Help students develop metacognitive skills.

Metacognition is a loosely defined concept that refers to the awareness and regulation of one's own cognitive processes (Flavell, 1976). Metacognitive knowledge includes information about ourselves as learners, the kinds of tasks we encounter, and the strategies we employ to influence the outcome of cognitive activities (see Baker & Brown, 1984; Flavell, 1976; Flavell & Wellman, 1977). In other words, metacognitive awareness means that learners are thinking about the effectiveness of the learning strategies they are using during learning activities. For example, if students are memorizing the order of the planets from the sun, they could be asked to describe how they did it. If the students are metacognitively aware, then they would know whether they used a repetition strategy or a mnemonic strategy. Because metacognitive strategies and reflective thinking are not learned automatically, students need to be engaged in activities that teach and support the use of metacognitive skills (von Wright, 1992). Activities such as cooperative learning and reciprocal teaching (Palincsar & Brown, 1984), as well as the activities described by Scardamalia *et al.* (1989) as related to computer-supported intentional learning environments, encourage and enhance the development and use of metacognitive strategies, high-level reasoning, and interpersonal skills (Johnson & Johnson, 1990). REALs utilize these strategies to not only support students in their metacognitive skill development, but to extend students' overall responsibility for managing their own learning.

Metacognitive awareness is a skill that is associated with successful learners. Successful learners are able to analyze what they are doing—what strategies they are employing—and evaluate their value. Less successful learners never think to try different learning strategies because they don't realize that the techniques they are using are not as appropriate or effective for the task on which they are working.

The process of assessing metacognitive strategies should be made overt to help students become aware of what they are doing. Students should be expected to produce records about the processes and strategies they use, as well as products reflecting their knowledge. It is just as important to reflect the process of learning as well as the resulting products. Associative memory tasks should provide strategies for memorizing—mnemonics, or drill and practice. Problem solving should record overt evidence of participation in the problem-solving steps, including hypothesis generation, solution experimentation, and analysis of problem components, constraints, and resources.

Students should be frequently encouraged to reflect on the processes they are using during the learning process, to compare one strategy to another, and to evaluate the effectiveness of a strategy for the particular learning activity the students are engaged in. They should be stopped and asked, "What are you doing? Is it working? If it isn't, what are your other options?" In other words, students need to be given time to reflect on their thinking processes by asking themselves (or being prompted by the instructor or peers) questions, such as:

- Which strategies did you use? Which ones worked? Which ones didn't work?
- What would you do differently next time?
- What would you do similarly next time?
- What was your single, most important difficulty in solving the problem?
- Did you start by looking at the overall problem, or did you immediately break the problem down into smaller chunks?
- What would you do differently if you had more time and resources to work on the problem? Less time and resources?

Students should be encouraged to recognize frustration and blocks in the learning process. They should be taught to identify the source of that frustration and encouraged to seek help from other students and instructors. Teachers must keep a watchful eye for signs of frustration, but avoid telling students what to do next. Instead, instructors need to guide the students through the frustrations by helping them understand both the causes of the frustrations and the learning strategies they are employing. They should be taught to discriminate between frustration caused by problems and frustrations caused by inappropriate strategies.

Student responsibility is a crucial aspect of creating a rich environment for active learning (REAL). The primary idea behind a REAL is to create an environment where students create complex, rich knowledge structures that apply to a variety of problems. However, in order to become capable problem solvers, students must know how to learn and be willing and able to take responsibility for identifying learning deficits, setting goals, managing the learning process, and monitoring the learning strategies they use.

2. Situate Learning in Meaningful Contexts

"Why do I have to learn this stuff?"
"I'll never have to do this in the *real* world."
"What does this have to do with anything?"

Higher education instructors often find themselves bombarded with several "Why do we have to do this?" questions during instruction. Interestingly enough, these questions typically accompany one specific instructional activity: the introduction of new content presented out of context, such as introducing sentence structuring and diagramming without involving the students in writing activities; or introducing computer programming concepts without putting the students in front of computers.

In many situations, content is often presented to learners in simplified, decontextualized, isolated chunks that promote memorization rather than problem solving or higher-level thinking. This kind of instructional process makes it difficult to help students see interrelationships among content areas, the inherent complexity of the content, or the content's applicability to actual problems and meaningful situations. In order to make learning meaningful for students, two main instructional issues need to be addressed:

- How can we help students apply the information they learn?
- How can we make the need and reason to learn content apparent?

REALs address these issues by encouraging students to use their existing knowledge and by anchoring the instruction in meaningful, realistic contexts. The following guidelines describe how learning can be made more meaningful for students and presents the research that supports these prescriptions.

2.1. Make maximum use of existing knowledge.

Knowledge comes from a continuous process of construction that builds on existing knowledge structures, or what is already known. Taking a constructivist view of learning, the learner's knowledge representations "are constantly open to change, its structure and linkages forming the foundation to which other knowledge structures are appended" (Bednar et al., 1991, p. 91). Therefore, the learning of new material is facilitated by calling upon existing knowledge to serve as a point of reference and as a foundation from which new knowledge structures are built.

One question that is often asked in the higher education classroom is, "What does this have to do with what I already know?" Students want to understand and make the connections between existing and new knowledge not only because it facilitates new learning, but because, in general, students are more comfortable with what they are familiar with. Unfortunately, we often don't take the time to allow students to explore and determine these connections on their own. Therefore, in order to address this issue, it is necessary to engage students in classroom activities that allow them to consider how their new learning is related to and supported by their existing knowledge; in other words, we need to build opportunities for reflection on what they already know into learning activities.

One way to help students make use of their existing knowledge is to ask them to explicitly describe the relationships between new information and existing information through text, visuals, analogies, oral discussion, computer-based mind tools, and other instructional materials. Students must generate overtly the relationships between new and existing knowledge. It is necessary to allow students to elucidate the relationship themselves, while gently guiding them if they are on the wrong track. Again, one of the reasons for this is based on constructivism theory (Bednar et al., 1991). Constructivists believe that each student constructs an individual view of the reality being discussed or examined (Bednar et al., 1991). This does not necessarily deny the existence of common knowledge, but that common knowledge is developed through social interaction and negotiation. If this is the case, it is not very effective for instructors to relate a "common" view of new and old knowledge to students. Instead, students are better off relating their own understandings of the concepts and problems, with instructors assisting with misunderstandings and misrepresentations.

2.2. Anchoring instruction in realistic situations enhances the meaningfulness of the content.

Anchored instruction refers to instruction that reflects realistic, complex, ill-structured situations. Rather than separating new content into its component skills, the skills are taught holistically within a meaningful problem-solving context and with their links and interrelationships intact.

This guideline is based on an apprenticeship learning model (Brown, Collins, & Duguid, 1989), in which students actually learn by doing because they work on realistic tasks. This guideline directly addresses students' questions, "Why do we need to learn this stuff?" and "I'm never going to do this in the *real* world." When instruction is anchored in a meaningful and realistic context, the answers to these questions become obvious and apparent.

Anchored instruction does not imply that instruction needs to reflect actual situations with 100% fidelity. The maturity and ability of the learners and the nature of the content must be taken into consideration when creating a context for the instruction. The role of the instructor is contingent on how much complexity and detail is necessary to make the learning activities meaningful. Students have to learn to deal with a variety of stimuli within the context. Unfortunately, this is often a difficult leap for students because their typical higher education classroom-based problem solving activities have required them to deal with and handle only a limited set of stimuli in a decontextualized situation. In other words, students are used to solving the same simplified, decontextualized problems in the same way, over and over again. But, in anchored instruction, the students must learn to handle and work with authentic problems that have the natural complexity and ill-structuredness of actual problems. Therefore, the amount of scaffolding that the instructor must provide varies, depending on the previous problem-solving experiences students have been exposed to and the level of complexity and ill-structuredness of the problems they now have to tackle.

2.3. Provide multiple ways to learn content.

Meaningful learning can also be promoted by providing variety in the learning activities. Given that students are accepting more responsibility and that they are working in authentic contexts that relate to things they know, students must be free to pursue a variety of ways to learn. Some students learn better individually, others in groups. Some like to read, others like to listen. Some take notes, others sit listening. Some like to talk things out with others, while others need time to reflect. Still others prefer to approach a problem from the end rather than the beginning. If we believe that proposition, then we must give students more responsibility, then the responsibility must carry over into the ways they gather information and learn content—skills needed to be life-long learners.

Making learning meaningful has always been recognized as a critical element in learning. The primary idea behind a REAL is to create an environment where students create complex, rich knowledge structures that apply to a variety of problems. This cannot be done from decontextualized, lower level activities. To become capable problem solvers, instructors must provide students with a variety of learning activities that are anchored or situated in realistic problems, while showing them how to use their existing knowledge to address each new situation.

3. Engaging Students in Dynamic, High-Level Knowledge Construction

In order to bridge the classroom-workplace gap, students must be able to engage in on-the-job problem solving and decision making under ill-structured and complex circumstances, higher education students have to be involved in problems solving and higher-level thinking activities—referred to as *reflection-in-action* (Schön, 1983) or *dynamic knowledge construction*. Therefore, instead of being told what to know about specific content areas, an act that Bruner (1990) refers to as *imposing* understanding on someone, students must engage in their own active construction of knowledge in order to be prepared for and to live up to employers' expectations. In order to appropriately address this need, educators and instructional designers need strategies for creating learning environments that will enable dynamic knowledge construction by students.

3.1. Use activities that promote high-level thinking.

Glaser (1990) describes a shift in instructional theory from an emphasis on performance to an emphasis on learning due to the growing demand for people who are able to think and reason in novel settings. This shift focuses our attention on helping students to construct knowledge and understanding for themselves rather than teaching them specific information (Spiro & Jehng, 1990). Higher education teachers need to develop activities that encourage students to construct knowledge and understanding. While more successful students seem to be able to initiate these activities on their own, less successful students need a structure to help them learn and use higher-level thinking strategies for knowledge construction. REALs providing scaffolding and support so students become more comfortable with and skilled at tackling knowledge construction activities including ambiguous information; authentic, ill-structured problems; controversy and argumentation; and judgments and decision making.

- ambiguous information,
- authentic, open-ended problems with the natural uncertainty, complexity, and ill-structuredness intact,
- controversy and argumentation, and
- judgments and decision-making.

Making predictions, interpretations, and hypotheses. One way to engage students in higher-level thinking is to present them with an open-ended scenario and have them interpret the situation and predict what will happen next. Students also need to explain why they have made particular predictions, including what evidence presented in the scenario that led them to form their particular hypotheses. These types of activities can be conducted with students working individually or in small, collaborative groups. Either way, students need to explicitly present their predictions and hypotheses. Articulation is important because it is necessary for students to practice stating their positions, views, perspectives, ideas, and solutions in order to prepare them for what they will have to do once they leave school. Also, students must articulate their hypotheses to hear how others determined and justified their predictions. Besides managing the activity to ensure complete and equitable student participation, the instructor in the higher education classroom must reinforce the notion that there are many possible predictions that can be derived from one scenario.

Engaging in exploratory learning and experimentation. Another way to encourage students to become involved in higher-level thinking activities is to give them opportunities to explore content based on their own individually determined needs and desires, and allow them to experiment with new concepts. Students need to be encouraged to explore, alter, and manipulate the parameters of the content, problem, or environment, and to discover and examine all possible outcomes and solutions. Exploratory and experimentation learning activities provide students with opportunities that allow for the "rearranging or transforming (of) evidence in such a way that one is enabled to go beyond the evidence so reassembled to additional new insights...." (Bruner, 1961, p. 22). The students become explorers discovering and solving problems on their own (Schank & Jona, 1991).

3.2. Encourage students to revisit content and problems from different perspectives, given a variety of different constraints.

When successful students work on problems, they constantly refine their decisions in order to come up with more effective and efficient strategies, approaches, and solutions. They enjoy making revisions and have confidence in their own solutions. Less successful students tend to stop at one pass through information and usually only examine one viewpoint. They are reluctant to make revisions or to seek more efficient and effective solutions to problems. They have little confidence in their own ability and look for ways to give the instructors exactly what they think the instructors are looking for. So, in order to help students become effective higher-level thinkers and complex problem solvers, instructors must develop learning activities that encourage successful students to revisit new information and content by repeatedly considering how it can be applied in a number of different situations from a variety of perspectives (Spiro & Jehng, 1990).

3.3. Promote student articulation and presentation of ideas, perspectives, strategies and tactics, procedures and approaches, solutions, and creations and products.

Articulation requires students to do more than think or reflect on what they have learned. Articulation means that students must present their ideas, perspectives, solutions, and products available to others for reflection, review, criticism, and use. In fact, students have not really completed the knowledge construction process until they test their ideas on other students.

The notion of "presentation" is actually very important, considering one of the underlying reasons for implementing REALs in higher education classrooms: to help bridge the classroom-workplace gap. In the workplace, people are constantly making presentations to their employees, employers, customers, and colleagues, often in public forums (e.g., board rooms, company meetings, project development meetings, brain-storming sessions, manager retreats, sales room floors, training classrooms). Yet, in a typical higher education classroom setting, students are asked to present their ideas privately via a paper turned in to the instructor. Instead, REALs require students to demonstrate what they have learned in ways that authentically represent what they will have to do after completing formal schooling.

Facilitating active knowledge construction is a critical element in learning. The primary idea behind a REAL is to create an environment in which students create complex, rich knowledge structures that will apply to a variety of problems. This cannot be done using simplified, decontextualized, lower level activities. To become capable problem solvers, students must be exposed to complex, open-ended problems that are anchored or situated in realistic contexts.

In order for active knowledge construction to occur, students in higher education classrooms must be provided with opportunities to engage in high-level thinking, reflection, and articulation activities. REALs provide a structure that supports and scaffolds students in the pursuit of active knowledge construction so they are able to successfully engage in the types of knowledge construction activities (including decision making and problem solving) that are becoming a staple in today's workplace environment.

4. Implementing REALs in the Classroom: Supportive Strategies

In order to implement REALs in higher education classrooms that (1) extend students' responsibility, (2) promote meaningful learning, and (3) engage students in dynamic knowledge construction activities, there are a number of supportive strategies that need to be incorporated. These strategies are described below.

4.1. REALs need to provide appropriate scaffolding.

Learning environment support structures need to provide options from which students select the kind of mental activity in which they intend to engage. Providing options encourages metacognitive awareness and helps make the process overt by providing the means to make a conscious selection and then recording that selection for later discussion or analysis.

Learning environments, while striving for realism, must balance that realism with the needs, ability, and maturity of the audience. Learner analysis remains an important element of any design. In addition to the usual general and specific characteristics, learning environment design must also take into consideration how much experience students have had working in REALs.

The learning environment should be structured in a way that provides consistent, timely feedback from teachers and peers. The feedback should moderate frustration and keep students moving along on their tasks. Students should not be left to their own devices under the guise of responsibility and freedom. Constant monitoring and feedback is required.

A guiding structure to provide scaffolding is characteristic of learning environments. Rather than "telling" the student what do do, students must be "guided" through the learning activities. They should be encouraged to make their own decisions and to pursue directions that they decide upon. Instructors should help keep students from generating major misconceptions or from getting held up by major frustrations, but a moderate amount of mistakes and frustration must be expected and should be considered healthy and natural characteristics of active learning.

4.2. REALs require students to contribute to each other's learning through collaborative activities.

Collaboration needs to be an integral part of REAL implementation in a higher education classroom for four main reasons. First, collaboration gives students an opportunity to see and hear how other students approach and solve problems or make decisions. Because the students in a collaborative group are working closely together, students are able to share ideas and perspectives, as well as help each other clarify issues.

Second, when problems are very complex, students working together collaboratively can often successfully tackle problems that individual students working alone would not be able to handle; collaborative learning can "give rise synergistically to insights and solutions that would not come about without them (the members of the collaborative group)." (Brown *et al.*, 1989, p. 40) In other words, through collaboration students can potentially go beyond their individual problem solving abilities with the support of group members. Related to Vygotsky's (1978) "zone of proximal development," which proposes that students actively collaborating will be able to go beyond their current development levels, the collaborative component of complex, open-ended problem solving provides students with a supportive framework or scaffold that allows them to accomplish activities they would not have been able to accomplish on their own (Brown *et al.*, 1989).

Collaboration can also encourage students to help each other grow as thinkers and problem solvers by providing constructive, individualized feedback to each member of the collaborative group. The development of complex problem-solving abilities requires individualized feedback, an activity instructors in the higher education classroom are not always able to do because of time constraints and the number of students in the class. Students working collaboratively can help each other through the complex problem-solving process by taking on the responsibility of providing constructive, individualized feedback to all members of the group.

Finally, collaboration allows students to share the risk involved in problem solving. Complex, open-ended problem solving involves a lot of risk because for many students it is new and unfamiliar; because complex problems often require students to try new or unorthodox approaches and consider creative solutions, it is risky because there is the potential for "failure." Because students do not want to take sole responsibility for mistakes or "failures," collaboration provides students with a mechanism for spreading out the risk.

4.3. REALs must be nonthreatening, safe settings for learning.

This strategy is crucial to all aspects of REALs. Students are not going to be willing to take the risks necessary to assume responsibility if the environment punishes them for making mistakes. The instructor needs to encourage students to experiment and try different options. When a mistake is made, instructors need to emphasize an understanding of what went wrong rather than focusing on the creation of a mistake-free product. When students ask for help, instructors have to hold back from telling students the correct answer; instead, instructors need to ask students to perform the analysis themselves by gently guiding them through the analysis process.

Many students' previous experiences with learning activities, such as problem solving, may have included hearing comments such as "Boy, that's a dumb answer," "Don't you know how to do this?" and "WRONG!" So, there may be a certain level of fear associated with a variety of high level learning activities due to what peers and instructors may have said in the past. Plus, when attempting to tackle anything new, mistakes should be expected. However, students are acclimated to believing that mistakes are "bad" and should be avoided at all times. Therefore, REALs must encourage students to engage in trial-and-error.

Again, students must be trained and encouraged to take risks. This is a new element in learning for most students. The instructor is the primary person to encourage this kind of risk taking by providing positive and constructive feedback and encouragement, as well as modeling risk taking behavior.

4.4. REALs encourage students to reflect on the processes and outcomes of learning activities.

As stated throughout this article, students need to reflect on the processes and outcomes of learning activities in order to learn from and about their learning. This process of reflection is just as important as engaging in the high-level thinking activities themselves; in fact, reflection helps students refine and strengthen their high-level thinking skills and abilities through self-assessment. Reflection gives students an opportunity to think about how they answered a question, made a decision, or solved a problem; what strategies were successful or unsuccessful; what issues need to be remembered for next time; and what could be or should be done differently in the future. In other words, reflection gives students a chance to evaluate their high-level thinking performance, and take mental notes that can be used to adjust and refine subsequent performance.

Conclusion

REALs are one way of conceptualizing and applying constructivist principles to learning in order to help students to prepare for the expectations of a competitive world. It is one attempt to bring together thoughts, ideas, and theories in a way that will help teachers of all levels develop classroom environments that foster higher level thinking skills, especially reflection, problem solving, flexible thinking, and creativity. We owe our students a return on their investments by helping them to become flexible and creative problem solvers and life-long learners.

References

American Association for the Advancement of Science (1989). *Science for all Americans. A project 2061 report on literacy goals in science, mathematics, and technology.* Washington, DC: AAAS.

Baker, L., & Brown, A. (1984). Cognitive monitoring in reading. In J. Flood (Ed.), *Understanding reading comprehension*. Newark, DE: International Reading Association.

Bednar, A. K., Cunningham, D., Duffy, T. M., & Perry, J. D. (1991). Theory into practice: How do we link? In G. Anglin (Ed.), *Instructional technology: Past, present, and future.* Englewood, CO: Libraries Unlimited, Inc.

Bransford, J., Sherwood, R., Hasselbring, T., Kinzer, C., & Williams, S. (1990). Anchored instruction: Why we need it and how technology can help. In D. Nix & R. Spiro (Eds.), *Cognition, education, and multimedia: Exploring ideas in high technology* (pp. 115–142). Hillsdale, NJ: Lawrence Erlbaum Associates.

Brown, J., Collins, A., & Duguid, P. (1989). Situated cognition and the culture of learning. *Educational Researcher, 18*(1), 32–42.

Bruner, J. (1961). The act of discovery. *Harvard Educational Review, 31*(1), 21–32.

Bruner, J. (1990). *Acts of meaning*. Cambridge, MA: Harvard University Press.

Butterfield, E. (1988). On solving the problem of transfer. In M. Gruneberg, P. Morris, & R. Sykes (Eds.), *Practical aspects of memory* (Vol. 2) (pp. 277–318). New York: Psychological Dimensions.

Butterfield, E., & Nelson, G. (1989). Theory and practice of teaching for transfer. *Educational Technology Research and Development, 37*(3), 5–38.

CTGV (Cognition & Technology Group at Vanderbilt) (1992). The Jasper experiment: An exploration of issues in learning and instructional design. *Educational Technology Research and Development, 40*(1), 65–80.

CTGV (Cognition & Technology Group at Vanderbilt) (1993). Designing learning environments that support thinking: The Jasper series as a case study. In T. Duffy, J. Lowyck, & D. Jonassen (Eds.), *Designing environments for constructivist learning*. Berlin: Springer-Verlag.

Collins, A., Brown, J. S., & Newman, S. (1989). Cognitive apprenticeship: Teaching the crafts of reading, writing, and mathematics. In L. Resnick (Ed.), *Knowing, learning, and instruction: Essays in honor of Robert Glaser* (pp. 453–494). Hillsdale, NJ: Lawrence Erlbaum Associates.

Flavell, J. (1976). Metacognitive aspects of problem solving. In. L. Resnick (Ed.), *The nature of intelligence* (pp. 38–62). Hillsdale, NJ: Lawrence Erlbaum Associates.

Flavell, J., & Wellman, H. (1977). Metamemory. In R. Kail & J. Hagen (Eds.), *Perspectives on the development of memory and cognition*. Hillsdale, NJ: Lawrence Erlbaum Associates.

Forman, G., & Pufall, P. (Eds.). (1988). *Constructivism in the computer age*. Hillsdale, NJ: Lawrence Erlbaum Associates.

Fosnot, C. (1989). *Enquiring teachers, enquiring learners: A constructivist approach for teaching*. New York: Teachers College Press.

Gagné, R., Briggs, L., & Wager, W. (1992). *Principles of instructional design* (4th ed.). New York: Holt, Rinehart, & Winston.

Gay, G., & Mazur, J. (1989). Conceptualizing a hypermedia design for language learning. *Journal of Research on Computing in Education*, Winter 1989, 119–125.

Glaser, R. (1990). The reemergence of learning theory within instructional research. *American Psychologist, 45*(1), 29–39.

Goodman, N. (1984). *Of mind and other matters*. Cambridge, MA: Harvard University Press.

Honebein, P., Duffy, T., & Fishman, B. (1993). Constructivism and the design of learning environments: Context and authentic activities for learning. In T. Duffy, J. Lowyck, & D. Jonassen (Eds.), *Designing environments for constructivist learning*. Berlin: Springer-Verlag.

Johnson, D., & Johnson, R. (1990). Cooperative learning and achievement. In S. Sharan (Ed.), *Cooperative learning theory and research* (pp. 22–37). New York: Praeger.

Kinzie, M., & Berdel, R. (1990). Design and use of hypermedia systems. *Educational Technology Research and Development, 38*(3), 61–68.

Kyle, D., Dittmer, A., Fischetti, J., & Portes, P. (1992). *Aligning the Kentucky internship program with the Kentucky education reform act*. Frankfort, KY: Kentucky Department of Education.

Lave, J. (1988). *Cognition in practice: Mind, mathematics, and culture in everday life*. Cambridge: Cambridge University Press.

Lebow, D. (1993). Constructivist values for instructional systems design: Five principles toward a new mindset. *Educational Technology Research and Development, 41*(3), 4–16.

Lynton, E. (1989). *Higher education and American competitiveness* (working paper). National Center on Education and the Economy.

Lynton, E., & Elman, S. (1987). *New priorities for the university*. San Francisco, CA: Jossey-Bass.

National Council of Teachers of Mathematics (1989). *Curriculum and evaluation standards for school mathematics*. Reston, VA: NCTM.

Palincsar, A., & Brown, A. (1984). Reciprocal teaching of comprehension: Fostering and monitoring activities. *Cognition and Instruction, 1,* 117–175.

Perkins, D., & Salomon, G. (1988). Teaching for transfer. *Educational Leadership,* September, 22–32.

Presidential Task Force on Psychology in Education (APA & McREL) (1993). *Learner-centered psychological principles: Guidelines for school redesign and reform.* Washington, DC: American Psychological Association.

Putnam, R. (1991). Recipes and reflective learning: "What would prevent you from saying it that way?" In D. Schön (Ed.), *The reflective turn: Case studies in and on educational practice.* New York: Teachers College Press.

Resnick, L., & Klopfer, L. (Eds). 1989. *Toward the thinking curriculum: Current cognitive research.* Alexandria, VA: ASCD.

The Secretary's Commission on Achieving Necessary Skills. (1991). *What work requires of schools: A SCANS report for America 2000.* Washington, DC: U. S. Department of Labor.

Scardamalia, M., Bereiter, C., McLean, R., Swallow, J., & Woodruff, E. (1989). Computer-supported intentional learning environments. *Journal of Educational Computing Research, 5*(1), 51–68.

Schank, R., & Jona, M. (1991). Empowering the student: New perspectives on the design of teaching systems. *The Journal of the Learning Sciences, 1*(1), 7–35.

Schön, D. (1983). *The reflective practitioner.* New York: Basic Books.

Spiro, R.,, Feltovich, R., Jacobson, M., & Coulson, R. (1991). Cognitive flexibility, constructivism, and hypertext: Random access instruction for advanced knowledge acquisition in ill-structured domains. *Educational Technology, 31*(5), 24–33.

Spiro, R., & Jehng, J. (1990). Cognitive flexibility and hypertext: Theory and technology for the nonlinear and multidimensional traversal of complex subject matter. In D. Nix & R. Spiro (Eds.), *Cognition, education, and multimedia: Exploring ideas in high technology.* Hillsdale, NJ: Lawrence Erlbaum Associates.

Suchman, L. (1987). *Plans and situated actions: The problem of human-machine communication.* Cambridge: Cambridge University Press.

Von Wright, J. (1992). Reflections on reflection. *Learning and Instruction, 2,* 59–68.

Vygotsky, L. (1978). *Mind in society: The development of higher psychological processes.* Cambridge, MA: Harvard University Press.

Wilson, B., & Jonassen, D. (1989). Hypertext and instructional design: Some preliminary guidelines. *Performance Improvement Quarterly, 2*(3), 34–50.

Winn, W. (1993). Instructional design and situated learning: Paradox or partnership? *Educational Technology, 33*(3), 16–21.

Wittrock, M. (1974). Learning as a generative process. *Educational Psychologist, 11,* 87–95.

Wittrock, M. (1978). The cognitive movement in instruction. *Educational Psychologist, 15,* 15–29.

Joanna C. Dunlap is an instructional designer for the University of Colorado Health Sciences Center and an instructional technology lecturer at the University of Colorado at Denver. She is also a consultant specializing in the creation of authentic training environments using rich environments for active learning and problem-based learning. She is currently completing her dissertation at the University of Colorado at Denver.

R. Scott Grabinger is associate professor of Instructional Technology at the University of Colorado at Denver. He has published on a number of topics, including expert systems in education, instructional strategies and tactics, and screen design. His current research interests center around strategies for implementing constructivist learning, such as problem-based learning and rich environments for active learning (REALs).

7

Developing Statistical Reasoning Through Simulation Gaming in Middle School: The Case of 'The Vitamin Wars'

Helena P. Osana
Sharon Derry
Joel R. Levin

There is a general consensus among psychologists and educators that instruction in American schools is in need of reform. This book pertains to a philosophical and psychological movement in education called "constructivism," which is providing impetus for an active reform movement. The constructivist philosophy argues for a shift away from a "transmission" view of learning toward the view that learning is an "effort after meaning" (Bartlett, 1932) and is often best achieved through a process of social negotiation that is embedded within meaningful, goal-oriented activity (e.g., Confry, 1991; Lave & Wenger, 1991). Within the constructivist framework, teachers take on roles as mentors who facilitate their students' construction of knowledge in the context of authentic shared problem-solving activity (e.g., Brown & Campione, 1990; Brown, Collins, & Duguid, 1989; The Cognition & Technology Group at Vanderbilt, 1990; Cunningham, 1992; Lave, 1991; von Glasersfeld, 1990).

Constructivism is an educational philosophy for the information age (Commission on Standards for School Mathematics, 1989). With continual advances in technology and modes of communication, huge quantities of information are being disseminated rapidly everywhere around the globe. Hence, the abilities to selectively encode information from diverse sources and to use it to construct complex meanings have never been more important. Moreover, information and meaning construction must be brought to bear on critical social and scientific problems of ever-increasing complexity (issues such as AIDS, the environment, and overpopulation, just to name a few)—problems of such magnitude that they cannot be solved by individuals working alone. People need to become better collaborative reasoners. It is essential, therefore, that schools give children opportunities to become active problem solvers, effective negotiators, and critical evaluators and users of the information they will confront once they are members of the workforce and other sectors of adult society.

In recognition of these needs, there have been calls for implementing real-world curricula and applying principles of authentic activity in the classroom. For example, the Commission on Standards for School Mathematics (1989), in its *Curriculum and Evaluation Standards for School Mathematics,* claims that the mathematics curriculum must reflect the needs of society within genuine problem-solving activities. Resnick (1987) argues for all instruction, not just mathematics instruction, to incorporate real-world practice. She suggests "a general need to redirect the focus of schooling to encompass more of the features of successful out-of-school functioning" (p. 19). It is believed that creating lifelike environments in everyday school activity can provide students with the skills that they will need in order to tackle the types of problems they will face once they leave school. Resnick maintains that school is "a place to prepare people for the world of work and everyday practical problems" (p. 19).

Although increasingly prevalent, calls for constructivist approaches are far from new. They are reminiscent of Dewey's (1938) Progressive philosophy, which advocated a child-centered experiential curriculum that attempts to extend adult society and the roles and responsibilities found there. Constructivist leanings are also found in the work of Whitehead (1925), who believed that instruction which emphasizes the passing on of factual information results in students acquiring useless, inert knowledge.

Our contribution to this book describes an attempt by our research group to introduce authentic, interdisciplinary, problem-solving, constructivist approaches to teaching into middle-school classrooms. Specifically, we designed and implemented a three-week simulation-based instructional activity that engaged students in argumentation, social problem solving, and collaborative product development not unlike that found within genuine "cultures of practice" (e.g., Lave & Wenger, 1991) in adult society. The simulation was designed specifically to help develop students' statistical reasoning.

A number of researchers have stressed the importance of being able to think statistically (Kahneman & Tversky, 1973; Kuhn, 1991; Nisbett & Ross, 1980). The ability to use statistical concepts as tools for reasoning about complex issues has been an increasingly studied topic in recent years. Reasoning with probability and uncertainty, understanding the fundamentals of scientific research (such as sampling issues and randomness), and evaluating evidence are some of the skills that are becoming vitally important for the lay person when deciphering and thinking about life's ill-structured problems.

General Goals

Our project had several broad research objectives. First, we wanted to better understand some of the issues and problems associated with attempting to introduce and implement educational reform based on constructivist philosophy. From another perspective, we wanted to design and try out reusable materials and procedures that would engage middle-school students in an interesting, real-world problem and provide a context for developing their reasoning abilities, argumentation skills, understanding of statistical concepts, and social problem-solving skills. A related research goal was to create classroom contexts for qualitative study of the social discourse that takes place within such environments, and to examine such discourse for evidence that reasoning and argumentation capabilities can be developed by simulation-based instruction. Finally, we wanted to observe the extent to which students remained engaged, productive, and motivated throughout the simulation.

Goals for the students. As we designed the simulation, we had in mind a great many (perhaps too many!) specific goals for students. First, we wanted to enhance students' tendencies and abilities to view the world statistically. We felt that this should include mastering the distinction between deterministic and probabilistic thinking. Konold (1989) describes those people who think deterministically (or those with an "outcome approach") as not being able to think of a particular event as a member of a larger set of events. Shaughnessy (1992) states that, when making predictions, "outcome-oriented people may believe that their task is to correctly decide for certain what the next outcome will be, rather than to estimate what is likely to occur" (p. 476). On the other hand, those people who think probabilistically (or those who possess "aleatory" views of the world) are better able to understand that predictions based on previous occurrences should be determined by considering any one event as a single instance of a number of events. Decisions must therefore be made according to laws of probability.

A related idea motivating instructional design was to help students develop an awareness of the uncertainties in daily world events and issues. To reason appropriately about social issues means to understand that very little can be determined with 100% certainty, and that it is necessary to employ certain fundamental laws of probability in the reasoning process. For example, there is a possibility that a medical treatment that has been shown to have a positive effect in one or a few instances may in fact have no effect at all over repeated observation. A pregnancy test is not absolute proof positive; an eye-witness account contains shades of uncertainty. There are varying probabilities associated with the occurrence of almost any event, and it is important to take this into account when making decisions and solving problems in the social domain.

Connected to the idea of uncertainty are various statistical concepts that help to judge the reasonableness of a statement, argument, or conclusion. Along these lines, another goal of the activity was to help students understand that a given conclusion, even if reached as a result of a scientific test, is not necessarily the "truth," or a "proof." There is always the chance of a Type I error (or the probability of claiming an effect exists when in fact it does not), as well as a Type II error (making the claim that an effect does not exist when in reality it does).

Another goal was to teach students basic ideas about sampling and experimental design. For example, it was hoped that through the instructional simulation, the students would come to realize how and why conclusions based on randomly constituted treatment groups are more solidly founded than those based on nonrandomly constituted treatment groups, self-selected "treatment groups," or subjectively identified single cases. The objective here was to encourage the students to base their arguments on what Kuhn (1991) terms "genuine evidence." Hence, a curricular objective was to help students to judge the validity of the experimental evidence cited in support of their arguments, and the arguments of others, and to assess the reliability of the sources.

Another goal of instructional design was to help students decipher the elements that make an argument convincing, and to help them learn to evaluate the strength of an argument using such criteria. There exists a clear distinction between the logically sound and reliable evidence used to marshal support for a position, and the rhetoric involved in making a case persuasive. A goal of our simulation activity was to help students see that better arguments are both logical and rhetorically persuasive.

Finally, it was hoped that as a result of the simulation, the students would develop skills related to collaborative problem solving. The classroom was designed so that it mimicked a real-world society, a culture complete with many of the resources necessary for meaningful problem solving. Students were asked to assume true-to-life responsibilities consistent with their classroom roles. Both within and across groups, students were encouraged to investigate issues, share knowledge, and negotiate understandings together.

Goals for the teachers. It was hoped that participating in this project would expose the teachers to reform-oriented instructional principles, and that they would be more likely to implement related techniques in their future lesson plans. More specifically, it was hoped that from their experience working with university researchers on this project, the participating teachers would acquire new and useful knowledge about designing and mentoring authentic, collaborative problem-solving activities that foster argumentation, metacognitive skills, and the social construction of knowledge.

Procedure

The project was conducted in a large midwestern middle school which, though predominately middle class, is attended by students from a broad spectrum of ethnic and social backgrounds. Two eighth-grade teachers and one seventh-grade teacher participated. This team of three teachers formed an interdisciplinary group; their subject specialties were history, science, and mathematics. The history and science classes were not tracked with respect to ability. The mathematics class was a "standard" (average) ability class.

The teachers and their learning coordinator met with project researchers throughout the summer. Hence, the middle-school teachers and a school administrator were involved in every phase of designing the materials and implementing the instructional activity.

The topical issue chosen to serve as the problem context for the simulation was government regulation of the vitamin and dietary supplement industry. This particular topic was selected (in collaboration with the participating teachers) for several reasons. First, it was—and still is—an important national issue. Second, it had great potential for teaching statistical and scientific thinking, as well as science and social science content. Third, the researchers and teachers felt that it could be turned into an interesting and motivating topic for seventh- and eighth-grade students. Finally, and importantly, it was a topic that was acceptable to both teachers and parents, and one that was not as potentially explosive as other seemingly more engaging topics (e.g., drugs, steroids, gangs, crime, AIDS).

Each class was divided into small groups. Certain groups were made up of students role playing people who opposed federal regulation of the vitamin industry; other groups consisted of people who favored regulation; and some groups contained people who held a balanced position on the issue. Students in each group were given roles that represented various members of the community: doctors and other health officials, vitamin consumers, manufacturers, government officials, members of the press, and so on. In each of the three classes, the students' roles were assigned by the teacher.

Students studied data and other evidence made available by the researchers, they developed arguments and counter-arguments, and they designed presentations to support their positions on the issue. Presentations and arguments were made during a four-day mock legislative hearing wherein the fate of a vitamin regulation bill (written by students playing roles as legislators) was decided. The specific classroom activities for each of the three participating classes were as follows:

Days 1-7: Introduction and discussion of relevant issues.

- Days 1–4: Discussion-based showing of the movie, *Lorenzo's Oil*. This film, shown in short segments each day by laserdisc, provided contexts for introducing various topics related to statistics, medical research, and scientific reasoning with statistics. A Socratic teaching method was used by the teacher and the researchers to encourage discussion in the classroom. Following the film, a medical researcher from the local university (who had actually been depicted as a character in the film), visited classrooms and gave a presentation and answered questions concerning research issues depicted in the film.
- Days 5–7: Rotating 70-minute instructional units on the following topics:
  1) *Ways to present a position:* Models, graphs, charts. This unit was taught by the eighth-grade science teacher in collaboration with a project researcher.
  2) *Scientific and statistical credibility:* In the eighth grade, this was taught by a project researcher; in the seventh grade math class, this unit was taught by the teacher herself.
  3) *Thinking as evidential argument:* This unit included concepts of covariation and correlation, and was taught by the eighth-grade social studies teacher in collaboration with a project researcher.

Days 8–15: Classroom research and hearing.
- Days 8–11: Student research and presentation preparation, done in small-group settings. Each group of students was closely mentored by a project researcher, or by the teacher. The mentoring consisted of helping students to stay on track, to work collaboratively, and to develop more sophisticated metacognitive strategies. The mentors also attempted to encourage the students to think statistically, as well as to think correctly about evidence.
- Days 12–15: Mock legislative hearings on proposed regulatory bill.

Results

Assessment and videotaped data were collected to permit the investigation of both qualitative and quantitative questions about the instructional intervention. At this point, however, it is possible for the researchers to report only their informal observations about the experience, as the data collected during and following the instructional intervention have not yet been analyzed.

Here we summarize several broad observations made by researchers while working with students and teachers during the project:

In all classes there were moments of intense, energetic argumentation that were highly engaging for all participants. Many students adopted their assigned roles and positions and played them out with great vigor, prompting us to dub our instructional materials package as "Vitamin Wars" (Long, 1993). We speculate that the combining of role playing and situated argumentation is a potentially powerful motivational and instructional strategy that should be investigated further. However, such activity can sometimes erupt in unexpected ways, since anger and other emotions can be triggered.

Some sophisticated statistical argumentation did take place. The classroom activities were structured in such a way so as to encourage the students to weigh evidence and consider counter-arguments, and in fact, these components of the reasoning process were seen. For example, there were some students who challenged the evidence of their classmates on certain sampling and statistical issues (such as sample size, replicability, and causality) and the reliability of the source. Some students' graphs, charts, overhead slides, illustrations, and played-out scenarios during their formal "legislative hearing" arguments were highly imaginative and effective. Group interviews with students after the simulation revealed some recognition of the distinction between a persuasive delivery and the logical support of an argument.*

We observed clearly that the particular roles played by students were very important in determining their levels of engagement in research and group

---

*As was just noted, however, and consistent with the caveats given to our middle-school students about research evidence and scientific credibility, we remind the reader that we have not yet systematically determined: (1) whether the proportion of students who developed such skills was substantial; and (2) the extent to which the sophisticated argumentation observed can be traced directly to the instructional intervention. It is similarly unknown at this point whether students who were exposed to statistical-reasoning instruction and experiences were better able to transfer them to novel statistical-reasoning situations.

collaboration. For example, in all classes, students who played roles as members of the press appeared to spend much more time off task. Also, students in certain roles became highly influential at certain points in the activity by virtue of their assigned position in the simulated society. For example, in two classes, members of the legislature were authoritative and thus positively influenced the quality of their hearings by setting and maintaining rules of conduct, fairness, and pace. In these classes, the hearings were very productive. In the third class, however, the legislators exerted little influence and control. The hearing in this classroom did not proceed smoothly and emotional arguments sometimes were allowed to dominate reason.

We noted with interest many other ways in which students and teachers from different classrooms responded very differently to the instructional simulation. For example, one eighth-grade class and the seventh-grade class became immediately engaged in the project and assumed their roles rather quickly and took them seriously. These students worked in an orderly fashion, and apparently displayed more sophisticated forms of reasoning. The other eighth-grade class needed a great deal more guidance from the teacher and the university researchers. The students in this class were not as interested in marshaling logical support for their arguments, seeming instead more attentive to the persuasiveness and the esthetic elements of presentations. Not surprisingly, neither the teacher nor students in this class evaluated the activity positively, although teachers and students in the other two classes reacted very positively. Such classroom differences, whether resulting from the student composition, the teachers' operational styles, or certain situational effects of the instruction, serve to underscore the reality of methodological and statistical arguments about within-classroom nonindependence and the appropriate "units" that should accompany classroom-based research interventions of this kind (e.g., Levin, 1985, 1992).

Our final observation for now is that students who participated in the instructional intervention learned much more than statistics and in fact did not regard statistics as the primary learning outcome of the project. Preliminary analyses suggest that the students learned a great deal about the *content* about which they were reasoning. Classroom observations and student questionnaires indicated that after the three-week intervention, the students knew a great deal more about vitamins and their effects, the legislative process, and the roles and functions of various community, political, and professional people.

Concluding Comments

In the past, innovative teachers have attempted to apply constructivist principles in their classrooms. Formal implementations and evaluations of programs such as this one, however, are just beginning. Theoretical ideas that center around constructivism, situated social cognition, and authentic activity have been discussed and debated widely in recent years. The ways in which these principles can inform practice, however, are infinitely less clear. The project described here was an attempt to apply abstract psychological and educational ideas in the classroom, and to observe the types of thinking and learning that occurred as a result.

Many detailed studies have been conducted examining the nature and acquisition of statistical reasoning. In that regard, this project is nothing new. The goal of the project, however, was to address research questions in a setting that was less contrived and not as isolated from authentic practice. The expectation was that such a situated-simulation approach would yield results that would help to: (a) inform researchers of the ways in which students actually think about social issues; and (b) refine current instruction, and to design other types of classroom activity that help middle-school students develop more sophisticated reasoning abilities.

Whether or not these expectations were borne out has yet to be determined. However, it is clear that much additional work in the field of educational psychology in general is required to obtain a more complete understanding of the theoretical ideas described in this volume, as well as the finer details involved in school reform of this genre—and ambitiousness.

References

Bartlett, F. C. (1932). *Remembering*. Cambridge: Cambridge University Press.

Brown, A. L., & Campione, J. C. (1990). Communities of learning and thinking, or a context by any other name. *Human Development, 21*, 108–125.

Brown, J. S., Collins, A., & Duguid, P. (1989). Situated cognition and the culture of learning. *Educational Researcher, 18*(1), 32–42.

Confry, J. (1991). Steering a course between Vygotsky and Piaget. *Educational Researcher, 20*(8), 28–34.

The Cognition & Technology Group at Vanderbilt. (1990). Anchored instruction and its relationship to situated cognition. *Educational Researcher, 19*(6), 2–10.

Commission on Standards for School Mathematics. (1989). *Curriculum and evaluation standards for school mathematics*. Reston, VA: National Council of Teachers of Mathematics.

Cunningham, D. J. (1992). Beyond educational psychology: Steps toward an educational semiotic. *Educational Psychology Review, 4*, 165–194.

Dewey, J. (1938). *Experience and education*. New York: Collier Books.

Kahneman, D., & Tversky, A. (1973). On the psychology of prediction. *Psychological Review, 80*, 237–251.

Konold, C. (1989). Informal conceptions of probability. *Cognition and Instruction, 6*, 59–98.

Kuhn, D. (1991). *The skills of argument*. New York: Cambridge University Press.

Lave, J. (1991). Situated learning in communities of practice. In L. B. Resnick, J. M. Levine, & S. D. Teasley (Eds.), *Perpectives on socially shared cognition* (pp. 63–84). Washington, DC: American Psychological Association.

Lave, J., & Wenger, E. (1991). *Situated learning: Legitimate peripheral participation*. Cambridge, England: Cambridge University Press.

Levin, J. R. (1985). Some methodological and statistical "bugs" in research on children's learning. In M. Pressley & C. J. Brainerd (Eds.), *Cognitive learning and memory in children*. New York: Springer-Verlag.

Levin, J. R. (1992). On research in classrooms. *Mid-Western Educational Researcher, 5*, 2–6, 16.

Long, P. (1993, May/June). The vitamin wars. *Health*, 45–54.

Nisbett, R., & Ross, L. (1980). *Human inference: Strategies and shortcomings of social judgment*. Englewood Cliffs, NJ: Prentice-Hall.

Resnick, L. B. (1987). Learning in school and out. *Educational Researcher, 16,* 13–20.

Shaughnessy, J. M. (1992). Research in probability and statistics: Reflections and directions. In D. A. Grouws (Ed.), *Handbook of research on mathematics teaching and learning* (pp. 465–494). Reston, VA: National Council of Teachers of Mathematics.

von Glasersfeld, E. (1990). An exposition of constructivism: Why some like it radical. In R. B. Davis, C. A. Maher, & N. Noddings (Eds.), Constructivist views on the teaching and learning of mathematics. *Journal for Research in Mathematics Education: Monograph 4,* 19–30.

Whitehead, A. N. (1925). *Science and the modern world.* New York: Macmillan.

Funding for this project was provided by the National Center for Research in Mathematical Sciences Education, Wisconsin Center for Educational Research. We are grateful to Velma Bell Hamilton Middle School teachers Tom Bauer, Kim Vergeront, Joan Unmacht, and Doris Dubielzig for their substantial contributions. Dr. Leona Schauble is thanked for her considerable service as an advisor and guest lecturer, and Dr. Ian Duncan for being a guest speaker. Correspondence concerning this article should be addressed to Sharon Derry, Department of Educational Psychology, 1025 W. Johnson St., University of Wisconsin, Madison, WI 53706.

Helena Osana is a doctoral student in the Department of Educational Psychology at the University of Wisconsin, Madison. Her doctoral research pertains to the influence of prior knowledge on the development of statistical reasoning skills.

Sharon Derry is Professor of Educational Psychology at the University of Wisconsin, Madison. Her research interests involve application of cognitive science theories, social constructivist philosophies, and advanced computer technologies to the educational problem of helping students develop better problem solving, judgment, and decision making skills.

Joel R. Levin is Professor of Educational Psychology at the University of Wisconsin, Madison. His research interests include students' cognitive and metacognitive skills (and strategies for fostering their development), as well as methods for improving the quality of educational research and statistical analysis.

8

From Constructivism to Constructionism: Learning *with* Hypermedia/Multimedia Rather Than *from* It

David H. Jonassen
Jamie M. Myers
Ann Margaret McKillop

Constructivism to Constructionism

This chapter, we believe, focuses on the distinction made by Papert (1990) between instructionism and constructionism. Instructionism, he claimed, is the dominant method of learning in schools. With instructionism, students are passive receptacles for the information and knowledge that the teacher imparts to them. Instructionism has also been referred to as the *sponge* method of teaching (Schank & Jona, 1991) and the *banking* concept of learning (Freire & Macedo, 1987), where the goal of learners is to absorb and accumulate what they are given until the examination, at which time the information is wrung out of them. The alternatives to instructionism, Papert argues, are constructivism and constructionism. Is there a difference?

> The word with the v expresses the theory that knowledge is built by the learner, not supplied by the teacher. The word with the n expresses the further idea that this happens especially felicitously when the learner is engaged in the construction of something external or at least sharable...a sand castle, a machine, a computer program, a book. (Papert, 1990, p. 3)

Constructivism is the more generic concept. While it clearly supports the production of external products, constructionism argues that constructivism is most readily manifested when learners become constructors and producers of personal products that can be shared with others. Although we believe that learners can construct meaningful personal representations without producing external, physical products, constructivist processes are more evident when students collaborate to produce and share representations of their understandings of the world. This position is supported by Bruner (1986) when he explains his own changes in thought over the years about the best structure for learning in schools:

> Some years ago I wrote some very insistent articles about the importance of discovery learning—learning on one's own, or as Piaget put it later (and I think better), learning by inventing. What I am proposing here is an extension of that idea, or better a completion. My model of the child in those days was very much in the tradition of the solo child mastering the world by representing it to himself in his own terms. In the intervening years I have come increasingly to recognize that most learning in most settings is a communal activity, a sharing of the culture. It is not just that the child must make his knowledge his own, but that he must make it his own in a community of those who share his sense of belonging to a culture. It is this that leads me to emphasize not only discovery and invention but the importance of negotiating and sharing—in a word, of joint culture creating as an object of schooling and as an appropriate step en route to becoming a member of the adult society in which one lives out one's life. (Bruner, 1986, p. 127)

Our belief is that producing hypermedia and multimedia products is among the most complete and engaging of the constructivist/constructionist activities. Therefore, we contend that rather than using hypermedia and multimedia as information sources that learners access in order to acquire knowledge in the *sponge* or *banking* way, learners benefit most from socially constructing hypermedia/multimedia knowledge bases that reflect their own, and their community's understandings of content being studied. Additionally, we shall show that the process of researching, organizing, and constructing such knowledge bases necessarily engages learners in higher-order, critical thinking and literacy. We shall argue that control of the technology should be taken away from the teachers and instructional designers and invested in the learners, because meaning accrues more readily from constructionist than instructionist activities.

A Rationale for Constructing Hypermedia/Multimedia

The reasons why we believe that learners should be hypermedia/multimedia constructors follow.

Knowing as Designing

Perkins (1986) argues that knowledge acquisition is a process of design, that it is facilitated when learners are actively engaged designing knowledge rather than interpreting and encoding it. Learners become designers when they focus on the purpose for acquiring information, its underlying structure, generating model cases, and using the arguments entailed by the subject matter to justify the design. The people who learn the most from instructional materials are the designers. Jonassen, Wilson, Wang, and Grabinger (1993) reported this discovery while developing expert system advisors that were designed to supplant the thinking required by novice instructional designers. The process of articulating their knowledge about the domain of instructional design (with the purpose of providing advice, identifying numerous cases, and especially elucidating the arguments in the form of rules) forced them to reflect on that knowledge in new and meaningful ways. We have all stated at one time or another that the quickest way to learn about subject matter is to have to teach (design) it.

Goodlad (1983) identified two major deficiencies existing in school curricula, which support the need to define learning as a design activity:

> The first is a failure to differentiate and see the relationships between facts and the more important concepts facts help us to understand. The second, closely related to the first, is a general failure to view subjects and subject matter as merely turf on which to experience the struggles and satisfaction of personal development. (p. 15)

Students cannot distinguish ideas from the supporting facts because they seldom engage in the design activities which would require them to organize information and personal experience to represent together and for others knowledge about the world.

Knowledge Construction, Not Reproduction

The primary rationale for learners as authors is constructivist. Although constructivism is the general topic of this book, let us briefly summarize our assumptions about it. Constructivism is concerned with the process of how we *construct* knowledge. The knowledge that we construct depends upon what we already know, which depends on the kinds of experiences that we have had, how we have organized those experiences into knowledge structures, and what we believe about those experiences. We construct our understandings of the world through interpreting our experiences in the world. However, reality does not exist completely in an objective world or in an individual's subjective world. The teacher cannot map his or her representation onto the learner, because they don't share an isomorphic set of experiences and interpretations. Rather, reality (or at least what we know and understand of reality) resides in the mind of each knower, who interprets the external world according to his or her own experiences, beliefs, and knowledge. Yet, there is an objective world that does conform to certain predictable laws. We simply want to emphasize that our view of constructivism is not extreme, but rather functional. Nor does our conception mean, as some designers fear, that learners can only comprehend their own interpretations of reality. We socially construct meaning through our everyday interactions with others in which we represent back and forth to each other our negotiated sense of reality. Learners should be capable of comprehending a variety of interpretations in that social process and using others' ideas in arriving at their own interpretations of the world. Knowing is a process of negotiating sense, not transmitting fully developed truths.

Constructivist models of instruction (Duffy & Jonassen, 1992) strive to create environments in which learners actively participate in ways that are intended to help them construct their own understandings, rather than having the teacher interpret the world and insure that students understand the world as he or she has told them. In constructivist environments, learners are actively engaged in perceiving different perspectives and organizing and representing their own interpretations reflecting their sense of the communities in which they belong. This is not "active" in the sense that learners actively listen and then mirror the *one* correct view of reality, but rather "active" in the sense that learners must participate and interact with the surrounding environment in order to invent and negotiate their own view of the subject.

Learning *with* Hypermedia/Multimedia, Not *from* It

Educational technologies have traditionally been conceived as conveyors of information, communicators of knowledge, or tutors of students. Instruction is conceived as a process where learners perceive messages encoded in the medium and sometimes "interact" with the technology, meaning students input responses to pre-programmed queries, the technology engages in some form of answer judging, and then the technology presents a scripted response.

> Thinking about learning in this way, we are virtually forced to strategize about education through schemes of decomposition and reconstruction, to break apart the stream of human activity—into skills, schemes, behaviors, rule systems, subroutines, procedures—and then recompose a more sophisticated system. We are virtually forced into pedanticism. (Newman, Griffin, & Cole, 1989, p. xiv)

The distinction between hypermedia/multimedia as tutors or teachers vs. hypermedia/multimedia as construction tools is also expressed by Salomon, Perkins, and Globerson (1989) as the effects *of* technology versus the effects *with* computer technology. The former refers to the effects *of* multimedia on the learner, as if the learner has no input into the process. The effects of learning *with* multimedia refers to learners entering into an intellectual partnership with the technology. Learning with hypermedia/multimedia requires "the mindful engagement of learners in the tasks afforded by these tools and that there is the possibility of qualitatively upgrading the performance of the joint system of learner plus technology." In other words, when students construct multimedia, rather than being controlled by it, they enhance the capabilities of the technology while the technology enhances their thinking and learning. The results of this intellectual partnership with the technology is that the whole of learning becomes greater than the sum of its parts.

Distributing Cognitive Processing

Technologies should be thought of as tools to help learners transcend the limitations of their minds, such as memory, thinking, or problem-solving limitations (Pea, 1985). Computer-based hypermedia and multimedia may also function as cognitive technologies for amplifying and reorganizing the way that learners think. When learners use technologies as partners, they off-load some of the unproductive memorizing tasks, allowing them to think more productively (Perkins, 1993). Our goal in using technologies should be to allocate to the learners the cognitive responsibility for the processing they do best while we allocate to the technology the processing that it does best. Rather than using the limited capabilities of the computer to present information and judge learner input (neither of which computers do well) while asking learners to memorize information and later recall it (which computers do with far greater speed and accuracy than humans), we should assign cognitive responsibility to the part of the learning system that does it the best. Learners should be responsible for recognizing and judging patterns of information and then organizing them, while the computer system should perform calculations, and store and retrieve information. Constructionist applications of technology better distribute cognitive responsibilities between the learner and the technology.

Having argued for hypermedia and multimedia as knowledge design and construction tools, rather than neutral containers and transmitters of information, let us now describe some cases in which learners have used the technology to construct representations of their world.

Examples of Hypermedia/Multimedia as Design

Authoring Multimedia with Mediatext

The Highly Interactive Computing Environments (Hi-CE) Group at the University of Michigan has developed a multimedia composition tool called Mediatext (Hays, Weingard, Guzdial, Jackson, Boyle, & Soloway, 1993). They believe that rather than using media to deliver instruction to learners, learners should use the media to generate their own instruction and in so doing, learn more about the content by creating multimedia documents containing text, graphics, sounds, animation, and links to external technology devices such as videodisc players. When learners actively construct knowledge from multimedia, they acquire cognitive, metacognitive, and motivational advantage over learners who attempt to absorb knowledge.

Mediatext is a composition tool for constructing multimedia. Rather than a presentation tool, Mediatext is to various media as a word processor is to text (Hays *et al.*, 1993). Word processors are tools for creating or generating text. Mediatext is a tool for creating and generating multimedia which includes a word processor, MediaLink, that links other media (videodiscs, QuickTime movies, graphics, sounds, etc.) to the document, and many Media Workshops (tools), including the Videodisc and Compact Disc Workshops, the Graphics Workshop, the Sound Workshop, the Animation Workshop, and Link Workshops (enabling Mediatext documents to be linked to other documents, applications, or Mediatext documents).

The Hi-CE group has researched high school students creating Mediatext stories (see Figure 8.1), biographies, or instructional aids, as well as multimedia essays. Students have learned to use techniques, such as mentioning, directives, titling, and juxtaposition, to integrate their documents. They have found that as their experiences with Mediatext increase, their documents become more integrated rather than merely annotated text. Students have been very enthusiastic about being constructionists, believing that they are learning more because they understand the ideas better.

HyperComposition

Another tool, HyperAuthor, has been developed to engage eighth graders in designing history lessons (Lehrer, 1993). Lehrer agrees with Perkins (1986) that knowledge is a process of design and not something to be transmitted from

> It was a cold day at Loveland valley resort. The wind whipped across the valley like a roller coaster. The sky was a deep, crystal-clear blue. The snow sparkled like recently polished diamonds. The air was clean and fresh as it blew across the faces of the excited skiers. The metal on the chairs was as cold as the inside of a freezer as they grabbed it to steady their uphill flight. However, the cold did not dampen the spirits of the people. They were all eager to get on the slopes again.
>   About ten miles down the road, two skiers were driving in. Their names were Cody Brown and Todd Barber. They were both skilled skiers and had been skiing a fairly long time. As Cody and Todd got closer to the mountain, they noticed that it was a busy day, but there was one slope that no one was occupying. This was Psychopathics Gulch, a name which accurately described the type of run it was. As long as Cody and Todd had been skiing, they had never seen anyone on it. It was a dangerous run; people were often cautioned about it.
>   When Cody and Todd arrived they quickly bought tickets, then they hit the slopes. They were having a great day until around their tenth run. They were taking the lift to Parson's Bowl, which goes right above Psychopathic Gulch. The warm Colorado sun was soaking into their skin. The lift ride was about half way over when Cody decided to hang his poles on the side of the lift. As he was doing this, his pole suddenly
>
> *Clear Day on Slopes*
> *Trail Map*
> *Cody & Todd*
> *Lift Ride*

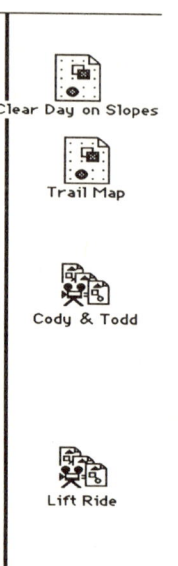

Figure 8.1. Excerpt from a Mediatext story written by a junior high school student.

teacher to student. So he developed a hypermedia authoring tool, HyperAuthor, to engage students in HyperComposition, which involves transforming information into concept maps, segmenting information into nodes, linking the information segments by semantic relationships, and deciding how to represent ideas. This is a highly motivating process because authorship results in ownership of the ideas in the presentation.

Lehrer (1993) has generated some exemplary research to document the intellectual result of this motivating process. He investigated high and low ability eighth graders developing hypermedia programs on the Civil War. They conducted library research and found pictures and video clips to exemplify many of the points they wanted to make. The students enjoyed assuming control of their learning and began to see history more as a process of interpretation than memorization. In the process, they acquired knowledge "that was richer, better connected, and more applicable to subsequent learning and events" (p. 221), and the students worked harder, were more interested and involved, and collaborated and planned more (Carver, Lehrer, Connell, & Erickson, 1992).

Lehrer, Erickson, and Connell (in press) conducted another study with ninth grade students, developing hypermedia on World War I, lifestyles between 1870-1920, immigration, and imperialism. They found similar results: on-task behavior increased over time; students perceived the benefits of the planning and transforming stages of development, such as taking notes, finding information, coordinating with other team members, writing interpretations, and designing the presentation. Figure 8.2 presents a montage of graphics that the learners created to illustrate ideas in their presentations, including charts to show the probability of soldiers returning home safely, the balance of powers among the competing countries, corsets illustrating contemporary vs. past lifestyles of women, and a helmet to illustrate the fight for women's rights.

Constructing Cultural Representations

The ACCESS Project (American Culture in Context: Enrichment for Secondary Schools) focuses on the subject-matters commonly taught in high school, such as United States history, American literature, and American Studies courses. The project began in 1988 with teachers assembling a collection of textual, pictorial, audio, and video materials to supplement their courses. Initially, students used and benefited from the materials for information retrieval (Spoehr, 1994; Spoehr, 1992; Spoehr & Shapiro, 1991). The researchers found that students who made more extensive use of the conceptual structure organization which was built into the system benefited more than the students who used the system like a linear, electronic book. They also found that hypermedia's effectiveness depends on the extent to which students can internalize the important conceptual structures in a subject matter as they browse.

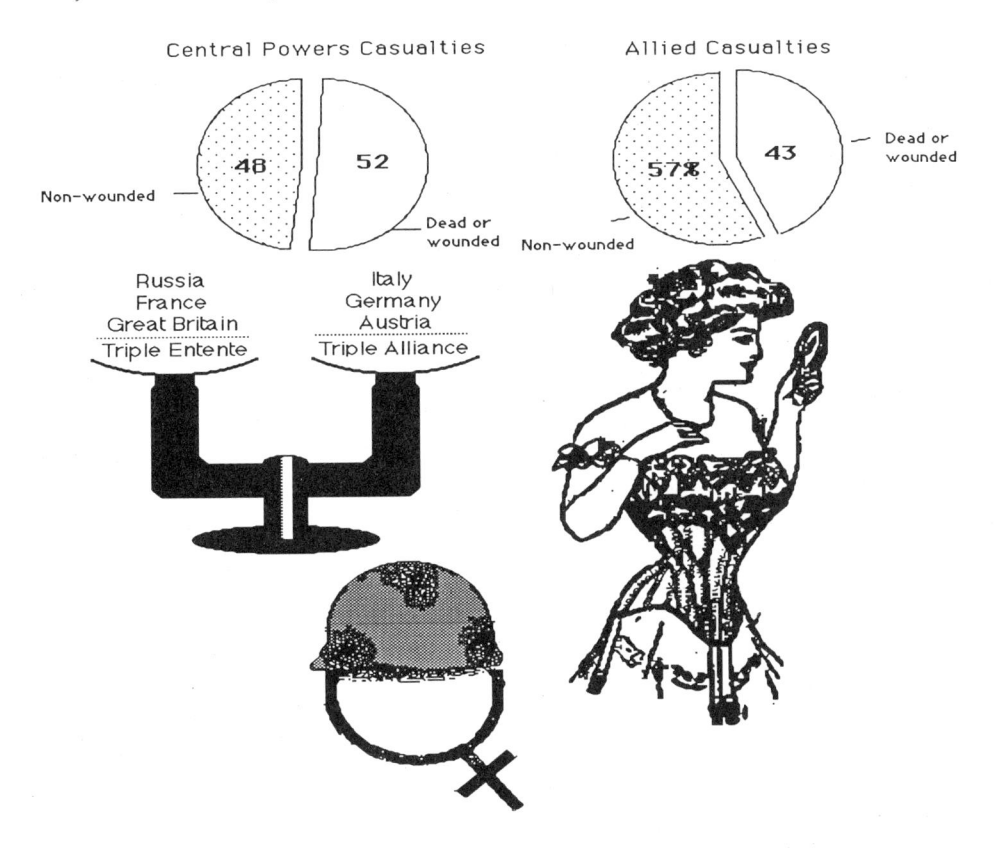

Figure 8.2. Icons used to illustrate ideas in HyperAuthor presentations (reprinted with permission of the author).

The project shifted its focus recently by having students create their own hypermedia projects. Students build their own conceptual links for material which they add to the system. In order to make it easy for students to create hypermedia projects, the researchers developed an authoring tool which includes a mouse-driven authoring tool palette to permit student authors to rapidly carry out authoring activities. After practicing with small authoring projects, students later take on one or more major hypermedia development projects.

Perhaps the most important characteristic of any hypermedia product is its overall organization and structure. Most students quickly learn to develop more complex information models with topics divided into subtopics which are divided into sub-subtopics, and so on. Figure 8.3 shows a relatively sophisticated tree-representation for a student project on John Donne with a sample screen from that project. The example is one in which the student uses both the interactive capability of hypermedia (the bold-face text appears only when the user clicks on the light-bulb button) and sound (the student-author is heard reading Donne's poetry).

There are many ways in which the hypermedia authors appeared to benefit from their computer-based experiences, all of which fall roughly into the category of superior knowledge representation and thinking skills. Research shows that students who build and use hypermedia apparently develop a proficiency to organize knowledge about a subject in a more expert-like fashion; they represent multiple linkages between related ideas and organize cluster of concepts into meaningful clusters (Spoehr, 1993). Superior knowledge representations then support more complex arguments in written essays. And, most importantly, the conceptual organization skills acquired through building hypermedia are robust enough to generalize to material students acquire from many other sources.

Multimedia Construction as a Whole Language Experience

At Penn State University, preservice teachers in English Education construct multimedia representations about ideas that they believe are important in works of adolescent literature. At the beginning of the semester, they read three or four novels about culturally diverse life experiences. As they read these novels, they are asked to look deeply into their own life-worlds and find "texts" which connect to the novels. They bring in popular songs, movies, television shows, poetry, photographs, all somehow bearing an intertextual connection between the lives of those in the novel and their own lives. These multimedia texts are digitized and maintained in a database, which small groups of students then use to author hypermedia using an authoring tool called Textbook Toolbox. Textbook Toolbox allows the small groups to annotate the text in a HyperCard stack with illustrations, QuickTime movies, sounds, and pop-up notes. The students in each small group collaborate to focus on a particular idea which cuts across the novels and their own lives, write the text about the focus idea on several successive cards, and illustrate their text with the digitized media from the class database. Each digitized "text" has the potential to appear in each small group stack in a different interpretive way. How these "texts" are used differently becomes one focus of the sharing of products which helps students

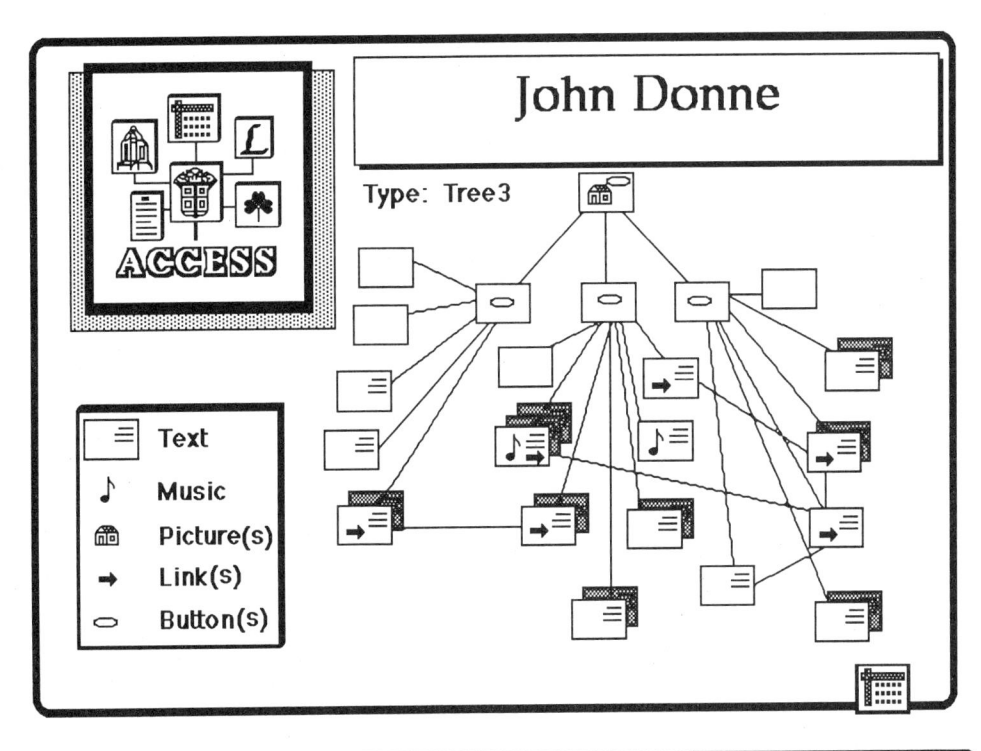

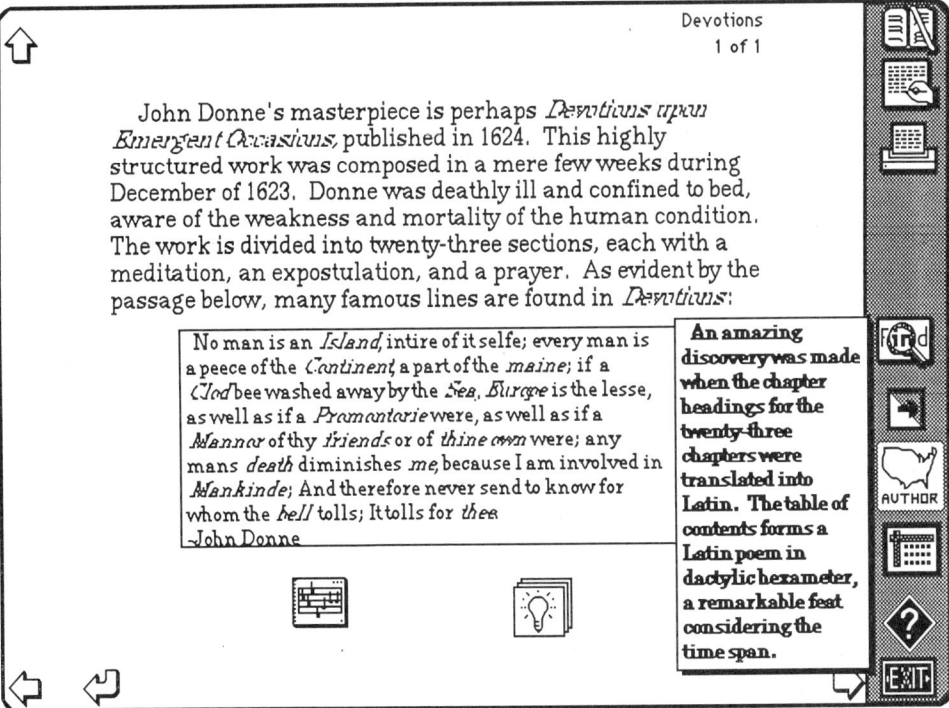

From Constructivism to Constructionism: Learning with Hypermedia/Multimedia   101

Figure 8.3. Tree representation for a student project.

begin to think about literacy and media as interpretive and not a neutral transmitter of ideas.

Indicative of the potential for personal and collaborative knowledge construction are the titles of the stacks and individual cards within the stacks. Overall titles include "Identity," "Injustices," "Power," "Racism," and "Stages." Individual card topics include power, separation, family values, war, racism, trust, judgment, and tragedy. Figure 8.4 illustrates some of the connections between texts and among themselves that students negotiated.

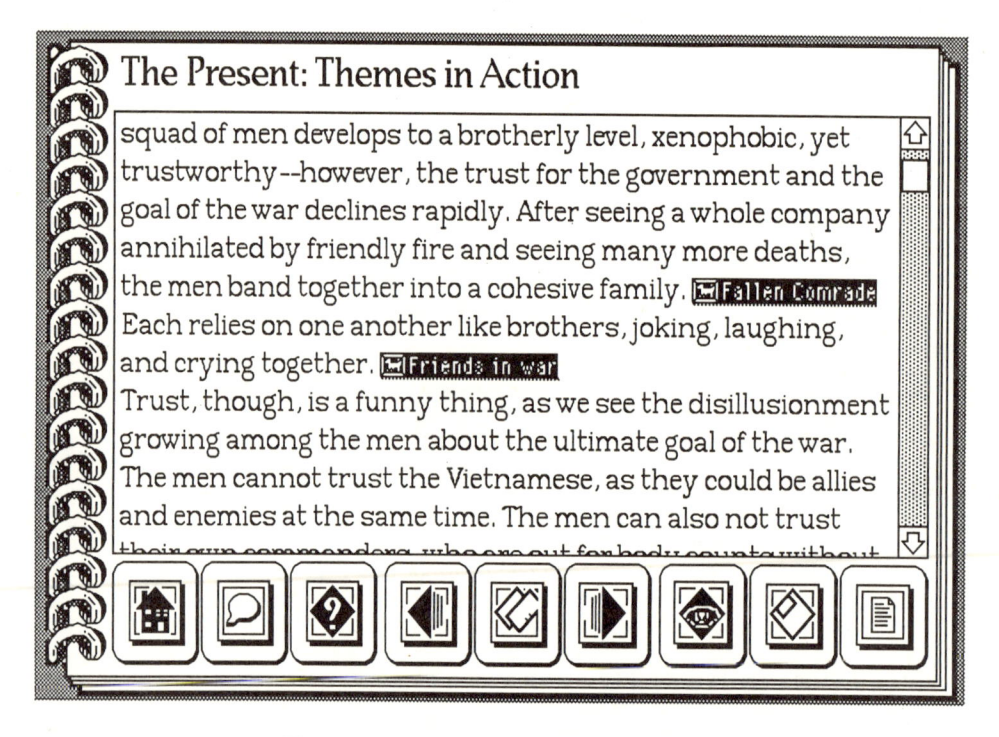

The Present: Themes in Action

squad of men develops to a brotherly level, xenophobic, yet trustworthy--however, the trust for the government and the goal of the war declines rapidly. After seeing a whole company annihilated by friendly fire and seeing many more deaths, the men band together into a cohesive family. [Fallen Comrade] Each relies on one another like brothers, joking, laughing, and crying together. [Friends in war] Trust, though, is a funny thing, as we see the disillusionment growing among the men about the ultimate goal of the war. The men cannot trust the Vietnamese, as they could be allies and enemies at the same time. The men can also not trust

Figure 8.4. Textbook Toolbox screen.

As the experience progressed, interesting patterns emerged. One of the books the students read was about the Vietnam conflict. Several students have parents who saw active duty in Vietnam. However, for a few of them, discussions at home about Vietnam were taboo. Thus, the hypermedia became a way for them to begin to explore unresolved issues. Others were reluctant to bring in artifacts. But as the actual creation of the hypermedia continued, the influx of artifacts increased dramatically. Students commented that they needed to really see where their project was heading before they could connect the ideas to outside media. Then it became easy.

Students generally believed the experience to be fruitful, both for them personally and potentially for their future students. Several regarded hypermedia as a tool that would help foster creativity: "I think hypermedia could be a very big help in the classroom. Kids would really love composing their own projects and I think it gives them an opportunity to get really creative." Others cited the links that could be forged between various media: "I think it is beneficial for adolescents to see how literature they read can be related to each other and related to more modern forms of media." One student summed up the entire project like this: "It seems like a great way for students to explore a topic, theme, or piece of literature...at the same time creating their own piece of work that acts as a valuable learning tool. It also gets them to think in terms of present day applications and artifacts, and allows them to cross several genres and forms of media." One final student comment—"I thought the whole project was incredible."

Thinking Engaged by Hypermedia/Multimedia Constructionism

Why should we have learners create hypermedia and multimedia programs? In addition to engaging learners in meaning making (as described above), designing multimedia presentations engages learners in many critical thinking skills. Carver *et al.* (1992, pp. 388–389) listed some of those thinking skills that learners need to use as designers:

Project Management Skills
- Creating a timeline for the completion of the project.
- Allocating resources and time to different segments of the project.
- Assigning roles to team members.

Research Skills
- Determining the nature of the problem and how the research should be organized.
- Posing thoughtful questions, and determining structure, model, cases, values, and roles.
- Searching for information using text, electronic, and pictorial sources of information.
- Developing new information with surveys, interviews, questionnaires, and other original information sources.
- Analyzing and interpreting all of the information collected to find and interpret patterns.

Organization and Representation Skills
- Deciding how to segment and sequence information to make it understandable.
- Deciding how the information will be represented (text, pictures, movies)
- Deciding how the information will be organized (hierarchy, sequence) and how it will be linked.

Presentation Skills
- Mapping the design onto the presentation, implementing the ideas in multimedia.
- Attracting and maintaining the interest of the audience.

Reflection Skills
- Evaluating the program and the process used to create it.
- Revising the design of the program using feedback.

This list of skills offers educators a pedagogical framework of objectives to use as support as they lobby for the funds to establish hypermedia/multimedia centers within school classrooms, libraries, and computer labs. Currently, our world is one in which meanings are represented through multiple media, but our classrooms remain dominated by printed books, many of which present lists of facts unseparated from ideas and uncritical of underlying cultural beliefs. School lessons too often focus on reading and memorizing the information in these printed texts, marginalizing other forms of representing knowledge, other cultural identities, and leaving students relatively unsophisticated in their interpretation of mass produced images. Students have the ability to demonstrate the skills listed above, but very few of them experience the classroom activities and learning tools which would support the development of these knowledge construction skills. Hypermedia/multimedia development is one vehicle for aiding the accomplishment of these skills.

Conclusion

The classic school textbook and test are tools which have limited value, even in yesterday's world. They are most often contextualized within a view of knowledge as objective, outside the individual, and beyond the shared experience of the students' social community. This instructionist context has been well documented by educational researchers across this century. "The picture is of students passively listening, reading textbooks, completing assignments, and rarely initiating anything—at least in the academic subjects" (Goodlad, 1983, p. 10). And, long before, Dewey (1938) found it problematic that "the subject matter of education consists of bodies of information and of skills that have been worked out in the past; therefore, the chief business of the school is to transmit them to the new generation" (p. 17). Hypermedia/multimedia tools—not just the technology, but the technology as a tool—has the potential to reorganize classroom learning activity and support the active participation of students in the gathering of facts, the building of concepts, the negotiation of interpretations, the invention of representations, and the critique of shared products of knowledge. The use of these tools may help us make the critical shift in defining language and literacy as the continuous act of inventing and creating meaning in our social interactions with others, and leave behind the mistaken idea that language and literacy only act as a conduit by which already formed ideas travel between minds.

Multimedia books and lectures, however, also pose a danger because the technology might only replace the old-style authorized textbook. Instead of lecturing from notes to give the correct interpretation of the printed text, the teacher can now project the notes illuminated with the appropriate images and sounds, and the correct sequence of illustrative examples. The power of visual media, which has long been limited in the classroom, will suddenly become valued by teachers, but it will be embedded in maintaining the practice of transmitting and testing "correct" knowledge. The student would remain passive with respect to the construction of the knowledge carefully linked by the media design expert. There is little about many current multimedia books on CD-ROM and multimedia lectures which encourage the student to examine how the various media excerpts were selected and organized, or to interrogate the interpretations which underlie the whole and contextualize the meaning of each single media part. The hypermedia/multimedia tool alone may not change much about school instructional practice, if we do not at the same time work to refocus the evaluation of student knowledge from the academic game of reproducing the right answers, to the participation in socially interactive situations in which students construct, share, negotiate, and critique representations of subject matter inquiries (Myers, 1992).

For hypermedia/multimedia to enlighten our age, students must become authors, not consumers, of multimedia knowledge bases. As readers only, they are less likely to examine and understand the experiential truth of images and sounds that appear to be the same first-hand experience as everyday life, when actually these excerpted "texts" are constructed interpretations of reality. To be capable of deconstructing the potential meanings of a single hypermedia/multimedia experience, students must be able to see "texts of knowledge" as constructions in which authors purposefully select and exclude images and representations in relation to all of the other cultural media and experiences that they connect. By engaging in the design and construction of knowledge representations using hypermedia/multimedia tools, students can become fully and critically literate in our multimedia-multicultural society. We have long recognized that writers learn to write better by writing and that better writers become more astute and critical readers. So too, for our children of the electronic age, to become full participants in our cultural meanings, they must learn to author their ideas in hypermedia/multimedia. We cannot be satisfied as educators with mesmerized eyes.

References

Bruner, J. (1986). *Actual minds, possible worlds*. Cambridge, MA: Harvard University Press.

Carver, S. M., Lehrer, R., Connell, T., & Ericksen, J. (1992). Learning by hypermedia design: Issues of assessment and implementation. *Educational Psychologist, 27*(3), 385–404.

Dewey, J. (1938). *Experience and education*. New York: Macmillan.

Duffy, T. M., & Jonassen, D. H. (1992). *Constructivism and the technology of instruction: A conversation*. Hillsdale, NJ: Lawrence Erlbaum Associates.

Freire, P., & Macedo, D. (1987). *Literacy: Reading the word and the world*. South Hadley, MA: Bergin & Garvey.

Goodlad, J. I. (1983, April). What some schools and classrooms teach. *Educational Leadership*, 8–19.

Harel, I., & Papert, S. (1990). Software design as a learning environment. *Interactive Learning Environments, 1*, 1–32.

Hays, K.E., Weingard, P., Guzdial, M., Jackson, S., Boyle, R.A., & Soloway, E. (1993, June). *Students as multimedia authors*. Paper presented at the Ed Media conference, Orlando, FL.

Jonassen, D. H., Wilson, B. G., Wang, S., & Grabinger, R. S. (1993). Constructivistic uses of expert systems to support learning. *Journal of Computer Based Instruction, 20*(3), 86–94.

Lehrer, R. (1993). Authors of knowledge: Patterns of hypermedia design. In S. P. LaJoie & S. J. Derry (Eds.), *Computers as cognitive tools*. Hillsdale, NJ: Lawrence Erlbaum Associates.

Lehrer, R., Erickson, J., & Connell, T. (in press). Learning by designing hypermedia documents. *Computers in Schools*.

Myers, J. (1992). Curricular designs that resonate with adolescents' ways of knowing. In R. Lehrer (Ed.), *Early adolescence: Perspectives on research, policy, and intervention* (pp. 191–206). Hillsdale, NJ: Lawrence Erlbaum Associates.

Newman, D., Griffin, P., & Cole, M. (1989). *The construction zone: Working for cognitive change in school*. Cambridge: Cambridge University Press.

Papert, S. (1990). Introduction. In I. Harel (Ed.), *Constructionist learning*. Boston: MIT.

Pea, R. D. (1985). Beyond amplification: Using the computer to reorganize mental functioning. *Educational Psychologist, 20*, 167–182.

Perkins, D. N. (1993). Person-plus: A distributed view of thinking and learning. In G. Salomon (Ed.), *Distributed cognition: Psychological and educational considerations* (pp. 88–110). Cambridge: Cambridge University Press.

Salomon, G., Perkins, D. N., & Globerson, T. (1989). Partners in cognition: Extending human intelligence with intelligent technologies. *Educational Researcher, 20*(3), 2–10.

Schank, R. C., & Jona, M. Y. (1991). Empowering the student: New perspectives on the design of teaching systems. *Journal of the Learning Sciences, 1*(1), 7–35.

Spoehr, K. T. (1992, April). *Using hypermedia to clarify conceptual structures: Illustrations from history and literature*. Paper presented at the annual meeting of the American Educational Research Association, San Francisco.

Spoehr, K. T. (1993, April). *Profiles of hypermedia authors: How students learn by doing*. Paper presented at the annual meeting of the American Educational Research Association, Atlanta.

Spoehr, K. T. (1994). Enhancing the acquisition of conceptual structures through hypermedia. In K. McGilly (Ed.), *Classroom lessons: Integrating cognitive theory and classroom practice*. Cambridge, MA: MIT Press/Bradford Books.

Spoehr, K. T., & Shapiro, A. (1991, April). *Learning from hypermedia: Making sense of a multiply linked database*. Paper presented at the annual meeting of the American Educational Research Association, Chicago, IL.

David H. Jonassen is Professor of Instructional Systems; **Jamie M. Myers** is Assistant Professor of Language and Literacy; and **Ann Margaret McKillop** is a doctoral student, all at Penn State University.

9

Epistemic Fluency and Constructivist Learning Environments

Donald Morrison
Allan Collins

Introduction

In a synthesis of the centuries-old debate about the relative merits of "teacher-centered" vs. "child-centered" views of education (Cuban, 1990), many researchers and practitioners have begun to view the classroom as a place in which teachers and students construct knowledge and negotiate meanings *together* (Edwards & Mercer, 1989; Pea, 1994). Although the degree to which these conversations are or should be teacher-directed or teacher-supported is debatable (Perkins, 1992; Scardamalia & Bereiter, 1991), it is useful, for many, to think of the school as a special kind of "knowledge-building community" (Scardamalia & Bereiter, 1991), "community of practice" (Lave & Wenger, 1991), or "community of learners" (Brown, 1992). Within such a community, learning is an "intermental process" (Edwards & Mercer, 1989; Vygotsky, 1978) that takes place in the context of real-time discourse—what Pea calls "conceptual learning conversations" (1992, 1993) or "transformative communication" (1994).

The practical implications of these views of learning are just beginning to be explored. Researchers have been studying what it means to "talk science" both in the classroom (Lemke, 1990) and among practicing scientists (Kraut, Egido, & Calegher, 1990). Others have been devising ways to help students learn how to take part in various kinds of productive learning conversations (King, 1994; Scardamalia, Bereiter, & Steinbach, 1984). Still others have been at work designing technology environments that in various ways attempt to support the social construction of knowledge (Edelson & O'Neill, 1994; Pea, 1994; Scardamalia & Bereiter, 1991).

Our purpose in this chapter is to take a closer look at what it means to "construct knowledge" as a member of a community of practice. In particular, we wish to introduce the notion of *epistemic fluency* into the discussion about the nature of "constructivist" learning environments.

Our argument runs like this:
1. Our culture supports numerous ways of constructing knowledge—some domain-specific, and some more general.
2. These different ways of constructing knowledge, which we call *epistemic games*, are culturally patterned.
3. Different contexts (communities of practice) support different ways of knowing, and therefore different kinds of epistemic games. People are more or less fluent epistemically, depending largely on their contextual experiences, i.e., the sorts of subcultures and communities of practice in which they have participated.
4. An important goal of school is to help people become epistemically fluent, i.e., be able to use and recognize a relatively large number of epistemic games.
5. A key question to ask about particular environments is whether they tend to foster (or inhibit) epistemic fluency. It seems likely that an infrastructure that combines relatively open, epistemically neutral environments with environments that provide various kinds of scaffolding will be more likely to foster epistemic fluency than environments that are dedicated only to particular kinds of knowledge construction.

Epistemic Complexity

In a complex, multicultural society such as ours, truth takes many forms. Different contexts and different subcultures support different ways of constructing knowledge, and different ways of understanding what it means to "know" something (Belenky, Clinchy, Goldberger, & Tarule, 1986; Morrison, Crowder, & Théberge, 1994; Perry, 1970). What passes for truth at one family's dinner table may be dismissed as hearsay at another. Scientists of different stripes have different methods of building and testing theory.

The culture's large repertoire of tools for understanding and knowing is both enriching—and potentially confusing and frustrating to those who find themselves communicating *across* epistemic divides. Consider, for example, the conversation reported by Minner (1994), involving what he describes as a "culture clash" between a university professor (himself) and a school teacher colleague in a field-based training program. The teacher had been discussing the advantages of multi-age classroom arrangements. In response, the professor described a recent meta-analytic study of multi-age groupings which had found very little evidence that these groupings had any positive impact on learning. Minner reports the ensuing conversation like this:

> *My colleague's reaction was a strong one...She simply chose not to believe the results. They were counterintuitive, she claimed. They were inconsistent with her personal experiences—experiences that were powerful and important to her. I saw this as a perfect segue into how teachers' perceptions sometimes differed from those of*

university professors. One must try to go beyond one's own biography, I suggested. Sometime one's personal experiences are not consistent with what is known to be true. The idiosyncrasies of one's own life should not distract one from the truth. My colleague's response was a classic one. "You're wrong," she said.

What is interesting here is the communication gap, based not on the lack of a shared language (although in a sense the two are speaking different languages), as on the lack of a shared epistemological framework. The teacher *might* have responded simply that her own experience was not consistent with the findings of the meta-analysis. The professor *might* have acknowledged that practitioner experience in particular situations is useful evidence, that the teacher's definition of a successful outcome may have been different from the outcome measures used in the meta-analysis, and so forth. Instead, both continued to make conversational moves based on an apparent inability or unwillingness to share or even acknowledge the other's epistemological frame of reference. We take this as an apparent case of interlocuters lacking *epistemic fluency*, defined as the ability to identify and use different ways of knowing, to understand their different forms of expression and evaluation, and to take the perspective of others who are operating within a different epistemic framework (Morrison, Crowder, & Théberge, 1994). The next few sections of the chapter explain more precisely what we mean by this, and why we think such cases are relevant to discussions of "constructivist learning environments."

Epistemic Forms and Games

It is axiomatic in sociocultural views of learning that knowledge is not some amorphous entity or collection of isolated facts that can be transmitted from one person to another like pieces of mail. Knowledge has a structure, and learning to construct knowledge (learning to learn), and to co-construct it with others, requires learning how to use the knowledge-building structures that one's culture makes available. What are these structures, and how are they used?

Collins and Ferguson (1993) introduce two related concepts for studying the construction of knowledge: *epistemic forms* and *epistemic games*. Epistemic forms are "target structures" that guide inquiry. Examples include lists, stage models, hierarchies, systems-dynamics models, and axiom systems. Epistemic games are sets of moves, constraints, and strategies that guide the construction of knowledge around a particular epistemic form.

The *list game*, for example, focuses on the construction of a simple list (of causes, solutions, instances, etc.). People often make lists as part of carrying out their day-to-day activities, but they also make lists in an attempt to understand the world. Every list is implicitly the answer to a question. Some epistemic questions might be "What are the basic substances things are made of?" "What are the different forces in the world?" and "What were the causes of the French Revolution?" If the answer to these questions must be discovered, rather than recalled or looked up, then the list-making process is an inquiry process and the resulting list constitutes new knowledge.

List-making can be elaborated by adding constraints on the contents of the list. These constraints are the rules of the game and serve two purposes. They cause the resulting list to be more focused and they facilitate the finding of ideas. The constraints established by the list-making game that we have identified are: *similarity, coverage, distinctness, multiplicity,* and *brevity*. Similarity is the requirement that the items in the list be of the same general form: the same scale, the same kind of thing, of the same importance, and so on. Coverage means that all possible answers to the question are covered by the items on the list. Distinctness requires that no two items overlap or are difficult to distinguish. Multiplicity means that a list must have more then one element. Brevity refers to the fact that short lists are generally better than long ones, because they constitute more succinct answers to the inquiry.

Each of these constraints leads to useful list-constructing strategies in the form of auxiliary questions that may help to guide the inquiry. Similarity provokes the question: "Is one of these things not like the others?" Coverage asks, "Has anything been left out?" or "Is every example I can think of covered by one of the items in the list so far?" Distinctness leads to asking, "Do any of these items overlap or mean the same thing?" Multiplicity is a definitional constraint and really only leads to the question, "Am I really seeking a list?" when only one item can be thought of. Finally, brevity (when a list begins to grow too large) prompts questions like, "Should I be using more abstract categories?" or "Can the elements of this list be partitioned in some way?" The questions generated by violations of the brevity constraint often lead to major shifts in the nature of what is being listed. The magnitude of the developing list may push one into deciding to use much larger classes, or to change games altogether by trying to form a hierarchy or a table.

In addition to constraints, Collins and Ferguson (1993) have identified four other characteristics of epistemic games:

> *Entry conditions:* The entry conditions of an epistemic game determine when it is appropriate to play that game. The list game is appropriate when the question is of the form "What is the nature of X?," where X is decomposable into subsets or constituents. The list game is also appropriate early in an inquiry process, since it requires little to get it started, and since it often provides a basis for playing more powerful games as the inquiry proceeds.
>
> *Moves*: The moves in an epistemic game are the actions that can be taken at different points in the game. In the list game the basic moves are: (1) add a new item, (2) combine items, (3) substitute an item, (4) split an item, and (5) remove an item. There is another kind of move: changing the question. For instance, changing the question from "What are the things I can do to prevent pollution?" to "What are the things that anyone can do to prevent pollution?" Question alteration is a basic part of inquiry (Schank, 1986).
>
> *Transfers*: As we suggested above, sometimes the best move is to transfer to a different epistemic game. If an inquiry began as a list-making game, then transfers to the hierarchy game, the table game, or the primitive-elements game are possible.
>
> *The target epistemic form*: The desired result of any epistemic game is the completion of an epistemic form that satisfies the inquiry. Each epistemic

game produces a characteristic form. Because of this correspondence, the names of the games and forms are often similar—the list-making game produces lists, the system-dynamics game produces system-dynamics models, and compare and contrast produces a comparison table. But the same form may be produced by more than one game; for example the primitive-elements game also produces lists.

Epistemic games are described in Collins and Ferguson (1993):

compare-and-contrast game
spatial-analysis game
cost-benefit-analysis game
primitive-elements game
table or cross-product game
hierarchy or tree-structure game
axiom-system game
critical-event-analysis game
cause-and-effect game
problem-analysis game
form-and-function game
systems-dynamics game
aggregate-behavior game
trend-and-cycles game
situation-action game
constraint-system game

If you are thinking of other examples, or wondering if all the items on this list are really "epistemic games," then you are playing the list game with us. You may also be thinking that while it is possible to make a list of exemplars, the set of epistemic games is ill-defined. They are essentially "fuzzy" phenomena. You can make a case for a given set of epistemic games being vital for construction of knowledge in a technological society—Collins and Ferguson (1993) present a list of reasonably convincing ones—but one cannot be confident that any given list is not flawed by serious omissions. The same can be said for any attempt to list the moves of a particular game. Also, while it is theoretically helpful to identify basic games such as the compare-and-contrast game or the cost-benefit game, it seems clear that these games are never played in isolation. Rather, participants in natural face-to-face conversation constantly transfer from one game to another, continually negotiating and re-negotiating the name of the game, the rules and moves, etc.

This leads to another important point. While it is possible to play the list game or the tree structure game with names of epistemic games (as we are doing here), it is predictable that someone will eventually argue that lists or tree structures do not adequately capture the relationships between different games.

Thus, although it seems safe to say that there are indeed certain basic schemas with game-like qualities that make the social construction of knowledge possible, we do not claim to have anything like a working grammar, nor are we confident that it is possible to construct one. At this point, our argument for the importance of this notion is based more on its utility as a framework for analysis than on the psychological reality of these structures.

Epistemic Games in the Classroom: An Example

To see how epistemic game theory may be used in understanding classroom discourse, consider the fragment of conversation reported in Morrison, Crowder, and Théberge (1994). Aaron, a sixth-grader, has just provided an account of seasonal change based on the accepted "tilted earth" model.

Teacher: Aaron, can you give evidence of this theory of yours?

Aaron: Yeah, what happens is the sun is over here [left fist] okay, say this is the sun. When it goes around, say this is summer and this is winter [pointing to the hemispheres of the globe].

Teacher: But what's your evidence?

Aaron: When it goes around, [moves the globe in arc around his left fist] now this is summer and this is winter [his back is to the camera, blocking the view of the globe and his hands].

Teacher: I know. You're showing me a model, but is there evidence? Would you be able to prove that?

Aaron: How? What do you mean?

Teacher: Well, that's exactly what I mean. Could you prove it? Are there ways that you can prove this? Or is this just kind of a theory that you think sounds good?

Aaron: No, no, no, this is what happens, I know.

Viewed in terms of the framework described here, Aaron and the teacher are playing two different games. Aaron's moves may be interpeted as characteristic of a sort of spatial-analysis game, where the target structure is a model showing the form and function of a physical system (consisting of a globe, his hands, etc.) that accurately depicts some aspect of the functioning of a natural system (the solar system). The teacher, on the other hand, while apparently recognizing Aaron's game (*I know. You're showing me a model...*), attempts a transfer to what might be called the "theory and evidence" game—performed by his repeated requests for evidence.

Interestingly, Aaron seems unmoved by the illocutionary force of the teacher's moves. He does *not* say, as he might have, *I'm not trying to prove a theory, I'm just trying to describe the dynamics of the model*, which would be the equivalent of saying "I understand that you have transferred to the theory-and-evidence game, but I want to keep playing the physical model game." One way of explaining this is to say that Aaron is somehow incapable of distinguishing conceptually between theory and evidence (*cf.* Kuhn, 1989). However, one might also say that in this instance Aaron simply fails to respond to a theory-and-evidence move.

Epistemic Game Theory and Other Paradigms

We are not, of course, the only ones to point to higher level structures involved in the creation of knowledge. For example, King (1994), summarizing Brown & Campione (1986), and Brown, Bransford, Ferrara, and Campione (1983) refer to "procedures" that help people "reformulate new information or restructure their existing knowledge." These procedures include drawing inferences about new information, elaborating by adding details, and generating relationships between new material and material already in memory. Pea (1994) defines a central activity of learning as the "construction and refinement by learners of documents, problem interpretations, models, analyses, and so on." Hammer (1994) talks about the purpose of science instruction being not merely the learning of "facts and established theories" but also developing "habits and attitudes for inquiry" and refining "reasoning practices and abilities." In a teaching strategy that King (1994) calls guided cooperative questioning, students are taught to use a set of "thought-provoking" questions such as "What are the strengths and weakness of…? "What would happen if…?" and "Why is…important?" In all of these cases, we suspect a significant overlap in what we are calling epistemic forms and games, and what others call knowledge-building strategies, procedures, habits of mind, and so forth. A chief attraction of epistemic game theory is that allows a relatively more fine-grained description than is currently available of what it means to "construct knowledge" in the midst of actual conversations. In this emerging theory, the conversational moves of discourse analysis become the building blocks of knowledge construction.

In fact, from the perspective of discourse analysis, epistemic forms might be seen as special *frames* (Minsky, 1975), *scenarios* (Sanford & Garrod, 1981), or *schemata* (Anderson, 1977; van Dijk, 1981) that are used to construct and interpret certain kinds of text—both written and spoken (Brown & Yule, 1983). For example, just as in listening to a story about A Day in Court we expect to hear about the *judge*, the *accused*, *witnesses*, *lawyers*, and so on, so in listening to someone describing a process, we expect to hear about the *phases* or *stages* in the process, what *triggers* the transition from one stage to the next, the *duration* of the process, etc. The prior existence of these structures, which we have somehow stored away in our heads, helps us construct meaning from what might otherwise be a jumble of unrelated chunks of language. They also allow us to take part in the social construction of meaning with others. For example, once we have established that our interlocutor is playing some sort of category game, we can ask for exemplary cases, argue that the categories are not discrete, and so forth.

By highlighting the game-like qualities of knowledge construction, and especially its interactional nature, we believe it is possible to arrive at a more precise understanding of these structures and the role they play in the give and take of natural conversation. This kind of work may help bridge the gap between theories of conceptual change and sociolinguistic theories of language use (see Pea, 1994, p. 293).

Development of Epistemic Fluency

Stated in terms of epistemic game theory, epistemic fluency is the ability to recognize and practice a culture's epistemic games, with their associated forms (target structures), goals, rules, and strategies. How does this kind of fluency develop?

To answer this question, we think it is essential to recognize that epistemic forms and games are language-based. Although epistemic forms may be represented graphically (e.g., as tree structures, causal loop diagrams, etc.), the forms are themselves meaningless without reference to semantic structures encoded in human language. Otherwise they are just boxes and arrows. Similarly, while you can play epistemic games by yourself, in the private arena of internal cognition (as now, while thinking and reading), you cannot do so without language, any more than you can escape your identity as a social creature.

Understanding the linguistic and sociocultural basis of epistemic-game theory allows us to postulate how epistemic fluency is acquired. Following the work of Vygotsky and others (Vygotsky, 1978; Newman, Griffin, & Cole, 1989), it seems reasonable to assume that epistemic fluency, like language in general, develops in the context of social interactions with other members of a community of practice, including those who are at least slightly more expert at playing these games. This means you learn how to play the theory-and-evidence game, or the cost-benefit game, or the cause-and-effect game, simply and only by playing these games with people who are already relatively more fluent than you are—and who, crucially, are willing to gradually *pull you up* to their level of expertise by letting you play with them.

The Role of Technology

What role, if any, can technology play in the development of epistemic fluency? Can software environments and communication tools enrich opportunities to learn and play a large variety of epistemic games? Our simple answer to this question is yes—but only if the software environments support, and are supported by, a community of practice in which the social construction of knowledge in the context of authentic goal-directed projects is the dominant activity. If the community is oriented toward some other, more limited purpose—say, the accumulation of "correct answers"—or if there is insufficient *human* expertise in the system, then no software environment, no matter how sophisticated, will help students develop true epistemic fluency.

For example, while it is often claimed that technology improves access to information, simple access to information probably contributes about as much to epistemic fluency as watching a tennis match does to learning how to play the game. Wittrock's (1990) model of generative learning predicts that deep understanding (true knowledge construction) is more likely to occur when individuals actively transform information and integrate it into existing cognitive structures. In our model, this means that one must play epistemic games *with* the information. Assuming that this is the case—that learners *participate* in the information they have access to—then a rich source of information potentially supports the development of epistemic fluency.

We see at least three basic ways that technology can contribute to the people's understanding and use of epistemic games: (1) as communication environments, (2) as tools for constructing theories, and (3) as simulation environments to play epistemic games. We briefly describe these possibilities below:

Communication Environments

One claim for technology is that it allows users to manipulate symbols and organize textual information in new ways. Environments such as CSILE (Scardamalia & Bereiter, 1991), and CoVis (Edelson & O'Neill, 1994; Edelson, Gomez, Polman, Gordin, & Fishman, 1994) are specifically designed to support certain ways of constructing knowledge, or, in our terms, epistemic games. For example, the CoVis "page types"—*information, commentary, question, conjecture, evidence for, evidence against, plan,* and *step in plan,* which structure student interaction with the software—may be seen as corresponding to moves in the theory-and-evidence game.

This approach can be generalized to other epistemic games. For example, students might be supported in constructing stage models by prompts for each stage of a process or event, and with additional prompts for: (1) specific dimensions that characterize the different stages; (2) interrelationships between the dimensions; and (3) the reasons for each transition between stages. Epistemic games all have a specific set of constraints that can act as prompts in such a communication environment.

Tools or Construction Kits

Yet another function of technology lies in the use of various kinds of tools or "construction kits" (Perkins, 1992) that support people in carrying out tasks. Examples include physical construction sets, such as Legos and Tinker Toys, but also computer languages, mathematical modeling environments (such as *Mathematica*), and spreadsheets. One such tool is the commercially-available program called *Stella* that is a construction kit for building systems-dynamics models (i. e., playing the systems-dynamics game). *Stella* provides the user with the ability to construct very complex models of systems using a few basic concepts developed in system-dynamics modelling. When the models are constructed, they can then be run to see their effects.

Such tools could be constructed for a number of epistemic games. *Mathematica,* for example, enables users to construct complex sets of constraint equations (i. e., to play the constraint-system game) and solve them. There are also a number of graphical analysis tools that can be used for constructing trend-and-cycle models. It would be helpful if such tools had expertise built into them for effectively playing these epistemic games, so that they could provide advice to novice users.

Simulations or "Phenomenaria"

Perkins (1992) identifies "phenomenaria" as a separate category from construction kits, including models, simulations, and "microworlds" such as *SimCity* and *ThinkerTools* (White & Horwitz, 1987). For example, *RelLab* (Horwitz, Taylor, & Hickman, 1994) is an interactive computer environment that allows users to construct thought experiments involving paradoxes of relative motion at both everyday and relativistic speeds. Users create "scenarios" by placing objects like spaceships, trains, cars, etc., in a *RelLab* window, setting them in motion, and having them emit light, sound, or particles (explosion fragments) at particular points in spacetime. Scenarios can be viewed in different frames of reference. The program lends itself to construction of knowledge about relative motion using an epistemic game that might be called the thought-experiment game as contextualized in the domain of relativity—characterized by moves such as the following: *Is it the same time or a different time in the frame of the spaceship? How fast is the car going relative to the oncoming truck? The speed of light is the same in every frame, so the clock on the spaceship must be slower.*

In a sense, *RelLab* constitutes a sort of flexible epistemic form, a target structure or set of schemas with which the thought-experiment game can be played, just as a chess board and its pieces allow and invite one to play chess. The clocks and velocity indicators that attach to the objects, the frame of reference indicator, the rulers, and the expanding circles that represent emissions of light, sound, or particles are all available for use in playing the thought-experiment game. Although the software is specifically designed to support this game, it will not teach you how to play it. For this you need a human who is willing to play the game with you. In classrooms in which *RelLab* was piloted, the teacher posed a weekly paradox, "stimulated" initial discussion, acted as a "research advisor" to students working with the software, and chaired periodic "research conferences" at which student groups reported and discussed their findings (Horwitz, Taylor, & Hickman 1994, p. 81). In our interpretation, this teacher helped organize a community of practice in which "playing the though-experiment game" was a central activity, supported by the structure of the software (the game board), and, at the discourse level, by the teacher's shaping of the discourse.

Perhaps the most important aspect of the *RelLab* example is that it forces us to extend the perimeter of the "constructivist learning environment" beyond confines of the software environment to include the community of practice that uses the environment as a construction set.

Summary and Conclusion

In this chapter we have introduced epistemic-game theory as a framework for thinking about the design of "constructivist" learning environments. Epistemic forms are the target structures that humans use to construct knowledge. Epistemic games are the sets of moves, constraints, and strategies associated with particular forms. Epistemic fluency is the ability to recognize and practice a culture's epistemic games, to understand their different forms of expression and evaluation, and to take the perspective of interlocutors who are operating within different epistemic frameworks.

Viewed from the perspective of epistemic-game theory, a constructivist learning environment is a community of practice that has access to some particular set of epistemic forms and games. Relatively rich environments provide frequent opportunities for participants to play these epistemic games with each other, and, crucially, with members of the community who are relatively more expert. While software environments can be useful in helping students develop expertise in certain *kinds* of epistemic games, it is much less clear that it is possible to construct a single software environment that is suitable for helping students develop real fluency. It seems more likely that schools will benefit from environments that support a wide variety of different tools, including simulations, construction sets of all kinds, and communication tools that extend the community of practice to include participants from beyond the school walls.

References

Anderson, R. (1977). The notion of schemata and the educational enterprise. In R. Anderson *et al.* (Eds.), *Schooling and the acquisition of knowledge*. Hillsdale, NJ: Lawrence Erlbaum Associates.

Belenky, M., Clinchy, B., Goldberger, N., & Tarule, J. (1986). *Women's ways of knowing*. New York: Basic Books.

Brown, A.L. (1992). Design experiments: Theoretical and methodological challenges in creating complex interventions in classroom settings. *Journal of the Learning Sciences*, 2(2), 141–178.

Brown, A. L., Bransford, J. D., Ferrara, R. A., & Campione, J. C. (1983). Learning, remembering, and understanding. In J. Flavell & E. M. Markman (Eds.), *Handbook of child psychology* (4th ed.). *Cognitive development* (Vol. 3, pp. 515–629). New York: John Wiley & Sons.

Brown, A. L., & Campione, J. C. (1986). Psychological theory and the study of learning disabilities. *American Psychologist*, 41(10), 1059–1068.

Brown, G., & Yule, G. (1983). *Discourse analysis*. Cambridge: Cambridge University Press.

Collins, A., & Ferguson, W. (1993). Epistemic forms and epistemic games: Structures and strategies to guide inquiry. *Educational Psychologist*, 28(1), 25–42.

Cuban, L. (1990). Reforming, again, again, and again. *Educational Researcher*, January, 3–13.

Edelson, D., Gomez, L., Polman, J., Gordin, D., & Fishman, B. (1994). Scaffolding student inquiry with collaborative visualization tools. Paper presented at the Annual Meeting of the American Educational Research Association, New Orleans.

Edelson, D., & O'Neill, D. (1994). The CoVis Collaboratory Notebook: Computer support for scientific inquiry. Paper presented at the Annual Meeting of the American Educational Research Association, New Orleans.

Edwards, D., & Mercer, N. (1989). Reconstructing context: The conventionalization of classroom knowledge. *Discourse Processes*, 12, 91–104.

Gee, J. (1990). *Social linguistics and literacies: Ideology in discourses*. London: Falmer Press.

Hammer, D. (1994). Epistemological considerations in teaching introductory physics. Paper presented at the annual meeting of the American Educational Research Association, New Orleans.

Horwitz, P., Taylor, E. F., & Hickman, P. (1994, February). "Relativity readiness" using the RelLab program. *The Physics Teacher*, 32, 81–86.

King, A. (1994). Guiding knowledge construction in the classroom: Effects of teaching children how to question and explain. *American Educational Research Journal*, 31(2), 338–368.

Kraut, R., Egido, C., & Calegher, J. (1990). Patterns of contact and communication in scientific research collaboration. In *Intellectual teamwork: Social and technological foundations of cooperative work*. Hillsdale, NJ: Lawrence Erlbaum Associates.

Kuhn, D. (1989). Children and adults as intuitive scientists. *Psychological Review*, 96(4), 674–689.

Lave, J., & Wenger, E. (1991). *Situated learning: Legitimate peripheral participation.* Cambridge: Cambridge University Press.

Lemke, J. L. (1990). *Talking science.* Norwood, NJ: Ablex Publishing Corp.

Minner, S. (1994). When "cultures" clash: How small things subvert university-school collaborations. *Education Week,* April 13.

Minsky, M. (1975). A framework for representing knowledge. In P. H. Winston (Ed.), *The psychology of computer vision.* New York: McGraw-Hill.

Morrison, D., Crowder, E., & Théberge, C. (1994). The development of sense-making as a way of knowing and talking: A modest longitudinal study. Paper presented at the Annual Meeting of the American Educational Research Association, New Orleans.

Newman, D., Griffin, P., & Cole, M. (1989). *The construction zone: Working for cognitive change in school.* Cambridge: Cambridge University Press.

Pea, R. (1992). Augmenting the discourse of learning with computer-based learning environments. In E. de Corte, M. Linn, H. Mandl, & L. Verschaffel (Eds.), *Computer-based learning environments and problem-solving* [NATO Series, subseries F: Computer and System Sciences] (pp. 313–343). New York: Springer-Verlag.

Pea, R. (1993). Practices of distributed intelligence and designs of education. In G. Salomon (Ed.), *Distributed cognition* (pp. 47–87). New York: Cambridge University Press.

Pea, R. (1994). Seeing what we build together: Distributed multimedia learning environments for transformative communications. *Journal of the Learning Sciences, 3*(3), 285–299.

Perkins, D. (1992). Technology meets constructivism: Do they make a marriage? In T. Duffy & D. Jonassen, (Eds.), *Constructivism and the technology of instruction.* Hillsdale, NJ: Lawrence Erlbaum Associates. Originally in *Educational Technology,* 1991, *31*(5).

Perry, W. (1970). *Forms of intellectual and ethical development in the college years.* New York: Holt, Rinehart, & Winston.

Richards, J., Barowy, W., & Levin, D. (1992). Computer simulations in the science classroom. *Journal of Science Education and Technology, 1*(1), 67–79.

Sanford, A., & Garrod, S. (1981). *Understanding written language.* Chichester: John Wiley & Sons.

Scardamalia, M., & Bereiter, C. (1991). Computer support for knowledge-building communities. *Journal of the Learning Sciences, 1*(1), 37–68.

Scardamalia, M., Bereiter, C., & Steinbach, R. (1984). Teachability of reflective processes in written composition. *Cognitive Science, 8,* 173–190.

Schank, R.C. (1986). *Explanation patterns.* Hillsdale, NJ: Lawrence Erlbaum Associates.

Stanovich, K. (1994). Reconceptualizing intelligence: Dysrationalia as an intuition pump. *Education Digest, 23*(4), 22–23.

Sternberg, R. (1994). What if the construct of dysrationalia were an example of itself? *Education Digest, 23*(4), 22–23.

van Dijk, T. (1981). Review of R. O. Freedle (Ed.), 1979. *Journal of Linguistics, 17,* 140–148.

Vygotsky, L. (1978). *Mind in society: The development of higher psychological processes.* Cambridge, MA: Harvard University Press.

Wittrock, M. (1990). Generative processes of comprehension. *Educational Psychologist, 24,* 345–376.

White, B., & Horwitz, P. (1987). *ThinkerTools*: Enabling students to understand physical laws. In the *Proceedings of the Ninth Annual Meeting of the Cognitive Science Society.* Hillsdale, NJ: Lawrence Erlbaum Associates.

Donald Morrison, a Scientist at Bolt Beranek and Newman Inc., currently serves as Co-Principal Investigator for the NSF-supported Conditions for Sense-making project, and co-leads the Assessment Team on the Co-NECT Schools project at BBN.

Allan Collins is Principal Scientist at Bolt Beranek and Newman Inc. and Professor of Education and Social Policy at Northwestern University. He was Co-Director of the Center for Technology in Education from 1991 to 1994, and currently co-directs the assessment effort for the Co-NECT School project.

10

Implementing Jasper Immersion: A Case of Conceptual Change

Michael F. Young
Bonnie K. Nastasi
Lynette Braunhardt

Whenever an educational research project is exported to a real classroom in the form of teacher training or an implementation study, it is expected that the classroom teacher will change to accommodate the new theoretical perspective of the research project. The researchers' theoretical conceptions, fundamental to the design of the project, are considered to be more stable—less likely to change. Yet, from a constructivist perspective, one might expect the interaction of theory with practice to inform and alter both. This is precisely what we experienced in implementing a constructivist design in a constructivist manner. We observed a conceptual change in classroom teaching regarding the nature of learning. In addition, research hypotheses were re-conceptualized and fundamental theoretical concepts were revised. This duality, potentially a hallmark of implementing constructivist designs, is presented from the perspective of situated cognition.

Perspectives of Situated Cognition

Recent cognitive psychology has developed the view that all learning should be considered "situated"; that is, co-determined by the attributes of the context along with the attributes of the people involved. The theoretical basis for situated cognition is grounded in the perceptual psychology of James Gibson (1979/1986) that defines the attributes of the context as the information specifying the affordances of an environment (e.g., books afford reading, doors afford opening, windows afford looking through). In parallel, the attributes of the people are defined by the activities in which they are capable of engaging, their effectivities. Note the duality of this definition in which books would only afford reading for an agent with the ability (effectivity) to read.

The co-determined nature of situated cognition's description of thinking caused us to focus on the interactions going on within classrooms. Classrooms that provided only lecture, text, and worksheets appeared quite impoverished from this perspective in that they did not afford the rich multiple interactions that exist in everyday activities (e.g., Rogoff & Lave, 1984). We believed that interactive videodisc technology could enrich the classroom by providing contrived yet realistic situations with high fidelity (Cognition & Technology Group at Vanderbilt, 1990, 1992, 1993; Young, 1993).

Yet one important aspect of any student's environment is a knowledgable adult with expertise in a domain relevant to the context established by the videodisc—in our case, a mathematics teacher. From the perspective of situated cognition, the teacher must be prepared to manage the interaction among groups of students and the problem space presented by the videodisc problem. To do this, the teacher must know the problem and its solution, plus the common errors, preconceptions, and misconceptions that arise. In addition, teachers must be prepared for students noticing attributes of the rich, realistic context that had not been attended to before, and for the possibility of novel solutions. Teachers must also be prepared to guide student interactions as they work cooperatively to solve complex problems that no one student could manage alone.

It should be noted that situated cognition differs from constructivism (e.g., Duffy & Jonassen, 1992) by rejecting the solely internal nature of the understandings that are constructed. Situated cognition emphasizes perception over memory. Understanding is considered to be directly related to current contexts and not retrieved and assembled from memory. Meaning is described as arising directly from a match between current personal goals and the actions the present environment afford, rather than as a match between stored information and incoming information. Specifically, learning and understanding are inherently interactions that arise on the fly in a specific context, not the property of an individual stored in memory.

For situated learning, a critical component of any "realistic" complex problem is the need for collaboration (Young & McNeese, in press). From our perspective, students' active engagement in collaborative problem solving (i.e., characterized by cooperation and shared decision making) encouraged negotiation of perspectives and consensus building, a process referred to as *reciprocal sense making* (Nastasi & Clements, 1991, 1992). Within such a context, students have opportunities to pose and resolve discrepant viewpoints (conflicts of ideas, or *cognitive conflicts*). Engagement in both consensus building and resolution of cognitive conflicts have been linked to better understanding (e.g., Bearison, 1982; Bearison, Magzamen, & Filardo, 1986; Doise & Mugny, 1984; Johnson, Johnson, Pierson, & Lyons, 1985; Johnson, Brooker, Stutzman, Hultman, & Johnson, 1985; Nastasi & Clements, 1992, 1993; Nastasi, Clements, & Battista, 1990). Interactions that appear to be especially critical are resolution of cognitive conflict in which partners participate equally, discuss the quality of ideas, and attempt to reconcile or integrate their divergent perspectives (Bearison, 1982; Nastasi & Clements, 1992, 1993; Nastasi et al., 1990). Thus, instructional environments that foster consensus building and equitable resolution of discrepant viewpoints may be particularly important for fostering cognitive growth and learning. In addition, such contexts provide opportunities to examine the interaction between social problem solving and mathematical problem solving.

Our situated cognition conception of learning suggested that the affordances of the videodisc problem can only be understood as they interact with a particular problem-solving student dyad in the context of a particular classroom. Thus, our question was not how technology can be applied, or what is the impact of the Jasper problem on students, but rather, what interactions are established when these students encounter these materials. Our research attempted to establish an environment that would foster problem-solving interactions and assess the nature of the interactions that occurred.

Implementation Method

Prior to the intervention described in this chapter, there was a history of interactions between the school and participating university researchers. The first author had worked closely with the classroom teacher on more limited classroom interventions for the preceding two years. Also, a conscious effort had been made by the school administrator to target the fifth grade for this intervention. The classroom teacher had also completed a graduate seminar on the topic of situated cognition taught by the first author. Two researchers and two classroom teachers collaborated to implement the immersion intervention.

Parental consent was required for the implementation of such a special program taking place across a significant amount of time. In addition to initial parental consent, a parents' night was organized at which an explanation of the Jasper immersion program was given. Several parents elected to visit the classroom during the first few weeks of the intervention. Parents who had initial reservations about taking time away from preparation for the statewide standardized testing became supporters of the program by the end of the year.

We took three months in the Fall from traditional text instruction to engage students in "anchored instruction," using the problem-solving videodisc series "Jasper" (for a description of anchored instruction, see the Cognition & Technology Group at Vanderbilt, 1990, 1992; and Young, 1993). Instead of lectures, worksheets, and homework problems on decimals and measurement, the students were immersed into a complex, realistic problem-solving situation. In three months, the students solved three problems. Each problem represented a realistic situation in which middle school mathematics, planning, information-finding, and cooperative group problem solving could be used to solve an everyday kind of problem. Students were immersed in these problems and, after solving them, were engaged in related activities that enriched the problem context. This was problem solving in depth rather than the development of fluency with mathematical procedures across hundreds of worksheet problems. Our goal was to emphasize problem solving and other higher order thinking skills, such as planning for complexity and information finding across distributed sources, along with fifth grade mathematics topics such as decimals, ratios, and measurement. The content of the problems took us across traditional subject domains, from mathematics to science, geography, reading, writing, and physical education. Interactive videodisc technology and telecommunications played a key role. In the following Spring, the students solved a fourth videodisc problem and completed a project related to problem-solving stories.

Instruction included viewing three computer-interactive "Jasper Series" videodisc problem situations (available from Optical Data Corp.), problem solving in dyads, two lectures using direct instruction on the topics of decimals and measurement, plus classroom and follow-up activities designed to extend and enhance the problems across the curriculum.

All three authors served in both capacities, as fifth grade teacher and educational researcher. The first and third authors worked most directly to manage daily problem-solving activities and lessons along with the regular classroom teacher. During the initial three months of the intervention, conversations occurred nearly every night on the topics of lesson planning, student progress, and the theoretical approach to teaching. But the second author's role in conducting ethnographic research afforded her an opportunity also to intervene directly with target dyads, involving her directly in instruction. The second and third authors then collaborated closely in analyzing the ethnographic data; quantitative assessments were developed, administered, and analyzed primarily by the first author.

In the summer following completion of the study, the second and third authors collaborated in coding videotapes for occurrences of cooperative (social) problem solving. They viewed and coded tapes together, using a coding scheme based on previous research by the second author (e.g., Nastasi & Clements, 1992, 1993; Nastasi, Bingham, & Clements, 1993), and discussed codes until they reached consensus. This procedure provided the context for both quantitative and qualitative analyses of interactive sequences, and for discussing implications for instruction. The coding scheme focused on both student–student and teacher–student interactions during dyadic or small group activity. Target interactions included reciprocal sense-making, cognitive (idea) conflict, and level of conflict resolution (ranging from unresolved or teacher-assisted to dyad/group resolution through dominance or negotiation). (Details regarding the coding scheme can be obtained from the second author.)

Quantitative and Qualitative Approach

In any constructivist or situated learning intervention, the issues of assessment are difficult. Students are learning and thinking not only in class, but at lunch, on the bus home, and at the dinner table at night. What students write or share in class is only a small portion of their thoughts about a complex problem worked in a broad social context. The dialogue between problem-solving partners also reveals student thinking, but analysis can focus on only a few such dialogues. In our case, we decided that assessment must be broad and that complete experimental control was impossible. For this reason we undertook both quantitative (control group comparisons) and qualitative (videotape and interview) assessments. Throughout the three months, all classroom work was videotaped, ethnographic field notes were taken on two target student dyads, and pretesting/posttesting was done on this class and a similar "control" class in the same school. Pretesting included interests, attitudes toward mathematics, and basic mathematical calculation ability. During the intervention, students' planning ability was assessed using "planning cards" that enabled student dyads to construct questions relevant to solving problems by piecing together phrases on the cards (e.g., "Does Jasper" + "have enough" + "fuel"). Posttests included conventional paper and pencil measures of reading comprehension for analogous content, mathematical problem solving, and transfer complex word problems. Posttesting also included several innovative assessments. Information-finding ability was tested by showing a short video segment, rich with mathematical information, asking 10 questions, repeating the video, and asking the same questions again. Creativity was assessed by asking students to generate uses for a common rubber band. Target dyads also completed a computer-based assessment, the "Jasper Planning Assistant."

Ethnographic procedures included daily participant observations (fieldnotes and videotapes), weekly interviews with target dyads, daily personal journals, and student artifacts of problem solving. Observations yielded both quantitative and qualitative data about students' cooperative and mathematical problem solving; journals, interviews, and artifacts yielded qualitative data about students' knowledge, attitudes, and behaviors related to both aspects of problem solving. Following the first two weeks of observations, two female dyads were selected for focused observations and interviews conducted throughout the remainder of the project. Dyads were chosen because of observed difficulty in balancing social and academic (mathematics) task demands. One pair exhibited apparent facility with social demands but considerable difficulty with mathematical aspects. The other pair had difficulty with social demands and, although not expert mathematical problem solvers, exhibited some facility with mathematical task requirements. The selection of these dyads permitted in-depth study of students who experienced considerable difficulty in either (but not both) social or academic task requirements. Such study was expected to provide information pertinent to the design of interventions to foster effective collaborative interactions. (A full description of ethnographic procedures can be found in Nastasi, Braunhardt, Young, & Margiano-Lyons, 1993.)

Weekly interviews were intended to inform classroom teachers about topics to cover and areas of student confusion. Researchers were both observing students and actively teaching in the classroom. Research hypotheses were being generated on the basis of unfolding classroom activities. In traditional linear research designs, these statements would constitute a list of confounds that restrict internal validity. But in the situated learning framework, instruction and research are modeled as nonlinear dynamic systems. Rather than a confound, the continual interplay of data collection and interpretation with instruction was a critical element in the implementation of the project. This approach is consistent with an action research model and embodies the concept of *praxis*. To quote Partridge (1985, p. 144), "the practitioner of *praxis* is embedded in the social reality to which the theory of *praxis* has reference, and in order to continue being so embedded must continually, constantly adjust both theory and activity." Ethnographic methods (e.g., participant observation, key informant interviewing) are particularly well suited to fostering the interweaving of theory, resarch, and practice (*cf.* Jacob, 1987; Partridge, 1985; J. J. Schensul, 1985; S. L. Schensul, 1985; Wolcott, 1987). As we have noted, implementation of the Jasper project involved a continual interplay of data collection and interpretation, and instruction. The tools for fostering the interplay were participant observations and interviewing of students and teachers. Both procedures occurred at formal and informal levels.

Conceptual Changes

As we began our implementation, it became immediately clear that our initial emphasis on mathematical problem solving had to be broadened to include social problem solving, work outside the classroom, and activities across the curriculum. The first of these, social problem solving, meant giving equal instructional time to strategies for working with a partner. Students needed instruction on how to cooperate with the dyad partner and with other dyads to access limited classroom resouces such as the lone videodisc and the teacher(s). Our intention to use journals to encourage students to be reflective about the problem-solving process changed its focus away from mathematics toward social problem solving, with a concomitant change in research focus.

Our research focus (through observations and interviews) on cooperative problem solving influenced the instructional focus in the classroom. That is, teachers' interactions with students included attention to social as well as academic task-related behavior. This may be attributed to the dyadic and group nature of students' work as well as the ongoing interaction between researchers and teachers regarding the nature of students' social interactions. For example, several weeks into the study, one teacher indicated to us that one target student had particular difficulty working with a student in another dyad. Discussion ensued regarding the nature of the social difficulty, characterized by repeated conflicts both cognitive (idea-focused) and social in nature. As a result of the conversation, both teacher and researcher intervened with the students in question. The teacher intervened (outside of the classroom) with the non-target student, whose social interaction difficulties extended outside the immersion problem-solving context. The researcher discussed the incidents with the target dyad during regularly scheduled interview sessions (the focus of these sessions typically included discussions about difficulties with social task demands). The focus of both teacher's and researcher's discussions with students was on ways to resolve the social difficulties. In addition, the next mathematics (Jasper) class session began with teacher-led discussion and journal assignments for the entire class focused on the following questions: "What is the teacher's role in cooperative problem solving? When does the teacher get involved? Regarding conflict, when do you work it out yourselves and when do you ask the teacher?" (Nastasi, Braunhardt, Young, & Margiano-Lyons, 1993, pp. 17–18). These changes resulted from the focus on cooperative problem solving but were not planned *a priori*, thus reflecting more of a serendipitous action research approach.

A second conceptual change occurred when several groups experienced difficulty with decimal mile markers and converting fractional time to decimals (e.g., seven minutes 30 seconds shown on the video screen, dialogue stating "seven and a half minutes" and the mathematical representation as 7.5 min.). Lessons prepared by the regular classroom teacher, initially considered antithetical to the situated learning approach, were integrated with the videodisc story content and extended with in-context problem generation. This activity, not pre-planned, emerged solely as the result of the interaction of teachers and researchers.

A third conceptual change arose from electronic mail interactions with other teachers using the Jasper materials. In one message a Washington State teacher mentioned a relay race related to a video episode timed mile. Integrating a sports activity into the immersion problem broadened the boundaries of the immersion intervention and expanded the theoretical model of anchored instruction.

A fourth conceptual change arose from another e-mail message suggestion that construction of aluminum boats had been undertaken related to one of the videodisc episodes. Creating our own version of the activity, on the fly, we asked students to construct boats using three sheets of aluminum foil, and then to predict and to explain which of the designs would hold the heaviest load. As a result, the immersion intervention was expanded to include science content on flotation as well as hypothesis testing and decision making.

A fifth conceptual change concerned the extent to which important mathematical problem solving took place outside the mathematic classroom. The classroom implementation had not initially envisioned the extent to which students would be engaged with the anchor problems outside of class. Researchers' conceptualization of the out-of-class dimension of immersion problem solving was enriched by interaction with parents in the context of the intervention. Parents initially concerned about taking time away from drill and practice got involved in the problems and reported to teachers and researchers about students discussions outside of class. The close attention to the program given by some parents enabled researchers to gain access to information about how the anchor problems were coming up in the context of family trip planning and breakfast conversation. This prompted us to ask all students journal questions about their interactions outside of class. These aspects of immersion problem solving were consistent with the theoretical model. However, the conceptual change on the part of the researchers was in re-conceptualizing the boundaries of the intervention to include interactions with parents and peers outside the classroom.

Only through direct involvement in a classroom trial was it possible for the researchers to re-conceptualize the types of scaffolding needed for anchored instruction (see Bruner,1986, for a description of scaffolding). While theoretically it was clear that problem-solving dyads would not be able to complete the problem without considerable guidance and assistance, it was unclear precisely how scaffolding should be structured. What emerged from the collaboration between researchers and the classroom teacher was a classroom system for consulting (shown in Figure 10.1), along with an enriched theoretical model of scaffolding as more than expert-novice support. Our conception of scaffolding was revised to include structure within the environment that constrained the types of interactions students could have with the problem, the local expert (teacher), and with one another.

Our theoretical model of situated cognition included the goal to create in the classroom a community of learners. Yet it was not until the intervention began that it was possible to determine the extent to which the broader community could be included in classroom activities. Community contacts of both students

Dyad Info-Finding Rules
Step 1. check video for clues
Step 2. check with partner
Step 3. check with other dyads
Step 4. check with teacher

Figure 10.1. A classroom system for consulting.

and teachers were explored, resulting in several members of the community participating in the intervention. Specifically, three community professionals with expertise related to the videodisc episodes visited the classroom to answer student questions. These included a local ultralight airplane pilot, a veterinarian, and a TV news editor. These community professionals assisted students with various aspects of their mathematical problem solving, story comprehension, and solution presentations. The broadening of the concept of a community of learners to include relevant professionals was the result.

During implementation of the project, ongoing conversations between teachers and researchers regarding students' interactions resulted in interventions to enhance student performance. As target dyads became the focus, observers reported their observations to teachers. In addition, teachers sought general and specific feedback from the observers. Related changes in instructional focus followed such interchanges. For example, as noted above, the exchange of information about collaboration difficulties for one student was followed by interventions with the target student, with members of other dyads, and the whole class regarding conflict resolution. In another instance, several observers conveyed to the teaching staff the academic difficulties of a target dyad. This interchange was followed by increased instructional intervention with this dyad. As revealed by classroom videotapes, multiple members of the teaching and research staff deliberately intervened with the pair to insure understanding and facilitate learning. What is most noteworthy about these events was the serendipitous nature of the research-practice link. Much of the ongoing interaction among teachers and researchers and decisions about subsequent interventions occurred informally.

Discussions about the interaction of research and practice extended beyond the classroom intervention phase. Indeed, discussions between the researchers and teachers continued for months later, particularly as videotapes were coded, data interpreted, and formal presentations made at conferences and to the local school board. These interchanges focused on the implications of our findings for informing instruction in the future and the importance of collaborative university-school projects for enhancing the research-practice link. We return to this topic in a later section.

Conceptual change was evident within the research design and research hypotheses as well. Not only did qualitative student interviews inform teaching, but interactions with teachers affected the focus and direction of the ethnographic aspect of the project. During the course of the project, both the content of instructional and target students' responses to instructional demands influenced the content and focus of interviews. That is, classroom observations and discussions with teachers provided scenarios that guided interview questions about students' understanding and experiences and that helped to change the interviews into contexts for intervention (i.e., focused on helping students to reflect on their social and academic experiences and to solve social interaction problems). Furthermore, the teacher's insights about target students and perspective on the instruction-learning process influenced the analysis and intepretation of observational and interview data. In particular, the teacher's participation in coding of videotapes influenced qualitative analysis and data interpretation. The collaborative coding and analysis of a subset of videotapes provided hypotheses and research questions to guide subsequent analysis of the full set of data and, as we discuss in a later section, influenced future research.

Summary of Findings

Comparison of group data suggested that students who are immersed in a few rich, realistic problem situations, provided through interactive video and extended through telecommunications, can develop mathematical and scientific knowledge along with higher level thinking skills (specifically planning), general skills (specifically creativity), and learning skills (specifically information finding). Immersion students also outperformed their peers on a test of reading comprehension, showing that immersion in a complex mathematical problem on video can benefit literacy skills—but this finding was restricted to reading analogous content (a story about a river) and was not shown for reading unrelated content (a story about horse racing).

Quantitative and qualitative results suggested that the Jasper Immersion class acquired more planning and problem-solving skills than the similar Control class. The Jasper Immersion class also showed significant positive change in attitude toward mathematics in general, and to problem solving specifically. The Jasper immersion class was able to construct a greater number and more diverse responses to the creativity (rubber band uses) test. Jasper immersion students were also able to retrieve more relevant information from the video on both first and second viewings on the test of Information Finding.

The data suggest that students who are immersed in a few rich, realistic problem situations, provided through interactive video and extended through telecommunications, can develop mathematical and scientific knowledge along with higher level thinking skills: specifically planning, creativity, and information finding. This success is attributed to the characteristics of complex realistic "situated learning" (e.g., Brown, Collins, & Duguid, 1989; Cognition & Technology Group at Vanderbilt, 1990, 1992; Collins, Brown, & Newman, 1989; Greeno, 1989). Situated learning is described as being based less on memory and more on the tuning of perception, drawing on the psychology of James Gibson (1979/1986). Such learning is argued to provide greater transfer from the learning context (classrooms) to the real world of everyday problem solving.

Preliminary analysis (quantitative coding and qualitative description) of videotapes of target dyads revealed a possible interplay between social and academic collaborative activity. We found that certain types of social and academic problem-solving interactions co-occurred. Reciprocal sense making and cognitive conflict (and its resolution) co-occurred with mathematical planning and conceptual analysis. In contrast, noncollaborative interaction (e.g., working in parallel) co-occurred with data retrieval. Furthermore, the teacher's interactions with dyads were typically focused on the academic aspects of the task but infrequently focused on the social aspects. That is, the teacher's focus was clearly on instruction and mathematical problem solving. Attempts to address social interaction difficulties were more likely to be indirect; for example, a conflict might be resolved by re-focusing attention on the task rather than addressing the conflict directly. In addition, when the teacher intervened, students often ceased collaborative activity and focused attention on the teacher rather than on the partner.

Our collaborative interpretative analysis of these interactions (through discussion) focused on the extent to which teacher intervention regarding social dynamics may be critical. For example, observations of one group revealed considerable difficulty with managing the social and academic demands of the given task, which required negotiating the viewpoints of four individuals to solve an open-ended planning task. In four sessions, 13 cognitive conflicts occurred. The group attempted unsuccessfully to negotiate resolution of the conflicts and frequently sought teacher assistance. They resolved only one conflict without teacher intervention. In another instance, we observed that a reticent student who failed to present her "correct" ideas for problem solution to her partners, did so with direct questioning from the teacher who later intervened. (For a full report of these findings, see Nastasi, Braunhardt, Young, & Margiano-Lyons, 1993.) Such instances suggest that instructional interventions directed only toward academic aspects of collaborative work are insufficient. Despite the deliberate focus on social interaction at a global classroom level (as we noted earlier), our observations revealed that more attention was warranted at a dyad or group level regarding specific difficulties. That is, our preliminary data suggested that teachers' scaffolding regarding academic content did not necessarily generalize to social dynamics. Furthermore, we concluded that videotaping provided a rich source of data for evaluating and enhancing instruction. Our collaborative interpretation had implications for future research-practice directions, as we discuss in the next section.

Future Implementations

No two implementations of situated learning will ever be identical. Yet the process of immersing students in complex, realistic contexts (Young, 1993) and simultaneously engaging in collaborative research appears to work. Situated learning for students has an analogous implementation for researchers and teachers. Traditional linear experimental designs are inadequate and must be replaced by nonlinear, highly interactive, even constructivist research designs that admit and take advantage of the interplay between implementers and researchers. In our case, we all served dual roles as implementer and researchers, to the benefit of both.

The experiences inherent in this project emphasized the importance of researcher-participant collaboration. In particular, the collaborative process of data intepretation holds promise for enhancing the research-practice link. Our discussions since the intervention clarified the importance of ongoing interaction around data for changing the nature of instruction and research. For example, the collaborative viewing of videotapes will become a critical technique in future action research projects focused on both staff and student development. That is, videotapes will be used to document and examine critical instructional or learning events, to discuss the depicted experiences with participants (students and teachers), and to instruct teachers and students in social dynamics. Thus, videotapes serve multiple purposes of evaluation, instruction, and data collection. Likewise, journals and interviews can serve similar mutiple purposes. That is, students/teachers relate experiences and reflections; these records are not only for data collection but become the focal point for collaborative data interpretation and instructional design. Such techniques are applicable to both action research and collaborative consultation models (*cf.* Nastasi, 1994).

In conclusion, constructivist and situated learning designs for student instruction have direct implications for educational research. Models of action research and situated cognition are needed to design, analyze, and report findings from immersion problem-solving contexts that are inherently nonlinear, complex, and intimately related to the context in which they occur. Issues of transfer for both instructional techniques and research findings rest on the ability to model and interpret nonlinear systems. In short, the future is complex, both in its underlying model of thinking and learning as well as in the path from here to there.

References

Bearison, D. J. (1982). New directions in studies of social interaction and cognitive growth. In F. C. Serafica (Ed.), *Social-cognitive development in context* (pp. 199–221). New York: Guilford Press.

Bearison, D. J., Magzamen, S., & Filardo, E. K. (1986). Socio-cognitive conflict and cognitive growth in young children. *Merrill-Palmer Quarterly, 32,* 51–72.

Brown, J. S., Collins, A., & Duguid, P. (1989, Jan.–Feb.). Situated cognition and the culture of learning. *Educational Researcher, 18*(1), 32–42.

Bruner, J. (1986). *Actual minds, possible worlds.* Cambridge, MA: Harvard University Press.

Cognition & Technology Group at Vanderbilt. (1990). Anchored instruction and its relationship to situated cognition. *Educational Researcher, 19*(6), 2–10.

Cognition & Technology Group at Vanderbilt. (1992). The Jasper experiment: An exploration of issues in learning and instructional design. *Education Technology Research and Development, 40*(1), 65–80.

Cognition & Technology Group at Vanderbilt. (1993). Anchored instruction and situated cognition revisited. *Educational Technology, 33*(3), 52–70.

Collins, A., Brown, J. S., & Newman, S. E. (1989). Cognitive apprenticeship: Teaching the crafts of reading, writing, and mathematics. In L. B. Resnick (Ed.) *Knowing, learning, and instruction: Essays in honor of Robert Glaser* (pp. 453–494). Hillsdale, NJ: Lawrence Erlbaum Associates.

Doise, W., & Mugny, G. (1984). *The social development of the intellect.* New York: Pergamon.

Duffy, T. M., & Jonassen, D. H. (Eds.) (1992). *Constructivism and the technology of instruction: A conversation.* Hillsdale, NJ: Lawrence Erlbaum Associates.

Gibson, J. J. (1979/1986). *The ecological approach to visual perception,* Hillsdale, NJ: Lawrence Erlbaum Associates.

Greeno, J. G. (1989). A perspective on thinking. *American Psychologist, 44,* 134–141.

Jacob, E. (1987). Qualitative research traditions: A review. *Review of Educational Research, 57*(1), 1–50.

Johnson, D. W., Johnson, R. T., Pierson, W. T., & Lyons, V. (1985). Controversy versus concurrence seeking in multi-grade and single-grade learning groups. *Journal of Research in Science Teaching, 22*, 835–848.

Johnson, R. T., Brooker, C., Stutzman, J., Hultman, D., & Johnson, D. W. (1985). The effects of controversy, concurrence seeking, and individualistic learning on achievement and attitude change. *Journal of Research in Science Teaching, 22*, 197–205.

Nastasi, B. K. (1994, March). *The relevance of ethnography to school psychology research and practice*. Paper presented at the annual convention of the National Association of School Psychologists, Seattle, Washington.

Nastasi, B. K., Bingham, A., & Clements, D. H. (1993, April). *Study of social processes in cooperative learning environments: The qualitative-quantitative mix*. Paper presented at the annual meeting of the American Educational Research Association, Atlanta, GA.

Nastasi, B. K., Braunhardt, L., Young, M., & Margiano-Lyons, S. (1993, October). *Cooperative and mathematical problem-solving in the Jasper context*. Paper presented at the 24th annual conference of the Northeastern Educational Research Association, Ellenville, NY.

Nastasi, B. K., & Clements, D. H. (1991). Research on cooperative learning: Implications for practice. *School Psychology Review, 20*, 110–131.

Nastasi, B. K., & Clements, D. H. (1992). Social-cognitive behaviors and higher-order thinking in educational computer environments. *Learning and Instruction, 2*, 215–238.

Nastasi, B. K., & Clements, D. H. (1993). Motivational and social outcomes of cooperative computer education environments. *Journal of Computing in Childhood Education, 4*(1), 15–43.

Nastasi, B. K., Clements, D. H., & Battista, M. T. (1990). Social-cognitive interactions, motivation, and cognitive growth in Logo programming and CAI problem-solving environments. *Journal of Educational Psychology, 82*, 150–158.

Partridge, W. L. (1985). Toward a theory of practice. *American Behavioral Scientist, 29*(2), 139–163.

Rogoff, B., & Lave, J. (1984). *Everyday cognition: Its development in social context*. Cambridge, MA: Harvard University Press.

Schensul, J. J. (1985). Systems consistency in field research, dissemination, and social change. *American Behavioral Scientist, 29*(2), 186–204.

Schensul, S. L. (1985). Science, theory, and application in anthropology. *American Behavioral Scientist, 29*(2), 164–185.

Wolcott, H. F. (1987). On ethnographic intent. In G. Spindler & L. Spindler (Eds.), *Intrepretive ethnography: At home and abroad* (pp. 37–57). Hillsdale, NJ: Lawrence Erlbaum Associates.

Young, M. F. (1993). Instructional design for situated learning. *Educational Technology Research and Development, 41*(1), 43–58.

Young, M. F., & McNeese, M. D. (in press). Beyond cognition: An ecological situated cognition approach to problem solving with implications for assessment. To appear in J. M. Flach, P. Hancock, J. Caird, & K. Vicente (Eds.), *The ecology of human-machine systems*.

Acknowledgments

Teacher: Trisha Proctor, and Graduate Assistants: Allison Bingham, Ching-Hui Chen, Sylvia Hackett, Kimberly Lawless, Charles Lounsbury, Suzanne Margiano-Lyons & Everett Smith.

Michael F. Young is at the University of Connecticut. **Bonnie K. Nastasi** is at the State University of New York at Albany. **Lynette Braunhardt** is at Mansfield Middle School, Connecticut.

11

Problem Based Learning: An Instructional Model and Its Constructivist Framework

John R. Savery
Thomas M. Duffy

It is said that there's nothing so practical as good theory. It may also be said that there's nothing so theoretically interesting as good practice.[1] This is particularly true of efforts to relate constructivism as a theory of learning to the practice of instruction. Our goal in this chapter is to provide a clear link between the theoretical principles of constructivism, the practice of instructional design, and the practice of teaching. We will begin with a basic characterization of constructivism, identifying what we believe to be the central principles in learning and understanding. We will then identify and elaborate on eight instructional principles for the design of a constructivist learning environment. Finally, we will examine what we consider to be one of the best exemplars of a constructivist learning environment—Problem Based Learning, as described by Barrows (1985, 1986, 1992).

Constructivism

Constructivism is a philosophical view on how we come to understand or know. It is, in our mind, most closely attuned to the pragmatic philosophy of Richard Rorty (1991). Space limitations for this chapter prevent an extensive discussion of this philosophical base, but we would commend to the interested

---

[1]This succinct statement was noted in Gaffney & Anderson (1991).

reader the work of Rorty (1991) as well as vonGlasersfeld (1989). We will characterize the philosophical view in terms of three primary propositions:

1. Understanding is in our interactions with the environment. This is the core concept of constructivism. We cannot talk about what is learned separately from how it is learned, as if a variety of experiences all lead to the same understanding. Rather, what we understand is a function of the content, the context, the activity of the learner, and, perhaps most importantly, the goals of the learner. Since understanding is an individual construction, we cannot share understandings, but rather we can test the degree to which our individual understandings are compatible. An implication of this proposition is that cognition is not just within the individual, but rather it is a part of the entire context, i.e., cognition is distributed.

2. Cognitive conflict or puzzlement is the stimulus for learning and determines the organization and nature of what is learned. When we are in a learning environment, there is some stimulus or goal for learning—the *learner* has a purpose for being there. That goal is not only the stimulus for learning, but it is a primary factor in determining what the learner attends to, what prior experience the learner brings to bear in constructing an understanding, and, basically, what understanding is eventually constructed. In Dewey's terms, it is the "problematic" that leads to and is the organizer for learning (Dewey, 1938; Roschelle, 1992). For Piaget it is the need for accommodation when current experience cannot be assimilated in existing schema (Piaget, 1977; von Glasersfeld, 1989). We prefer to talk about the learner's "puzzlement" as being the stimulus and organizer for learning, since this more readily suggests both intellectual and pragmatic goals for learning. The important point, however, is that it is the goal of the learner that is central in considering what is learned.

3. Knowledge evolves through social negotiation and through the evaluation of the viability of individual understandings. The social environment is critical to the development of our individual understanding as well as to the development of the body of propositions we call knowledge. At the first, or individual level, other individuals are a primary mechanism for testing our understanding. Collaborative groups are important because we can test our own understanding and examine the understanding of others as a mechanism for enriching, interweaving, and expanding our understanding of particular issues or phenomena. As vonGlasersfeld (1989) has noted, other people are the greatest source of alternative views to challenge our current views and hence to serve as the source of puzzlement that stimulates new learning. The second role of the social environment is to develop a set of propositions we call knowledge. We seek propositions that are compatible with our individual constructions or understanding of the world. Thus, facts are facts because there is widespread agreement, not because there is some ultimate truth to the fact. It was once a fact that the earth was flat and the sun revolved around the earth. More recently, it was fact that the smallest particles of matter were electrons, protons, and neutrons. These were facts because there was general agreement that the concepts and principles arising from these views provided the best interpretation of our world. The same search for viability holds in our daily life. In both cases, concepts that we call knowledge do not represent some ultimate truth, but are simply the most viable interpretation of our experiential world (see Resnick, 1987). The important consideration in this third proposition is that all views, or all constructions, are not equally viable. Constructivism is not a deconstructivist view in which all constructions are equal simply because they are personal experiences. Rather, we seek viability, and thus we must test understandings to determine how adequately they allow us to interpret and function in our world. Our social environment is primary in providing alternative views and additional information against which we can test the viability of our understanding and in building the set of propositions (knowledge) compatible with those understandings (Cunningham, Duffy, & Knuth, 1991). Hence we discuss social negotiation of meaning and understanding based on viability.

Instructional Principles

The constructivist propositions outlined above suggest a set of instructional principles that can guide the practice of teaching and the design of learning environments. All too often when we discuss principles of teaching we hear the retort, "But we already do that..." While that assertion may well be accurate, too often the claim is based on the principle in isolation rather than in the context of the overall framework. Indeed, everyone "does" collaborative groups; the real issue is what the goal is in using collaborative groups, since that determines the details of how they are used and how they are contextualized in the overall instructional framework.

We think Lebow (1993) has hit upon a strategy for summarizing the constructivist framework in a way that may help with the interpretation of the instructional strategies. He talks about the shift in values when one takes a constructivist perspective. He notes that:

> ...traditional educational technology values of replicability, reliability, communication, and control (Heinich, 1984) contrast sharply with the seven primary constructivist values of collaboration, personal autonomy, generativity, reflectivity, active engagement, personal relevance, and pluralism. (1993, p. 5)

We agree with Lebow and would propose that this value system serve to guide the reader's interpretation of our instructional principles as well as the interpretation of the problem based learning environment we will describe. The instructional principles deriving from constructivism are as follows:

1. Anchor all learning activities to a larger task or problem. That is, learning must have a purpose beyond, "It is assigned." We learn in order to be able to function more effectively in our world. The purpose of any learning activity should be clear to the learner. Individual learning activities can be of any type— the important issue is that the learner clearly perceives and accepts the relevance of the specific learning activities in relation to the larger task complex (Cognition & Technology Group at Vanderbilt, 1992; Honebein, Duffy, & Fishman, 1993).

2. Support the learner in developing ownership for the overall problem or task. Instructional programs typically specify learning objectives and perhaps even engage the learner in a project, assuming that the learner will understand and buy into the relevance and value of the problem (Blumenfeld, Soloway, Marx, Krajcik, Guzdial, & Palincsar, 1991). Unfortunately, it is too often the case that the learners do not accept the goal of the instructional program, but rather simply focus on passing the test or putting in their time. No matter what we specify as the learning objective, the goals of the learner will largely determine what is learned. Hence, it is essential that the goals the learner brings to the environment are consistent with our instructional goals.

There are two ways of doing this. First, we may solicit problems from the learners and use those as the stimulus for learning activities. This is basically what happens in graduate schools when qualifying exams require the student to prepare publishable papers in each of several domains (Honebein et al., 1993). Scardamalia and Bereiter (1991) have shown that even elementary students can initiate questions (puzzlements) that can serve as the foundation of learning activities in traditional school subject matter. In essence, the strategy is to define a territory and then to work with the learner in developing meaningful problems or tasks in that domain. Alternatively, we can establish a problem in such a way that the learners will readily adopt the problem as their own. We see this strategy in the design of the Jasper series for teaching mathematics (Cognition & Technology Group at Vanderbilt, 1992) and in many simulation environments.[2] In either case, it is important to engage the learner in meaningful dialogue to help bring the problem or task home to that learner.

3. Design an authentic task. An authentic learning environment does *not* mean that the fourth grader should be placed in an authentic physics lab, nor that he or she should grapple with the same problems with which adult physicists deal. Rather, the learner should engage in scientific activities which present the same "type" of cognitive challenges. An authentic learning environment is one in which the cognitive demands, i.e., the thinking required, are consistent with the cognitive demands in the environment for which we are preparing the learner (Honebein et al., 1993). Thus, we do not want the learner to learn about history but rather to engage in the construction or use of history in ways that a historian or a good citizen would. Similarly, we do not want the learner to study science—memorizing a text on science or executing scientific procedures as dictated—but rather to engage in scientific discourse and problem solving (see Bereiter, 1994; Duffy, in press; Honebein et al., 1993). Allowing the problem to be generated by the learner, an option discussed above, does not automatically assure authenticity. It may well require discussion and negotiation

---

[2]Let us hasten to add that many simulation environments are not designed to engage the learner in the problems they are addressing. This is a design issue, not a natural component of a particular instructional strategy.

with the learner to develop a problem or task which is authentic in its cognitive demands and for which the learner can take ownership.

4. Design the task and the learning environment to reflect the complexity of the environment they should be able to function in at the end of learning. Rather than simplifying the environment for the learner, we seek to support the learner working in the complex environment. This is consistent with both cognitive apprenticeship (Collins, Brown, & Newman, 1989) and cognitive flexibility theory (Spiro *et al.*, 1992) and reflects the importance of context in determining the understanding we have of any particular concept or principle.

5. Give the learner ownership of the process used to develop a solution. Learners must have ownership of the learning or problem-solving process as well as ownership of the problem itself. Frequently, teachers will give students ownership of the problem, but dictate the process for working on that problem. Thus, they may dictate that a particular problem solving or critical thinking methodology be used or that particular content domains must be "learned." For example, in some problem based learning frameworks, the problem is presented along with the learning objectives and the assigned readings related to the problem. Thus, the student is told what to study and what to learn in relation to the problem. Clearly, with this pre-specification of activities, the students are not going to be engaged in authentic thinking and problem solving in that domain. Rather than being a stimulus for problem solving and self directed learning, the problem serves merely as an example. The teacher's role should be to challenge the learner's thinking—not to dictate or attempt to proceduralize that thinking.

6. Design the learning environment to support and challenge the learner's thinking. While we advocate giving the learner ownership of the problem and the solution process, it is not the case that *any* activity or *any* solution is adequate. Indeed, the critical goal is to support the learner in becoming an effective worker/thinker in the particular domain. The teacher must assume the roles of consultant and coach. The most critical teaching activity is in the questions the teacher asks the learner in that consulting and coaching activity. It is essential that the teacher *value as well as challenge* the learner's thinking. The teacher must not take over thinking for the learner by telling the learner what to do or how to think, but rather teaching should be done by inquiring at the "leading edge" of the learner's thinking (Fosnot, 1989). This is different from the widely used Socratic method wherein the teacher has the "right" answer and it is the student's task to guess/deduce through logical questioning that correct answer. The concept of a learning scaffold and the zone of proximal development, as described by Vygotsky (1978), is a more accurate representation of the learning exchange/interaction between the teacher and the student.

Learners use information resources (all media types) and instructional materials (all media types) as sources of information. The materials do not teach, but rather support the learners' inquiry or performance. This does not negate any kind of instructional resource—it only specifies the reason for using the resource. Thus, if domain specific problem solving is the skill to be learned, then a simulation which confronts the learner with problem situations within that domain might be appropriate. If proficient typing is required for some larger context, certainly a drill and practice program is one option that might be present.

7. Encourage testing ideas against alternative views and alternative contexts. Knowledge is socially negotiated. The quality or depth of one's understanding can only be determined in a social environment where we can see if our understanding can accommodate the issues and views of others and to see if there are points of view which we could usefully incorporate into our understanding. The importance of a learning community where ideas are discussed and understanding enriched is critical to the design of an effective learning environment. The use of collaborative learning groups as a part of the overall learning environment we have described provides one strategy for achieving this learning community (CTGV, 1994; Cunningham, Duffy, & Knuth, 1991; Scardamalia *et al.*, 1992). Other projects support collaboration by linking learners over electronic communication networks as they work on a common task, e.g., CoVis (Edelson & O'Neill, 1994), LabNet (Ruopp *et al.*, 1993), provide an alternative framework.

8. Provide opportunity for and support reflection on both the content learned and the learning process. An important goal of instruction is to develop skills of self regulation—to become independent. Teachers should model reflective thinking throughout the learning process and support the learners in reflecting on the strategies for learning as well as what was learned (Clift, Houston, & Pugach, 1990; Schön, 1987).

In the next section we will explore how these eight instructional principles are realized in the problem-based learning approach.

Problem Based Learning

The instructional design principles, implemented within the framework of the values outlined by Lebow (1993), can lead to a wide variety of learning environments. A number of environments reflecting these principles are described in Duffy and Jonassen (1992) and Duffy, Lowyck, and Jonassen (1993). Further, the elaboration and application of these principles to specific contexts is described in Brooks and Brooks (1993), Fosnot (1989), and Duffy (in press). In our own examination of learning environments, however, we have found one application that seems to us to almost ideally capture the principles—the problem based learning model of Howard Barrows (1985, 1992).

Problem Based Learning (PBL), as a general model, was developed in medical education in the mid-1950's and since that time it has been refined and implemented in over sixty medical schools. The most widespread application of the PBL approach has been in the first two years of medical science curricula, where it replaces the traditional lecture based approach to anatomy, pharmacology, physiology etc.. The model has been adopted in an increasing number of other areas, including business schools (Milter & Stinson, 1994), schools of education (Bridges & Hallinger, 1992; Duffy, 1994); architecture, law, engineering, social work (Boud & Feletti, 1991); and high school (Barrows & Myers, 1993).

As with any instructional model, there are many strategies for implementing PBL. Rather than attempting to provide a general characterization of PBL, we would like to focus on Barrows' model (Barrows, 1992) to provide a concrete sense of the implementation of this process in medical school. First we will present a general scenario, using the medical environment as the focus, and then examine some of the key elements in some detail.

When students enter medical school, they are divided into groups of five, and each group is assigned a facilitator. The students are then presented a problem in the form of a patient entering with presenting symptoms. The students' task is to diagnose the patient and to provide a rationale for that diagnosis and a recommended treatment. The process for working on the problem is outlined in Figure 11.1. The following paragraphs cover the highlights of that process.

The students begin the problem "cold"—they do not know what the problem will be until it is presented. They discuss the problem, generating hypotheses based on whatever experience or knowledge they have, identifying relevant facts in the case, and identifying learning issues. The learning issues are topics of any sort deemed of potential relevance to this problem and which the group members feel they do not understand as well as they should. A session is not complete until each student has had an opportunity to verbally reflect on his or her current beliefs about the diagnosis (i.e., commit to a temporary position), and assume responsibility for particular learning issues that were identified. Note that there are no pre-specified objectives presented to the students. The students generate the learning issues (objectives) based on their analysis of the problem.

After the session, the students all engage in self-directed learning. There are no assigned texts. Rather, the students are totally responsible for gathering the information from the available medical library and computer database resources. Additionally, particular faculty are designated to be available as consultants (as they would be for any physician in the real world). The students may go to the consultants, seeking information.

After self-directed learning, the students meet again. They begin by evaluating resources—what was most useful and what was not so useful. They then begin working on the problem with this new level of understanding. Note that they do not simply tell what they learned. Rather, they use that learning in re-examining the problem. This cycle may repeat itself if new learning issues arise—problems in the medical school program last anywhere from a week to three weeks.

Milter and Stinson (1994) use a similar approach in an MBA program at Ohio University, and there the problems last between five and eight weeks (see also Stinson, 1994). In our own implementation, we are using one problem that lasts the entire semester. Of course, in the MBA program and in our own, the problems have multiple sub-problems that engage the students.

Assessment at the end of the process is in terms of peer- and self-evaluation. There are no tests in the medical school curriculum. The assessment includes evaluation (with suggestions for improvement) in three areas: self directed learning, problem solving, and skills as a group member. While the students must pass the Medical Board exam after two years, this is outside of the

STARTING A NEW CLASS
1. Introductions
2. **Climate Setting** (including teacher / tutor role)

STARTING A NEW PROBLEM
1. **Set the problem.**
2. **Bring the problem home** (students internalize problem)
3. **Describe the product / performance required**
4. **Assign tasks** (Scribe 1 at the board, Scribe 2 copying from the board, and reference person)

IDEAS (Hypotheses)	FACTS	LEARNING ISSUES	ACTION PLAN
Students' conjectures regarding the problem--may involve causation, effect, possible resolutions, etc.	A growing synthesis of information obtained through inquiry, important to the hypotheses generated	Students' list of what they need to know or understand in order to complete the problem task	Things that need to be done in order to complete the problem task

5. **Reasoning through the problem**
    What you do with the columns on the board

IDEAS (Hypotheses)	FACTS	LEARNING ISSUES	ACTION PLAN
Expand / focus	Synthesize & re-synthesize	Identify / justify	Formulate plan

6. **Commitment as to probable outcome** (although much may need to be learned)
7. **Learning issue shaping/assignment**
8. **Resource identification**
9. **Schedule follow-up**

PROBLEM FOLLOW-UP
1. **Resources used and their critique**
2. **Reassess the problem**
    What you do with the columns on the board

IDEAS (Hypotheses)	FACTS	LEARNING ISSUES	ACTION PLAN
Revise	Apply new knowledge and re-synthesize	Identify new (if necessary)	Redesign decisions

PERFORMANCE PRESENTATION

AFTER CONCLUSION OF PROBLEM
1. **Knowledge abstraction and summary** (develop definitions, diagrams, lists, concepts, abstractions, principles)
2. **Self-evaluation** (followed by comments from the group)
    - reasoning through the problem
    - digging out information using good resources
    - assisting the group with its tasks
    - gaining or refining knowledge

Figure 11.1. The Problem Based Learning process. Taken from Barrows and Myers (1993).

curriculum structure.[3] However, tests as part of the PBL curriculum are not precluded. For example, one high school teacher we know who uses the PBL approach designs traditional tests based on what the students have identified as learning issues. Thus, rather than a pre-specification of what is to be learned, the assessment focuses on the issues the learners have identified.

That is an overview of the process in the medical school. Now we will comment on a few of the critical features.

Learning goals. The design of this environment is meant to simulate, and hence engage the learner in, the problem solving behavior that it is hoped a practicing physician would be engaged in. Nothing is simplified or pre-specified for the learner. The facilitator assumes a major role in modeling the metacognitive thinking associated with the problem solving process. Hence this is a cognitive apprenticeship environment with scaffolding designed to support the learner in developing the metacognitive skills.

Within the context of this cognitive apprenticeship environment, there are goals related to self-directed learning, content knowledge, and problem solving. To be successful, students must develop the self-directed learning skills needed in the medical field. They must be able to develop strategies for identifying learning issues and locating, evaluating, and learning from resources relevant to that issue. The entire problem solving process is designed to aid the students in developing the hypothetico-deductive problem solving model which centers around hypothesis generation and evaluation. Finally, there are specific content learning objectives associated with each problem. Since the students have responsibility for the problem, there is no guarantee that all of the content area objectives will be realized in a given problem. However, any given content objective occurs in several problems, and hence if it does not arise in one, it will almost certainly arise in one of the other problems.

Problem Generation. There are two guiding forces in developing problems. First, the problems must raise the concepts and principles relevant to the content domain. Thus, the process begins with first identifying the primary concepts or principles that a student must learn. Milter and Stinson working in the MBA program and Barrows working with medical education polled the faculty to identify the most important concepts or principles in their area. This, of course, generates considerable debate and discussion—it is not a matter of a simple survey. In developing high school PBL curricula, Myers and Barrows (personal communication) used the learning objectives identified by the state for grade and content domains.

Second, the problems must be "real." In the medical school, the patients are real patients. Indeed, Barrows worked with the presenting physician in gathering the details on the case. Milter and Stinson in the MBA program use problems such as "Should AT&T buy NCR?" These problems change each year so as to address current business issues. At the high school level, Myers and Barrows have developed problems such as:

---

[3]PBL students do as well as traditional students in a variety of discipline areas on standard or Board qualifying exams. The PBL students seem to retain their knowledge longer after the exam than students in traditional classes (Boud & Feletti, 1991; Bridges & Hallinger, 1992).

- Do asteroids in space pose a problem, and if so, what should we be doing about it?
- What caused the flooding in the Midwest in 1993 and what should be done to prevent it in the future?

We are still developing problems and sub-problems for our Corporate and Community Education program. One of the problems currently being developed relates to the numerous PCB sites around Bloomington, Indiana, and the general public apathy about cleaning up these sites. The problem is basically:

- What do citizens need to know about the PCB problem and how should that information be presented to encourage them to be active citizens in the discussion?

There are three reasons why the problems must address real issues. First, because the students are open to explore all dimension of the problem, there is real difficulty in creating a rich problem with a consistent set of information. Second, real problems tend to engage learners more—there is a larger context of familiarity with the problem. Finally, students want to know the outcome of the problem—what is being done about the flood, did AT&T buy NCR, what was the problem with the patient? These outcomes are not possible with artificial problems.

Problem Presentation. There are two critical issues involved in presenting the problem. First, if the students are to engage in authentic problem solving, then they must own the problem. We have been learners with the Asteroid Problem and we have been facilitators in two contexts: with a group of high school students and with a group of our peers who were attending a workshop to learn about constructivism. In all three cases, the learners were thoroughly engaged in the problem. Frankly, we were amazed at the generality across these disparate groups. In presenting this problem, we used a 10-minute video that described asteroids and showed the large number of sites on earth where they have hit and the kind of impact they can have (the diamond fields in South Africa, the possibility that an asteroid caused the extinction of dinosaurs, Crater Lake, etc.). We also talked about recent near misses—one in Alabama within the last year and one three years ago that could have hit Australia or Russia. Thus, the problem clearly has potential cataclysmic effects (we have past history) and it is a current real problem (we have had near misses quite recently).[4] This step in the PBL process of "bringing the problem home" is critical. The learners must perceive the problem as a real problem and one which has personal relevance. Of course, also central is the fact that the learners have ownership of the problem—they are not just trying to figure out what *we* want.

A second critical issue in presenting the problem is to be certain that the data presented do not highlight critical factors in the case. Too often when problems are presented, the only information that is provided is the key information relevant to the desired solution (end-of-chapter "problems" are notorious for this). Either the case must be richly presented or presented only as a basic

---

[4]The potential value of real-world problems in terms of sustained learning and potential impact on interest in the news is illustrated in terms of the 1994 collisions of asteroids with Jupiter. Once having engaged in the asteroid "problem," news concerning asteroid events takes on considerably greater significance.

question. For example, Honebein, Marrero, Kakos-Kraft, and Duffy (1994) present all of the medical notes on a patient, while Barrows (1985) provides answers generated by the presenting physician to any of 270 questions the learners might ask. In contrast, Milter and Stinson (1994) present only a four-word question and rely on natural resources to provide the full context.

Facilitator Role. In his discussion of the tutorial process, Barrows states:
> The ability of the tutor to use facilitory teaching skills during the small group learning process is the major determinant of the quality and the success of any educational method aimed at (1) developing students' thinking or reasoning skills (problem solving, metacognition, critical thinking) as they learn, and (2) helping them to become independent, self-directed learners (learning to learn, learning management). Tutoring is a teaching skill central to problem-based, self-directed learning. (1992, p. 12)

Throughout a session, the facilitator models higher order thinking by asking questions which probe students' knowledge deeply. To do this, the facilitator constantly asks "Why?" "What do you mean?" "How do you know that's true?" Barrows is adamant that the facilitators' interactions with the students be at a metacognitive level (except for housekeeping tasks) and that the facilitator avoid expressing an opinion or giving information to the students. The facilitator does not use his or her knowledge of the content to ask questions that will lead the learners to the "correct" answer.

A second tutor role is to challenge the learner's thinking. The facilitator (and hopefully the other students in this collaborative environment) will constantly ask: "Do you know what that means? What are the implications of that? Is there anything else?" Superficial thinking and vague notions do not go unchallenged. During his introduction of the Asteroid Problem, Barrows noted for the group that saying nothing about another member's facts or opinions was the same as saying "I agree." Similarly, the responsibility for a flawed medical diagnosis was shared by everyone in the group. During the first few PBL sessions, the facilitator challenges both the level of understanding and the relevance and completeness of the issues studied. Gradually, however, the students take over this role themselves as they become effective self-directed learners.

Conclusion

Our goal in this chapter was to present PBL as a detailed instructional model and to show how PBL is consistent with the principles of instruction arising from constructivism. We sought to provide a clear link between theory and practice. Some of the features of the PBL environment are that the learners are actively engaged in working at tasks and activities that are authentic to the environment in which they would be used. The focus is on learners as constructors of their own knowledge in a context similar to that in which they would apply that knowledge. Students are encouraged and expected to think both critically and creatively and to monitor their own understanding, i.e., function at a metacognitive level. Social negotiation of meaning is an important part of the problem-solving team structure and the facts of the case are only facts when the group decides they are.

PBL, as we have described it, contrasts with a variety of other problem or case based approaches. Most case based learning strategies (Williams, 1992) use cases as a means for testing one's understanding. The case is presented after the topic is covered in order to help test understanding and support synthesis. In contrast, in PBL, all of the learning arises out of consideration of the problem. From the start, the learning is synthesized and organized in the context of the problem.

Other case approaches simply use the case as a concrete reference point for learning. Learning objectives and resources are presented along with the case. These approaches use the case as an "example" and are not focused on developing the metacognitive skills associated with problem solving or with professional life. The contrast is perhaps that the PBL approach is a cognitive apprenticeship focusing on both the knowledge domain and the problem solving associated with that knowledge domain or profession. Other problem approaches present cases so that critical attributes are highlighted, thus emphasizing the content domain, but not engaging the learner in authentic problem solving in that domain.

Finally, this is not a Socratic process, nor is it a kind of limited discovery learning environment in which the goal for the learner is to "discover" the outcome the instructor *wants*. The learners have ownership of the problem. The facilitation is not knowledge driven; rather, it is focused on metacognitive processes.

References

Barrows, H. S. (1985). *How to design a problem based curriculum for the preclinical years.* New York: Springer Publishing Co.

Barrows, H. S. (1986). A taxonomy of problem based learning methods. *Medical Education, 20,* 481–486.

Barrows, H. S. (1992). *The tutorial process.* Springfield, IL: Southern Illinois University School of Medicine.

Barrows, H. S., & Myers, A. C. (1993). *Problem based learning in secondary schools.* Unpublished monograph. Springfield, IL: Problem Based Learning Institute, Lanphier High School, and Southern Illinois University Medical School.

Bereiter, C. (1994). Implications of Postmodernism for science, or, science as progressive discourse. *Educational Psychologist, 29,* 3–12.

Blumenfeld, P. C., Soloway, E., Marx, R. W., Krajcik, J. S., Guzdial, M., & Palincsar, A. (1991). Motivating project-based learning: Sustaining the doing, supporting the learning. *Educational Psychologist, 26* (3&4), 369–398.

Boud, D., & Feletti, G. (Eds.) (1991). *The challenge of problem based learning.* New York: St. Martin's Press.

Bridges, E., & Hallinger, P. (1992). *Problem based learning for administrators.* ERIC Clearinghouse on Educational Management, University of Oregon.

Brooks, J. G., & Brooks, M. G. (1993). *In search of understanding: The case for constructivist classrooms.* Alexandria, VA: Association for Supervision and Curriculum Development.

Brown, J. S., Collins, A., & Duguid, P. (1989). Situated cognition and the culture of learning. *Educational Researcher, 18(1),* 32–42.

Clift, R., Houston, W., & Pugach, M. (Eds.), (1990). *Encouraging reflective practice in education.* New York: Teachers College Press.

Cognition & Technology Group at Vanderbilt. (1992). Technology and the design of generative learning environments. In T. M. Duffy & D. H. Jonassen (Eds.), *Constructivism and the technology of instruction: A conversation*. Hillsdale, NJ: Lawrence Erlbaum Associates. Originally in *Educational Technology*, 1991, 31(5).

Cognition & Technology Group at Vanderbilt. (1994). From visual word problems to learning communities: Changing conceptions of cognitive research. In K. McGilly (Ed.), *Classroom lessons: Integrating cognitive theory and classroom practice*. Cambridge, MA: MIT Press/Bradford Books.

Cohen, E. (1994). Restructuring the classroom: Conditions for productive small groups. *Review of Educational Research*, 64, 1–35.

Collins, A., Brown, J. S., & Newman, S. E. (1989). Cognitive apprenticeship: Teaching the crafts of reading, writing, and mathematics. In L.B. Resnick (Ed.), *Knowing, learning, and instruction: Essays in honor of Robert Glaser* (pp. 453–494). Hillsdale, NJ: Lawrence Erlbaum Associates.

Cunningham, D. J., Duffy, T. M., & Knuth, R. A. (1991). The textbook of the future. In C. McKnight, A. Dillon, & J. Richardson (Eds.), *Hypertext: A psychological perspective*. London: Horwood Publishing.

Dewey, J. (1938). *Logic: The theory of inquiry*. New York: Holt and Co.

Duffy, T. M. (1994). *Corporate and community education: Achieving success in the information society*. Unpublished paper. Bloomington, IN: Indiana University.

Duffy, T. M. (in press). *Strategic teaching frameworks: An instructional model for complex, interactive skills*. To appear in C. Dills & A. Romiszowski (Eds.), *Instructional development*. Englewood Cliffs, NJ: Educational Technology Publications.

Duffy, T. M., & Jonassen, D. H. (Eds.) (1992). *Constructivism and the technology of instruction: A conversation*. Hillsdale, NJ: Lawrence Erlbaum Associates.

Duffy, T. M., Lowyck, J., & Jonassen, D. H. (Eds.) (1993). *Designing environments for constructivist learning*. Berlin: Springer-Verlag.

Edelson, D., & O'Neill, D. K. (1994). *The CoVis collaboratory notebook: Computer support for scientific inquiry*. Paper presented at the annual meeting of the American Educational Research Association, New Orleans.

Fosnot, C. T. (1989). *Enquiring teachers, enquiring learners. A Constructivist approach to teaching*. New York: Teachers College Press.

Gaffney, J. S., & Anderson, R. C. (1991). Two-tiered scaffolding: Congruent processes of teaching and learning. In E. H. Hiebert (Ed.), *Literacy for a diverse society: Perspectives, practices, & policies*. New York: Teachers College Press.

Honebein, P., Duffy, T. M., & Fishman, B. (1993). Constructivism and the design of learning environments: Context and authentic activities for learning. In T. M. Duffy, J. Lowyck, & D. H. Jonassen (Eds.), *Designing environments for constructivist learning*. Berlin: Springer-Verlag.

Honebein, P., Marrero, D. G., Kakos-Kraft, S., & Duffy, T. M. (1994). *Improving medical students' skills in the clinical care of diabetes*. Paper presented at the annual meeting of the American Diabetes Association, New Orleans.

Johnson, D. W., & Johnson, R. T., (1990). Cooperative learning and achievement. In S. Sharan (Ed.), *Cooperative learning: Theory and practice*. New York: Praeger.

Kagan, S. (1992). *Cooperative learning*. San Juan Capistrano, CA: Kagan Cooperative Learning.

Lebow, D. (1993). Constructivist values for systems design: Five principles toward a new mindset. *Educational Technology Research and Development*, 41, 4–16.

MacDonald, P. J. (1991). Selection of health problems for a problem-based curriculum. In D. Boud & G. Feletti (Eds.), *The challenge of problem based learning*. New York: St. Martin's Press.

Milter, R. G., & Stinson, J. E. (1994). Educating leaders for the new competitive environment. In G. Gijselaers, S. Tempelaar, & S. Keizer S. (Eds.), *Educational innovation in economics and business administration: The case of problem-based learning*. London: Kluwer Academic Publishers.

Piaget, J. (1977). *The development of thought: Equilibrium of cognitive structures*. New York: Viking Press.

Resnick, L. B. (1987). Learning in school and out. *Educational Researcher, 16*, 13–20.

Rorty, R. (1991). *Objectivity, relativism, and truth*. Cambridge: Cambridge University Press.

Roschelle, J. (1992). *Reflections on Dewey and technology for situated learning*. Paper presented at annual meeting of the American Educational Research Association, San Francisco.

Ruopp, R., Gal, S., Drayton, B., & Pfister, M. (Eds.) (1993). *LabNet: Toward a community of practice*. Hillsdale NJ: Lawrence Erlbaum Associates.

Scardamalia, M., & Bereiter, C. (1991). Higher levels of agency for children in knowledge building: A challenge for the design of new knowledge media. *The Journal of the Learning Sciences, 1*, 37–68.

Scardamalia, M., Bereiter, C., Brett, C., Burtis, P. J., Calhoun, & Lea, N. S. (1992). Educational applications of a networked communal database. *Interactive Learning Environments, 2*, 45–71.

Schön, D. A. (1987). *Educating the reflective practitioner*. San Francisco: Jossey-Bass.

Slavin, R. (1990). *Cooperative learning: Theory, research, and practice*. Boston: Allyn and Bacon.

Spiro, R. J., Feltovich, P. L., Jacobson, M. J., & Coulson, R. L. (1992). Cognitive flexibility, constructivism, and hypertext: Random access for advanced knowledge acquisition in ill-structured domains. In T. M. Duffy & D. H. Jonassen (Eds.), *Constructivism and the technology of instruction: A conversation*. Hillsdale, NJ: Lawrence Erlbaum Associates. Originally in *Educational Technology*, 1991, *31*(5).

Stinson, J. E. (1994). *Can Digital Equipment survive?* Paper presented at the Sixth International Conference on Thinking, Boston, MA.

Williams, S. M., (1992) Putting case-based instruction into context: Examples from legal and medical education. *Journal of the Learning Sciences, 2*, 367–427.

vonGlasersfeld, E. (1989). Cognition, construction of knowledge, and teaching. *Synthese, 80*, 121–140.

Vygotsky, L. S. (1978) *Mind in Society: The development of higher psychological processes*. Cambridge MA: Harvard University Press.

John R. Savery is a Ph.D. candidate in Instructional Systems Technology at Indiana University. His dissertation research is examining issues of learner ownership in a problem based, cooperative learning environment. He has recently joined the DLS Group in Denver, Colorado, as a senior instructional designer.

Thomas M. Duffy is Professor of Instructional Systems Technology and in Language Education at the School of Education, Indiana University, and director of the undergraduate Corporate and Community Education Program. His interests are in the design of learner-centered learning environments with particular design emphasis on technology supports and a research emphasis on the collaborative practical reasoning process.

Part Three

Open, Virtual Learning Environments

12

Constructivism in the Collaboratory

Daniel C. Edelson
Roy D. Pea
Louis Gomez

Great attention has been paid recently to the capabilities of computers to provide environments in which active learners can construct their own understanding through open-ended interaction. Yet discussion of constructivist learning environments has commonly focused on the learner as an individual, learning in isolation from other learners. For example, Perkins (1991) characterizes a learning environment as being composed of five facets: information banks, symbol pads, construction kits, phenomenaria, and task managers. Each of these is a valuable resource for an individual learner but none provides a means for a learner to interact with, influence, or be influenced by other learners.

In our research, we start with a constructivist belief in the importance of an active learner interacting with a variety of resources, developing his or her own understanding through a mixture of experimentation, experience, and expert guidance. However, we supplement this constructivist outlook with a sociocultural commitment to the importance of communication and collaboration with other learners throughout the knowledge construction process. In this chapter, we describe a learning environment that we have developed that combines constructivist-inspired tools for open-ended investigation with communication and collaboration tools that support both expert guidance and multi-learner collaboration. We begin by presenting our rationale for this approach.

Communication and Collaboration in Constructivist Learning

Early approaches to the use of technology in education were based on a transmission model of instruction, in which technology (e.g., film and broadcast media) was simply used to transmit instruction in a more engaging fashion in some cases, and to larger numbers of students in others. This practice continues today in the form of distance education that uses phone lines, satellite links, and microwave to transmit static knowledge to wider audiences, with minimal opportunities for highly interactive conversations with instructors or other learners (Pea & Gomez, 1992). With the advent of the personal computer, technology took on new roles in learning, including, in the best cases, permitting students to interact with responsive, dynamic environments that support compelling, active learning. However, in many workplaces and other environments not specifically designed for education, computers have shown their greatest value to be in support of communication and collaboration, as in electronic mail and in groupware applications such as *Lotus Notes*. Increasingly, technology has assisted in broadening the form that collaboration takes to include not just discussion but the sharing of artifacts and cooperative work across time and distance. We believe that technologies with similar emphases can play a revolutionary role in supporting new forms of learning conversations in educational settings.

In thinking about educational reform, it is important to recognize that the math and science reforms of the 1960's that were most successful were not just those that emphasized the active nature of the learner through manipulables and hands-on inquiry, but also those that provided opportunities for students to talk, while they were engaged in learning interactions, about what they were learning, what they believed, and what they had difficulty understanding (Bruner, 1966; Bredderman, 1983; Shymansky, Kyle, & Alport, 1983). With that experience, it would be a mistake to be satisfied in the current era of reform with constructivist learning environments that only provide for solitary interaction.

The act of communication during learning can enhance the quality of the learning. Our view of communication is that it is more than simply passing static knowledge back and forth between participants. The act of communication transforms all the parties involved (Pea, 1994). In a conversation, the act of speaking requires an individual to place a structure and a coherency on his or her understanding that may lead the individual to recognize gaps in that understanding or forge new connections between formerly disconnected knowledge. The interaction between speaker and listener(s) in a conversation amplifies this process as they attempt to reconcile the differences in their perspectives, opinions, and experiences. The result of such conversations for the participants can be new knowledge, reorganized knowledge, or simply the awareness of a need for additional understanding. In each case, however, the social act of attempting to share and reconcile the knowledge of different individuals motivates learning in a way that is much rarer (although not unheard of, e.g., Chi *et al.*, 1989) among solitary learners.

In addition to this emphasis on the transformative nature of communication, we have been influenced in our approach by the belief that an important goal of learning is to gain entrance to or understanding of communities of practice (Lave & Wenger, 1991). In the research we describe here, we view the scientific community as a community of practice, shaped by shared language, activities, and values (D'Amico *et al.*, 1994). Lave and Wenger characterize the learning process associated with becoming a member of a community of practice as legitimate peripheral participation. This form of learning, closely allied to Brown,

Collins, and Duguid's (1989) cognitive apprenticeship learning, consists of authentic participation in the activities of the community at a level appropriate to the learner's current competency. As the learner's understanding and competence increase, he or she is able to participate in more central, and therefore less peripheral, practice until eventually the learner becomes an acculturated member of the community. In the research we describe here, we provide learners with the ability to join a scientific community of practice by providing them with access to the tools and activities employed by scientists and by providing them with the means to communicate and develop relationships with practicing scientists in the context of authentic scientific inquiry.

This orientation toward learning alters the role of the teacher significantly. Where some forms of solitary constructivist learning threaten to remove the teacher from active participation in students' learning, the form of constructivist learning in a collaborative social context that we are advocating places the teacher in a role of central importance. The teacher must be able to guide students as they engage in open-ended activities, but more importantly must be able to help students establish and maintain transformative learning conversations about these activities. To do so requires the teacher to establish a culture of communication about matters of substance in the classroom that includes the teacher as both participant and facilitator. The teacher as participant brings an expertise in the content area and in the learning process that he or she can share with students at appropriate moments. The teacher as facilitator must bring an expertise in fostering and even guiding learning conversations that ideally involves a diversity of participants and that includes not just students but members of relevant extramural communities.

The CoVis Collaboratory

Over the past two years, we have been attempting to place the approach described above into practice in high school science classrooms under the auspices of the Learning Through Collaborative Visualization (CoVis) Project.[1] The CoVis project is an NSF-funded educational networking testbed that is establishing a scientific learning collaboratory (Lederberg & Uncapher, 1989) that includes students, teachers, scientists, informal science educators, and educational researchers. In its approach to transforming science learning the CoVis Project has focused on three areas: (1) a project-enhanced science learning pedagogy (Ruopp *et al.*, 1993), (2) scientific visualization tools for open-ended inquiry, and (3) networked environments for communication and collaboration. The project's classroom innovation efforts in these three areas are being accompanied by an evaluative research effort aimed at both formative and summative evaluation.

The CoVis project began working with six earth and environmental science teachers at two Chicago-area high schools in the summer of 1992. In the fall of 1993, these teachers and their nearly 300 students began the school year with a new suite of applications that included scientific visualization tools for atmospheric sciences and an asynchronous collaboration environment, both

---

[1] Information about the CoVis Project is available via the world-wide web at the URL "http://www.covis.nwu.edu."

developed by the CoVis project, as well as desktop video teleconferencing, and a full set of Internet tools including e-mail, Usenet news, and Gopher. These applications are accessed using six Macintosh Quadra workstations in each classroom connected to a high-speed video and data network running over Primary Rate ISDN digital phone lines. As an ensemble, these applications provide a "collaboratory" environment that couples open-ended scientific inquiry tools with tools to support communication and collaboration.

Visualization Tools for Open-Ended Inquiry

A wide, and growing, range of microcomputer-based tools that support constructivist learning have been developed over the past decade, from microworlds, to modeling and simulation environments, to programming languages (see, for example, Hancock, Kaput, and Goldsmith, 1992; Harel & Papert, 1993; Lewis, Stern, & Linn, 1993; Papert, 1980; Resnick & Ocko, 1994; Roschelle, 1992; Smith, Snir, & Grosslight, 1992; Stewart et al., 1992; White, 1993). We have been exploring yet an additional type of software environment for constructivist learning, scientific visualization environments. Scientific visualization is a technique for data analysis that has revolutionized several fields of science. Scientific visualization received its definition from a landmark NSF report (McCormick, DeFanti, & Brown, 1987) that brought together diverse representatives from the disciplines of science, computer science, and the visual arts. While scientific visualizations from different disciplines of science vary dramatically, they generally share the use of color, shape, and motion to provide a visual window into the patterns and structure to be found in large, complex data. Scientific visualizations can generally be characterized by the following traits adapted from Gordin and Pea, 1994):

- They incorporate massive amounts of quantitative data.
- They aim for verisimilitude with the phenomena they represent.
- They attempt to represent entire phenomena holistically by interpolating from data.
- They employ color and shape to encode the magnitude of variables.
- They use animated sequences to show progression over time.
- They rely on high speed computation to generate images.

Scientific visualizations are often similar to digital photographs in that they contain a set of values that can be rendered by mapping each number to a particular color. However, unlike a digital photograph, the values composing a scientific visualization do not necessarily represent the intensities of visible light. Instead, they can represent any measured or derived quantities of scientific interest. For example, the data set might be collected from temperatures all over the world. These temperatures are then viewed as a digital image, where each number is mapped to a specific color. The variations and patterns of color allow a viewer to observe underlying processes. Through this strategic use of color and motion, scientific visualizations exploit the strengths of the human visual system.

We conjecture that the same advantages that scientific visualization holds for scientists also hold for students of science. Many of the troubles that students experience in science stem from difficulty in understanding the abstractions, formalisms, and quantitative terms of equation-based data representations. In taking advantage of powerful human visual perceptual capabilities, scientific visualization offers a different route to scientific understanding, and thus the possibility of reaching a group of students that have not been well-served by traditional science teaching. Scientific visualization also offers the possibility of opening up new domains for study that have been considered too complex for high school students because of their heavy reliance on formulae and abstract representations. Similarly, scientific visualizations can give students the ability to conduct direct investigations in areas to which they have only had indirect access before (e.g., global climate data; planetary biomass distribution; ocean temperature).

From the point of view of socioculturally-based constructivist learning, scientific visualization has three additional important characteristics. The first is that scientific visualization allows students to pose their own research questions, investigate them through direct manipulation of data, and create their own graphical images to first generate and then demonstrate their conclusions. Scientific visualization tools can, therefore, provide the active, open-ended exploration that characterizes constructivist learning. Second, the images produced by scientific visualization provide a basis for discussion among learners. Learners can engage in dialogues about the meaning and interpretation of visualization images that can help them to extend their understanding and reveal their partial understandings. Third, inquiry using scientific visualizations can link students with the actual practice of scientists. This step toward reducing the distance between the practices of scientists and those of students in the classroom gives students a valuable common ground with scientists. In a situation where students have direct access to practicing scientists, this common ground can support effective communication and scientist-student relationships. In this manner, the construction of scientific visualizations becomes a form of legitimate peripheral participation in the community of scientific practice.

A primary challenge of employing scientific visualization in educational settings is that visualization tools as now employed by scientists are difficult to use and rely on a great deal of expertise on the part of the user. In the CoVis project, we have worked very closely with researchers in the atmospheric sciences to adapt the tools they use in their research for use in high school science classrooms by creating "front-ends," novice scaffolds for working with the challenges of complexity. We have developed a four-step process for this purpose:

1. *Investigate science practice.* We observe the use of visualization tools and data sets by scientists. This step requires our development group to become reasonably expert, with the support of scientific advisors, in the content area and its research questions. The result of this step is a characterization of the sorts of questions the visualization tools and data sets can be used to investigate, and the ways in which the tools are employed in the course of inquiry.
2. *Identify tacit knowledge used in science practice.* We seek to articulate the tacit knowledge employed by scientists in their use of the visualization tools. This knowledge includes scientific principles, understanding of the limitations of the data collection process and the models used to enhance the data, and how-to knowledge concerning the use of the tools.

3. *Scaffold the science practice for students by making the tacit explicit.* We adapt these visualization tools so as to make the tacit knowledge exposed in the second step explicit, structuring the software interface and affiliated pedagogical activities to assist students to pursue meaningful questions.
4. *Refine the visualization tools in response to formative evaluations.* Through a combination of observation and direct user feedback, evaluate the patterns of use that emerge and use these evaluations to inform the redesign of the software.

As part of the CoVis Project, we have developed three visualization environments using this four-step process for building "front-ends" to scientific visualization tools and data sets, and we are about to embark on the development of a tool that will partially automate the development of these environments for a certain range of data sets. The visualization environments we have developed cover three aspects of atmospheric science and are called the Weather Visualizer (Fishman & D'Amico, 1994), the Climate Visualizer (Gordin & Pea, 1994; Gordin, Polman, & Pea, 1994), and the Greenhouse Effect Visualizer (Gordin, Edelson, & Pea, 1995). Each of these is built on top of a scientific visualization tool used by researchers (e.g., *Transform* from Spyglass, Inc.) and provides learners with a more structured and more supportive user interface.

The Weather Visualizer is an interface to the most recent hour's weather data for the United States. It enables students to view satellite images in both the visual and infrared spectrum, weather maps displaying graphical symbols corresponding to atmospheric conditions and local station reports, and six-panel, false-color images showing such variables as temperature, wind speed and direction, atmospheric pressure, dew point, and moisture convergence. This visual information is supplemented by textual reports and forecasts for all National Weather Service reporting stations in the country. All the data used by the Weather Visualizer are provided via the Internet from the Department of Atmospheric Sciences at the University of Illinois at Urbana-Champaign.

The major feature of this environment is that it enables students to construct their own weather maps, displaying the variables that they are interested in, for whatever portion of the country and at whatever altitude they desire. This graphical representation can then be compared to the pre-constructed satellite images and six-panel visualizations that the Weather Visualizer also provides.

The most common use of the Weather Visualizer by students has been for conducting "nowcasts" and forecasts. Nowcasting is an activity usually used by teachers to introduce students to the interpretation of weather maps and symbols. Students use the graphical representations to construct descriptions of the current weather in a particular location. Performing forecasts is a great deal more open-ended and gives students the opportunity to share hypotheses, discuss the processes by which they came to those hypotheses, and engage in scientific disputes. In addition, they have the ability to compare their own thought processes with more expert practitioners both through the CoVis network or by watching meteorologists on TV. Using a companion program to the Weather Visualizer called the Weather Graphics Tool (Fishman & D'Amico, 1994), students are able to express their forecasts in the form of weather maps they draw themselves. The Weather Graphics tool, a plug-in module for Aldus

SuperPaint, gives students the ability to draw weather maps almost identical to those produced by the Weather Visualizer by "stamping" weather symbols from an electronic stamp pad onto blank maps. In addition to nowcasting and forecasting, students have used the weather maps and satellite images for research into weather-related topics. For example, one student used archived weather maps as part of an investigation of the conditions that led to the disastrous wild fires in the Los Angeles area in the late fall of 1993.

Like the Weather Visualizer, the Climate Visualizer provides students with access to weather data. However, the Climate Visualizer draws from a data set that contains twenty-five years of data from the early 1960's to the late 1980's for most of the Northern Hemisphere. The Climate Visualizer allows students to display temperature as color, wind as vectors, and atmospheric pressure as contours. It has been augmented from the tool that climatologists use to examine the same data by adding several features. These features include: (1) geographic references such as latitude and longitude markings and a continent overlay, (2) the addition of units to all numerical values, e.g., degrees Fahrenheit or Celsius, and (3) an interactive color palette that displays the direct mapping between colors or symbols displayed in a visualization and the quantities they represent. It is a measure of the success of the tool's adaptation process that students are most often able to begin to make sense of visualizations in the Climate Visualizer immediately, without the extensive assistance that would have been required for them to look at the same variables using the scientists' tool. The Climate Visualizer provides students with the ability to modify the mappings from values to colors in order to accentuate features of interest, and it provides them with the ability to create new data by subtracting one image from another. Subtraction allows students to track trends over time, e.g., diurnal, seasonal, and annual. Because the data set includes monthly averages and averages for the same date over twenty-five years, students are also able to use subtraction to investigate anomalies.

Students have used the Climate Visualizer to conduct investigations into topics of their own choosing that include the effect of coastlines on local temperatures, the impact of volcanoes on weather, and what the climate will be like in California in 50 million years (taking into account geologists' predictions that it will separate from the mainland). One of the most interesting discoveries by students using the Climate Visualizer is an apparent flaw in the model used to generate the data that the students are using. This dataset has been created using a complex mathematical model to interpolate from sparse measurements. Students first observed that temperature values in the Himalayas in some years were surprisingly cold. Upon consideration, they realized that in that part of the world, there are mountains at the height in the atmosphere they were viewing. The values they were seeing, therefore, had to have been generated by a model, since it is impossible to measure atmospheric temperature in the interior of a mountain. The fact that these areas were so much colder than surrounding areas indicated that the model was probably flawed. This hypothesis gained more strength from the fact that the temperatures in that part of the world were only anomalous in certain years. This process of examining the source and reliability of the data they were working with was a valuable opportunity for the students to expand their understanding of the scientific process.

The Greenhouse Effect Visualizer is the newest visualization environment in the CoVis software suite. It allows students to visualize and manipulate data having to do with the balance of incoming and outgoing solar radiation in the earth's atmosphere. The Greenhouse Effect Visualizer is constructed around three alternative models of the earth-sun system. The first model treats the earth as a body with no atmosphere, the second treats the earth as a body with an atmosphere but no clouds, and the third includes the earth, the atmosphere, and clouds. The Greenhouse Effect Visualizer combines measured with derived data and provides students with access to variables such as incoming solar radiation (insolation), reflectance of the earth's surface (albedo), and surface temperatures of the earth. In pilot usage, students have used the Greenhouse Effect Visualizer to try to understand and demonstrate possible sources of global warming.

In using all of the CoVis visualizers, students have had the opportunity to generate their own questions, develop their own plans for identifying and exploring appropriate data, and create their own artifacts to generate and demonstrate findings. Both the visualization process and the visualizations themselves then become the topic of a scientific dialogue in which students, together with teachers, scientists, and other students, try to make sense of what they have done. While many dialogues lead to increased understanding of scientific concepts, others involve the sharing and even growth of significant misconceptions. To the extent that a teacher or scientist can help shape these dialogues, students' understanding of the underlying science can be improved. Regardless, the sharing of viewpoints and the examination of the inquiry process invariably brings students closer to an understanding of the practice of science in a social context.

Using Tools for Communication and Collaboration

The practice of science takes place mostly in communities, and relies increasingly on collaborations that span widely distributed institutions through the use of networking technologies to form "collaboratories" (e.g., Lederberg & Uncapher, 1989; Office of Science and Technology Policy, 1994). In developing collaborative learning environments, the CoVis project has taken technologies developed primarily to support collaboration in industrial and research settings and adapted them to high schools. These technologies enable students and others to work together within classrooms and across the country, at the same time (synchronously) or at different times (asynchronously).

To participate in synchronous collaboration, several individuals can sit together at the same computer, or—using CoVis-provided tools—work together at a distance as if they were sitting at the same computer. The functionality for establishing such "media spaces" is achieved through desktop video teleconferencing coupled with remote screensharing.[2] In the desktop videoconferencing set-up used by CoVis participants, a video monitor, camera, microphone, and speaker adjacent to a computer workstation allow an individual or group at one end to see and talk to partners at the other. Remote screensharing allows

---

[2]Desktop videoconferencing is conducted using the Cruiser and Touring Machine applications developed at Bellcore, and remote screensharing is performed using Timbuktu and Timbuktu Pro from Farallon Computing.

individuals at one end to view the contents of their partners' computer screen and to control the remote computer with their own keyboard and mouse. The result is the ability to have parties in two locations viewing and controlling the same computer as if they were in the same place. Combined with the ability to see and speak with each other, remote screensharing supports an interaction that is very similar to working together at the same computer. In the first year of CoVis operations in the schools, this synchronous collaboration environment was primarily used as a means for students to work with graduate students at Northwestern University playing mentoring roles for students' investigations.

Asynchronous collaboration in CoVis classrooms is supported both by conventional communication applications like e-mail and newsgroup discussions, and by a novel groupware application we have developed called the Collaboratory Notebook (Edelson & O'Neill, 1994a; Edelson & O'Neill, 1994b). Individual students or project teams use e-mail and newsgroups to contact remote experts and to post queries for information from both the CoVis community and the Internet community at large. They use the Collaboratory Notebook to record their activities, and to share their work with others. The Collaboratory Notebook is a networked, multimedia database that is structured to support learners through the inquiry process and provides them with a mechanism for working cooperatively with others. It is also designed to provide teachers and other mentors with a window into the thinking processes and activities of students. In its structure and goals, the Collaboratory Notebook shares attributes with other hypermedia collaboration environments designed for educational and research use, such as CSILE (Scardamalia & Bereiter, 1991), Project INQUIRE (Brunner, 1990; Hawkins & Pea, 1987), GroupWrite (Schank & Osgood, 1993) and the Virtual Notebook System (Gorry *et al.*, 1991).

In a prototypical use of the Collaboratory Notebook, a group of students might develop an idea for an investigation and begin by recording some questions and hypotheses. These may be followed by a plan for how to pursue these issues. A teacher or other mentor could read the students' questions, hypotheses and plans and add comments to help them focus their efforts or to alert them to resources that they might find useful. In the next stage, students might engage in separate research activities that they could individually record for the others to view. In doing so, they might store both data and analyses within the Notebook. Without needing to meet in person, students could exchange questions and comments on their findings. Once they have conducted their investigations, they could get further guidance from an instructor or a scientist mentor, and then use the information they have recorded to draw conclusions or initiate further investigations.

Loosely modeled on the metaphor of a scientists' notebook, the Collaboratory Notebook provides users with the ability to author pages individually or in groups and to read the pages authored by others. Pages are labeled according to the role they play in the inquiry process (e.g., question, plan, conjecture, evidence-for, evidence-against, commentary) and may be linked via a hypermedia interface to other pages according to the relationship between them. Thus, a conjecture may be linked to the question it answers, and evidence-against may be linked to a conjecture it contradicts. The limited set of pre-defined page and link types are designed to provide students with a helpful supporting structure in recording their thought processes and actions as they engage in open-ended inquiry and to help them to develop a model of the inquiry process. The page- and link-types serve a second role, which is to help establish reliable conventions within a community of contributors that help readers to navigate through the hypermedia database more efficiently.

The Collaboratory Notebook database is divided into individual notebooks that students and teachers may create to serve specific purposes. Thus, a student may create a private journal, a group of students might create a shared project notebook, and a teacher may create a discussion notebook in which all of his or her students can participate. Because the Collaboratory Notebook is a multimedia database, students are able to record text as well as tables, graphics, sound, video, and animation within their notebooks. The Notebook is implemented as a networked client connected to a central database, so it may be used from any location on the Internet. Taking advantage of this capability in the past year, one teacher at a Chicago-area school set up an activity using the Collaboratory Notebook in which students in his class entered information about topics in mineralogy, and scientist mentors at the University of Illinois at Urbana-Champaign and the Exploratorium museum in San Francisco interceded with questions designed to impel students to probe more deeply.

In the integrated CoVis software environment, the Collaboratory Notebook provides a mechanism for constructivist activities in a social context. It provides the mechanism for recording activities, storing artifacts, and sharing the working process with others. Its structure helps to make the inquiry process explicit and even to make it a topic of discussion. Coupled with the scientific visualization tools and other Internet investigation tools provided by the CoVis project, the Notebook supports the social process of constructing knowledge.

As an example of the integration of inquiry tools and collaboration tools, consider the following activity conducted by a CoVis teacher. Rather than directly instructing students about weather phenomena, he chose to let them learn about them through the process of making weather predictions. To do so, he created a discussion notebook using the Collaboratory Notebook software and instructed students to make 48-hour weather predictions and place them within that shared notebook. His students used the Weather Visualizer to create weather maps and satellite images of the current weather, which they could then store in the notebook as data. Working from these visualizations, they attempted to project forward forty-eight hours using their limited understanding of meteorology to make predictions. Their predictions could be expressed in the form of weather maps that they drew themselves with the Weather Graphics Tool.

Once student groups had entered their predictions and the rationale for them, they were able to view the predictions of the other groups and to argue for or against competing forecasts. Taking advantage of the teacher, each other, and other sources of information, students were able to improve their understanding of the underlying scientific processes through social interaction. One of the most compelling incidents that occurred in this relatively brief process took the form of a "hint" posted by one group of students. These students encouraged the other

Constructivism in the Collaboratory 161

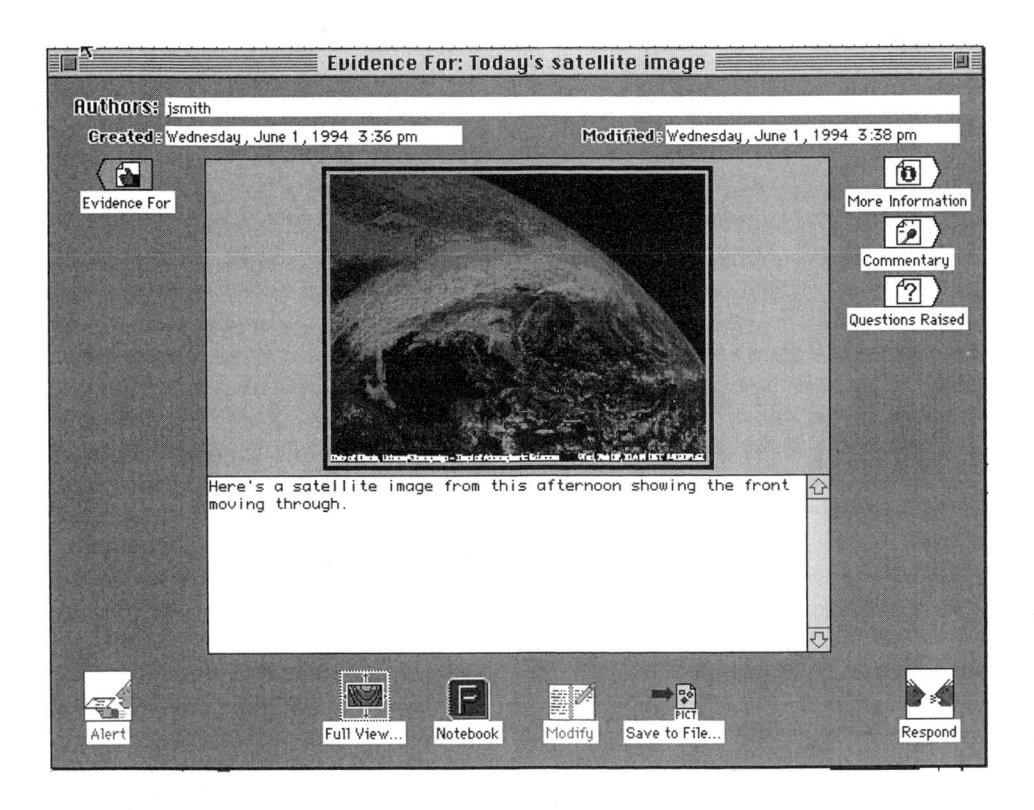

Figure 12.1. An "Evidence For" page from the Collaboratory Notebook showing a satellite image of the eastern United States generated by the Weather Visualizer. The arrow-shaped buttons at the left and right side of the window are used to link this page to other related pages in a notebook.

students to look at the wind speed in the upper atmosphere to help calculate the rate at which weather patterns would be moving. While it was the social environment established by the teacher that led the students to share this insight, the software provided them with the means to do so, and the nature of the activity made this piece of information valuable to the students involved. In the end, small pieces of information like these, shared and contextualized through meaningful activities, are the materials out of which learners are able to construct scientific understanding.

Conclusion

Constructivist learning environments have made great strides in moving away from the knowledge transmission model of learning toward an active learner model. However, active learning can be further enhanced through social interaction. The CoVis project has developed an integrated software environment that incorporates visualization tools for open-ended scientific investigations and communication tools for both synchronous and asynchronous collaboration. The visualization tools, modified versions of scientists' tools, enable students to participate in authentic scientific practice. The collaboration tools enable students to engage in this scientific practice in a social context that includes other students, teachers, and scientists. The resulting social interactions enhance the learning that students achieve through the transformative process of communication. Over the next several years, as the project grows to include more schools, we will be conducting in-depth studies within the participating classrooms to evaluate the character of the learning and the social interactions that take place there. Our experiences to date offer encouragement that practicing teachers are able to take advantage of these sorts of new technologies to provide their students with opportunities for active learning and meaningful social interaction about scientific subjects.

References

Bredderman, T. (1983). Effects of activity-based elementary science on student outcomes: A quantitative synthesis. *Review of Educational Research, 53,* 499–518.

Brown, J. S., Collins, A., & Duguid, P. (1989). Situated cognition and the culture of learning. *Educational Researcher, 18(1),* 32–42.

Bruner, J. S. (1966). *Toward a theory of instruction.* Cambridge, MA: Harvard University Press.

Brunner, C. (1990). *Designing INQUIRE.* New York: Bank Street College, Center for Children and Technology.

Chi, M. T. H., Bassok, M., Lewis, M. W., Reimann, P., & Glaser, R. (1989). Self-explanations: How students study and use examples in learning to solve problems. *Cognitive Science, 13,* 145–182.

D'Amico, L., Fishman, B., Gordin, D. N., McGee, S., O'Neill, K., & Polman, J. (1994). The atmospheric sciences: Six views into a community of practice. Unpublished manuscript.

Edelson, D. C., & O'Neill, D. K. (1994a). The CoVis collaboratory notebook: Computer support for scientific inquiry. Paper presented at the annual meeting of the American Educational Research Association, New Orleans.

Edelson, D. C., & O'Neill, D. K. (1994b). The CoVis collaboratory notebook: Supporting collaborative scientific inquiry. In *Recreating the revolution: Proceedings of the National Educational Computing Conference* (pp. 146–152). Eugene, OR: International Society for Technology in Education.

Fishman, B., & D'Amico, L. (1994). Which way will the wind blow? Networked computer tools for studying the weather. In T. Ottmann & I. Tomek (Eds.), *Educational multimedia and hypermedia, 1994: Proceedings of ED-MEDIA 94—World Conference on Educational multimedia and hypermedia* (pp. 209–216). Charlottesville, VA: Association for the Advancement of Computing in Education.

Gordin, D., & Pea, R. (1994). Prospects for scientific visualization as an educational technology. *Journal of the Learning Sciences.*

Gordin, D. N., Edelson, D. C., & Pea, R. D. (1995). The Greenhouse Effect Visualizer: A tool for the science classroom. *Proceedings of the Annual Meeting of the American Meteorological Society,* January, 1995.

Gordin, D., Polman, J., & Pea, R. (1994). The Climate Visualizer: Sense-making through scientific visualization. *Journal of Science Education and Technology, 3(4),* 203–225.

Gorry, A. G., Long, K. B., Burger, A. M., Jung, C. P., & Meyer, B. D. (1991). The Virtual Notebook System: An architecture for collaborative work. *Journal of Organizational Computing, 1*(3), 233–250.

Hancock, C., Kaput, J. J., & Goldsmith, L. T. (1992). Authentic inquiry with data: Critical barriers to classroom implementation. *Educational Psychologist, 27*(3), 337–364.

Hawkins, J., & Pea, R. D. (1987). Tools for bridging the cultures of everyday and scientific thinking. *Journal of Research in Science Teaching, 24*(4), 291–307.

Harel, I., & Papert, S. (1993). Software design as a learning environment. *Interactive Learning Environments, 1*(1), 1–32.

Lave, J., & Wenger, E. (1991). *Situated learning: Legitimate peripheral participation*. Cambridge: Cambridge University Press.

Lederberg, J., & Uncapher, K. (Co-Chairs). (1989). *Towards a national collaboratory: Report of an invitational workshop at the Rockefeller University, March 17–18*. Washington DC: National Science Foundation Directorate for Computer and Information Science.

Lewis, E. L., Stern, J. L., & Linn, M. C. (1993). The effect of computer simulations on introductory thermodynamics understanding. *Educational Technology, 33*(1), 45–58.

McCormick, B. H., DeFanti, T. A., & Brown, M. D. (Eds.) (1987). Visualization in scientific computing. *Computer Graphics, 21*(6).

Office of Science and Technology Policy. (1994). *High performance computing and communications: Toward a national information infrastructure: The FY 1994 U. S. research and development program*. A Report by the Committee on Physical, Mathematical, and Engineering Sciences, Federal Coordinating Council for Science, Engineering, and Technology. Washington, DC: Executive Office of the President.

Papert, S. (1980). *Mindstorms*. New York: Basic Books.

Pea, R. D. (1994). Seeing what we build together: Distributed multimedia learning environments for transformative communications. *Journal of the Learning Sciences, 3*(3), 285–299.

Pea, R. D., & Gomez, L. (1992). Distributed multimedia learning environments: Why and how? *Interactive Learning Environments, 2*(2), 73–109.

Perkins, D. N. (1991, May). Technology meets constructivism: Do they make a marriage? *Educational Technology, 31*(5), 18–23.

Resnick, M., & Ocko, S. (1994). LEGO/Logo: Learning through and about design. In S. Papert (Ed.), *Constructionism* (pp. 141–150). Norwood, NJ: Ablex.

Roschelle, J. (1992). Learning by collaboration: Convergent conceptual change. *The Journal of the Learning Sciences, 2*(3), 235–276.

Ruopp, R., Gal, S., Drayton, B., & Pfister, M. (Eds.) (1993). *LabNet: Toward a community of practice*. Hillsdale, NJ: Lawrence Erlbaum Associates.

Scardamalia, M., & Bereiter, C. (1991). Higher levels of agency for children in knowledge building: A challenge for the design of new knowledge media. *The Journal of the Learning Sciences, 1*(1), 7–68.

Schank, R. C., & Osgood, R. (1993). *The communications story*. Evanston, IL: Institute for the Learning Sciences, Northwestern University.

Shymansky, J. A., Kyle, W. C., Jr., & Alport, J. M. (1983). The effects of new science curricula on student performance. *Journal of Research in Science Teaching, 20*(5), 387–404.

Smith, C., Snir, J., & Grosslight, L. (1992). Using conceptual models to facilitate conceptual change: The case of weight-density differentiation. *Cognition and Instruction, 9*(3), 221–283.

Stewart, J., Hafner, R., Johnson, S., & Finkel, E. (1992). Science as model building: Computers and high-school genetics. *Educational Psychologist, 27*(3), 317–336.

White, B. Y. (1993). Intermediate abstractions and causal models: A microworld-based approach to science education. In *AI-ED 93: World Conference on Artificial Intelligence and Education* (pp. 26–33). Charlottesville, VA: Association for the Advancement of Computing in Education.

Acknowledgment

This material is based upon work supported by the National Science Foundation's Programs for Applications of Advanced Technology and Informal Science Education under Grant No. MDR-9253462. The CoVis project receives additional support from its industrial partners, including Ameritech, Bellcore, Apple Computer, Sony Corporation, Spyglass, Inc., Sun Microsystems, Aldus, and Farallon Computing.

The authors would like to thank Joe Polman for his assistance in preparing this chapter. In addition, we would like to acknowledge the major contributions to this research made by the entire CoVis project team at Northwestern: Laura D'Amico, Barry Fishman, Douglas Gordin, Stephen McGee, Kevin O'Neill, Joseph Polman, Phoebe Peng, Joey Gray, and Susan Rand. The Weather Visualizer was developed in cooperation with our collaborators at UIUC: Mohan Ramamurthy, Robert Wilhelmson, Steve Hall, and John Kemp. The Climate Visualizer was developed with assistance from Ray Pierrehumbert at the University of Chicago. Paul Forward and Ray Pierrehumbert assisted with the development of the Greenhouse Effect Visualizer. The CoVis teachers, Patty Carlson, George Dervis, Larry Geni, Mary Beth Hoffman, Ken Lewandowski, and Rory Wagner, have all provided valuable feedback in the development of the software described here and have been exceptional partners in innovation.

Daniel C. Edelson is Assistant Professor of Education and Computer Science, **Roy D. Pea** is Dean of the School of Education and Social Policy and John Evans Professor of Education and the Learning Sciences, and **Louis Gomez** is Associate Professor of Education and Computer Science, at the School of Education and Social Policy and Institute for the Learning Sciences, Northwestern University, Evanston, Illinois.

13

The Evolution of Constructivist Learning Environments: Immersion in Distributed, Virtual Worlds

Chris Dede

To date, uses of information technology to enhance constructivist learning environments have centered on creating computational tools and virtual representations that students can manipulate. For example, many of the chapters in this book describe information technology instantiations of Perkins' (1991) classification of constructivist paraphernalia: information banks, symbol pads, construction kits, phenomenaria, and task managers. As learners interpret experience to refine their mental models, computational tools that complement human memory and intelligence are made available. In parallel, transitional objects (such as Logo's "turtle") are used to facilitate translating personal experience into abstract symbols (Fosnot, 1992; Papert, 1988). Thus, technology-enhanced constructivist learning currently focuses on how representations and applications can mediate interactions among learners and natural or social phenomena.

However, the high performance computing and communications capabilities driving the deployment of the National Information Infrastructure create a new possibility. Like Alice walking through the looking glass, learners can immerse themselves in distributed, synthetic environments, becoming "avatars" who vicariously collaborate and learn-by-doing, using virtual artifacts to construct knowledge (Walker, 1990). Evolving beyond technology-mediated interactions between students and phenomena to technological instantiation of learners themselves and reality itself shifts the focus of constructivism: from peripherally enhancing how a student interprets a typical interaction with the external world to "magically" shaping the fundamental nature of how learners experience their physical and social context.

Immersing Learners in Distributed, Synthetic, Constructivist Worlds

Through underlying software models such as distributed simulation, a learner can be immersed in a synthetic, constructivist environment. The student acts and collaborates not as himself or herself, but behind the mask of an "avatar": a surrogate persona in the virtual world. Distributed simulation is a powerful educational delivery mechanism developed by the U. S. Department of Defense in the late 1980s. This instructional approach enhances students' ability to apply abstract knowledge by situating education in authentic, virtual contexts similar to the environments in which learners' skills will be used (Dede, 1992).

As one illustration, *SimNet* (Orlansky & Thorp, 1991) is a training application that creates a virtual battlefield on which learners at remote sites can develop collective military skills. The appearance and capabilities of graphically represented military equipment alter second-by-second as the virtual battle evolves. Complex data-objects that indicate changes in the state of the equipment are exchanged via a telephone network interconnecting the training workstations ("dial-a-war"). In the next generation of battle training simulations, learners will individually maneuver their virtual selves through weapons systems and landscapes populated by the avatars of friends and foes.

Via this type of information infrastructure, learners' collaborative interactions in synthetic constructivist environments can occur across distance, among avatars. In such virtual worlds, interpersonal dynamics provide leverage for learning activities in a manner rather different from typical face-to-face collaborative encounters. For example, participants in synthetic environments such as *SimNet* often feel as if the machine-based agents they encounter are real human beings, an illustration of the general principle that users tend to anthropomorphize information technologies. By using machine-based agents as synthetic personalities in a virtual corporate environment, the Advanced Learning Technologies Project at Carnegie Mellon University has taken advantage of anthropomorphization as a means to teach software engineering skills (Stevens, 1989). The agents provide both intellectual and psychosocial feedback to students, mimicking the types of interactions occurring in face-to-face constructivist learning (Dede, 1992).

As a complement to responding to knowbots as if they were human, participants in a virtual world interacting via avatars tend to treat each other as imaginary beings. An intriguing example of this phenomenon is documented in research on Lucasfilm's *Habitat* (Morningstar & Farmer, 1991). *Habitat* was initially designed to be an on-line entertainment medium in which people could meet in a virtual environment to play adventure games. Users, however, extended the system into a full-fledged virtual community with a unique culture; rather than playing pre-scripted fantasy games, they focused on constructing new lifestyles and utopian societies.

As an entertainment-oriented cyberspace, *Habitat* provided participants the opportunity to get married or divorced (without real-world repercussions), start businesses (without risking money), found religions (without real-world persecution), murder others' avatars (without moral qualms), and tailor the appearance of one's own avatar to assume a range of personal identities (e.g., movie star, dragon, invisible sprite). Just as *SimNet* enables virtual battles, *Habitat* and its successors empower users to construct artificial cultures. What people want from these virtual societies that the real world cannot offer is magic, such as the gender-alteration machine (Change-o-matic) that was one of the most popular devices in the *Habitat* world.

As in all constructivist learning, centralized, top-down planning fails in *Habitat*-like environments, because users prefer to design their own culture and artifacts. For example, Fujitsu's *Populopolis* (Japan's version of *Habitat*) has incorporated characteristics typical of Japanese society. As one illustration, *Populopolis* users make extensive use in written textual communication of a sign language they invented to provide the nonverbal context—usually conveyed through gesture, posture, and tone of voice—so important in Japanese culture (Yoshida & Kakuta, 1993).

Users learned more about their innermost needs and desires by participating in *Habitat* than they would have by spending an equivalent amount of time listening to psychology lectures. Similarly, social scientists are discovering more about utopias by studying *Habitat's* successors than they did by researching communes, which were too restricted by real-world considerations to meaningfully mirror people's visions of ideal communities. Giving users magical powers opens up learning in ways that educators are just beginning to understand. As with any emerging medium, first traditional types of content (e.g., instructionist approaches) are ported to the new channel; then alternative, more constructivist forms of expression—like *Habitat*—are created to take advantage of expanded capabilities for communication and education.

Beyond *Habitat*-like synthetic environments, another new form of virtual expression is what Rheingold (1993) terms "real-time tribes," the cross-cultural melange of written conversations proliferating under the technological medium of *Internet Relay Chat*. Stable identities, quick wit, and the use of words to construct an imagined shared context for interchange are the hallmarks of this environment, which is less formally structured than adventure-based worlds. As examples such as *Habitat* and *Internet Relay Chat* illustrate, synthetic simulation environments center on interaction and collaboration—unlike the passive, observational behavior induced by television and presentational multimedia—and are therefore well suited for constructivist experiences.

Virtual Cultures as a Lever for Constructivist Learning

Existing virtual communities provide a testbed for understanding what types of design heuristics attract and sustain students' interest in synthetic worlds for constructivist learning. Focusing on what participants want is very important to designing any type of learning environment, so researchers are now beginning to study the personality characteristics of users who find virtual environments of value. One such population is people who don't do well in spontaneous spoken interaction (e.g., shy, reflective, more comfortable with emotional distance), but who have valuable contributions to share with others. For this type of person, informal written communication is often more authentic than face-to-face verbal exchange. This may be a whole new dimension of learning styles orthogonal to the visual/auditory/kinesthetic/symbolic categories now underlying pedagogical approaches to individualization.

In addition, a wide range of participants are attracted to cooperative virtual environments because they gain something valuable by collaborating together. Social network capital (an instant web of contacts with useful skills), knowledge capital (a personal, distributed brain trust with just-in-time answers to immediate questions), and communion (psychological/spiritual support from people who share common joys and trials) are three types of "collective goods" that bind together virtual communities enabled by computer-mediated communication (Smith, 1992). Similar types of inducements to collaboration underlie face-to-face constructivist learning experiences.

One illustration of how people's behavior shifts in virtual worlds is exemplified by the ongoing overlay of textual commentary that establishes social context in current synthetic environments, such as Habitat or Internet Relay Chat. Historically, the social context cues that guide communication have been more physical than verbal (e.g., modes of dress, tone of voice, posture). In a world stripped of non-verbal context, users playfully recreate this context through written descriptions of props for a virtual culture: plans, recipes, rules, instructions for the governing of behavior (Reid, 1991). Developing a rhetoric for interchanges among avatars in distributed constructivist environments is vital to their educational effectiveness.

Perhaps because a synthetic social context is less mutually apparent than cohabiting a physical environment—and therefore less subject to consensual agreement—users experience both positive and negative disinhibition. Normally shy people speak out more, but usually polite people also "flame" more at others, hurling insults on-line that they would never use face-to-face (Sproull & Kiesler, 1991). While negative behavior must be channeled into isolated contexts that minimize damage to others, disinhibition is a potential lever for learning in constructivist environments, since this creates cognitive and emotional dissonance that can undercut suboptimal mental models.

Another psychosocial dynamic of virtual environments that opens opportunities to encourage learning is the fluidity of users' identity. Prior communications media (the printed word, the telephone, the television) dissolved social boundaries related to time and space. Synthetic environments based on text and computer graphics dissolve boundaries of identity as well, enabling communication about very personal things through a depersonalized medium (Rheingold, 1993). Many aspects of this openness are quite positive from a constructivist perspective, as people often reject new ideas because they feel that their own identities are contained in their existing mental models. However, the challenging side of personal revelation is that an avatar's authenticity is always questionable due to the masking and distancing properties of the medium.

One type of virtual environment that illustrates these challenges and opportunities of authenticity is Multi-User Dungeons (MUDs). These are magical, text-based worlds where users can assume fluid, anonymous identities and vicariously experience intriguing situations cast in a dramatic format. Beyond words as a vehicle for meaning, poses are also used; someone can leap on-stage, smirk, or disappear in a puff of smoke. The continual evolution of the shared environment based on participants' collaborative interactions keeps MUDs from becoming boring and stale. In contrast to standard adventure games, where one wanders through someone else's fantasy, the ability to personalize an environment and receive recognition from others for a widely appreciated addition to the shared context is attractive to users (as is also true in face-to-face constructivist learning environments).

This psychosocial fascination is not always positive for participants. Some users find MUDs so compelling a medium that they fall into addictive behaviors (Bruckman, 1992). Being able to have interesting conversations with people on demand—any time of the day or night, with your own identity fluid—can induce communications addiction in a significant number of participants. Moreover, access to desirable high-level magical powers (such as the ability to modify the simulation environment) often requires developing a detailed mastery of a MUD's lore and the rules collectively developed by its inhabitants—a process that can be both time-consuming and largely uncorrelated with learning.

The key psychological component underlying this type of addictive behavior may be need for mastery, competence in controlling one's environment (Turkle, 1984). People who feel that their self-image is based on exerting perfect control over their surroundings may seek refuge in simplistic virtual environments that provide an escape from the complexities and uncertainties of the real world. This is the opposite of a constructivist situation, in which learners deliberately expose themselves to challenge and paradox in search of new insights into order and meaning. A thin line separates being a virtuoso in a medium from being a prisoner addicted to a communications vehicle; promoting the former rather than the latter is a major issue in designing synthetic constructivist environments.

Magical media incorporating avatars are very seductive in inducing a desire for mastery because mimesis—feeling as if what happens to another is happening to you—is an ancient, powerful emotion at the heart of all drama (Laurel, 1991). While this can lead to escapism, as a dramatist knows, with good design the focus of mimesis shifts to playful exploration, learning by doing, and catharsis—all important processes for inducing constructivist learning. MUDs are gradually transforming into MUSEs (Multi-User Simulation Environments), which focus on shared learning within the computer-based world. Constructing utopian visions to empower transforming everyday reality has been historically powerful as a change mechanism; MUSEs are a new vehicle for accomplishing this goal.

Constructivist learning activities in MUSEs may empower finding one's identity rather than losing it in escapism and masking. Goffman's seminal work, *Presentation of the Self in Everyday Life* (1959), asserts that people are always onstage, creating a persona that they present to one audience or another. Some types of participants who are attracted to virtual communities (e.g., people denying unpleasant aspects of reality; people who present a persona to the world radically different than their internal self-image) are likely to have suboptimal learning behaviors as well. Synthetic constructivist environments provide a safe, anonymous opportunity to experiment with a new persona centered on a learning-centered lifestyle. For example, a person who feels ashamed of "being wrong"—and therefore is frightened of learning-by-doing situations—while masked within the context of a virtual community can safely risk making mistakes in the process of learning.

Evolving Mental Models
Via Immersion in Artificial Realities

The key capabilities that distributed synthetic environments for learning add to current educational media are:
- telepresence via avatars (perceived simultaneous presence in a virtual environment by geographically separated learners), and
- immersion (the subjective impression that a user is participating in a "world" comprehensive and realistic enough to induce the willing suspension of disbelief).

The induction of immersion and telepresence depends in part on actional and symbolic factors.

Inducing actional immersion involves empowering the participant in a virtual environment to initiate actions that have novel, intriguing consequences. For example, when a baby is learning to walk, the degree of concentration this activity creates in the child is extraordinary. Discovering new capabilities to shape one's environment is highly motivating and sharply focuses attention.

Inducing a participant's symbolic immersion involves triggering powerful semantic associations via the content of a virtual environment. As an illustration, reading a horror novel at midnight in a strange house builds a mounting sense of terror, even though one's physical context is unchanging and rationally safe. Invoking intellectual, emotional, and normative archetypes deepens one's experience in a virtual environment by imposing a complex overlay of associative mental models.

Distributed synthetic environments offer tremendous potential for actional and symbolic immersion. In fact, moderate-bandwidth environments such as *SimNet* may leverage more learning and behavioral change than interactions within high-bandwidth media (e.g., real-time videolinks) or low-bandwidth communication (such as electronic mail). Reflective asynchronous interaction, the playful re-creation of social context, the opportunity to try on a new persona, and catharsis are powerful levers for learning that may be optimally realized via a moderate-bandwidth communications channel.

The vignette below illustrates the potential for learning-by-doing in a distributed, synthetic environment that relies on actional and symbolic immersion for motivation. This constructivist learning experience takes place in a student's home, about 10:30 in the evening:

Vignette: Navigating Through Cyberspace

Roger was unobtrusively sidling across the Bridge of the Starship Enterprise when the Captain spotted him out of the corner of his eye. "Take the helm, Ensign Pulver," growled Captain Jean-Luc Picard, "and pilot a course through the corona of that star at lightspeed 0.999. We have astrophysical samples to collect. You'll have to guard against strange relativistic effects at that speed, but our shields cannot stand the radiation flux we would experience traveling less quickly."

As Picard glared at him from the screen of his home ITV *(interactive-television set)*, Roger drummed on his Cyberspace Console with his fingers and cursed quietly to himself. He had intended to sneak onto the Ecology Deck of the Starship and put in a little work on his biology class project in controlling closed-system pollution levels—but no such luck. Worse yet, Roger suspected that the Vulcan communications officer watching him while she translated a message in French was in fact the "avatar" *(computer-graphics representation of a person)* of a woman he admired who sat three rows behind him in his languages class. Of course, he could be wrong; she might be someone teleporting into this simulation from who knows where or could even be a "knowbot" *(a machine-based simulated personality used to simplify the job of the instructor Mage directing an constructivist simulation)*.

Buying a little time by summoning up the flight log, Roger glanced curiously around the bridge to see what new artifacts his fellow students had added since yesterday to this MUSE. In one corner, an intriguing creature was sitting in a transparent box, breathing a bluish-green atmosphere—maybe this was the long-awaited alien the university's anthropology and biology majors were creating as a mutual project. The 3-D goggles from his Nintendo++ set intensified the illusion that the lizard-like countenance was staring right at him.

"Impulse Engines to full speed, Mister," barked Captain Picard! "This Mage seems rather grumpy for a regular instructor," thought Roger, "maybe he's a visiting fireman from the new Net-the-Experts program." On his Console, Roger rapidly selected equations that he hoped would yield the appropriate relativistic corrections for successfully navigating through the star's corona.

Automatically, a cognitive audit trail of his actions began streaming to his factual-knowledge assessment file for physics. Each time he requested help from the computer-based coach, the performance score displayed on his Console dropped. "Why," said Roger sadly to himself, "couldn't I have lived in the days when students got to take multiple-choice tests..."

The potential interactions among avatars and virtual cultures in this hypothetical synthetic environment illustrate how shared evolution of physical/social context, fluidity of identity, disinhibition, and mimesis can empower distributed, constructivist learning.

Work in Progress: ScienceSpace

Beyond actional and symbolic immersion, advances in interface technology also enable physical immersion in artificial realities designed to enhance learning. Inducing a sense of physical immersion involves manipulating human sensory systems (especially the visual system) to enable the suspension of disbelief that one is surrounded by a virtual world. The impression is that of being inside an artificial reality rather than looking through a computer monitor "window" into a synthetic environment: the equivalent of diving rather than riding in a glass-bottomed boat.

A weak analog to physical immersion interfaces that many readers will have experienced is the IMAX motion picture theater, in which a two-story by three-story screen and high resolution images generate in the observer strong sensations of motion. Adding stereoscopic images, highly directional and realistic sound, tactile force-feedback, a visual field even wider than IMAX, and the ability to interact with the virtual world through natural physical actions produces a profound sensation of "being there," as opposed to watching. Because common sense responses to physical stimuli work in artificial realities, the learner quickly develops feelings of mastery, rather than the perception of helplessness and frustration typical when first attempting to use an unfamiliar computer interface or operating system.

With my colleague (R. Bowen Loftin at the University of Houston), my graduate students and I have recently begun the design of ScienceSpace, a series of artificial realities that explore the potential utility of physical immersion to enhance science education. One objective of this project is researching whether physically immersive constructivist learning can remediate typical misconceptions in the mental models of reality held by many students. Another is studying whether mastery of traditionally difficult subjects (e.g., relativity, quantum mechanics, molecular-orbital chemical bonding) is enhanced by physically immersive, collaborative learning-by-doing.

Most people's mental models include misconceptions that stem from misinterpreting common personal experiences with complex real-world phenomena, in which many forces are simultaneously acting. For example, the deceptively universal presence of friction makes objects in motion seem to slow and stop "on their own," undercutting belief in Newton's first law. As a result, most learners—including many science majors—have difficulty understanding physics concepts and models at the qualitative level, let alone the problems that occur with quantitative formulation (Reif & Larkin, 1991). These misconceptions, based on a lifetime of experience, are very difficult to remediate with instructionist pedagogical strategies.

We are studying whether physically immersive, shared artificial realities that allow users to alter the laws of nature can empower learners' constructivist evolution of mental models to correct pervasive misconceptions. Some of this work extends into physical immersion many ideas underlying 2-D constructivist microworlds for physics designed by researchers such as Barbara White (1993) and Andrea diSessa (Sherin, diSessa, & Hammer, 1993). Also, Sachter's research (1991) on how learners construct sophisticated mental models of 3-D space is providing valuable design heuristics for developing the interface to these immersive environments.

In incipient form, our ScienceSpace "worlds" for learning mechanics and dynamics in physics provide support for altering the magnitude and direction of gravitational acceleration, as well as the magnitudes of atmospheric drag, frictional coefficients between surfaces, and objects' coefficients of restitution. In addition, observations and measurements are made possible by controls that "freeze" the passage of time while objects are positioned and given initial velocities. Visualization, sonification, and tactilization features help learners sense attributes of objects in motion; and a display provides time, displacement, velocity, and acceleration data.

Of course, remediating misconceptions is not the only role that artificial realities designed for constructivist learning can play in science and technology education. Subjects such as quantum mechanics, relativity, and molecular bonding are difficult to teach in part because learners cannot draw analogies to personal experience that provides a metaphor for these phenomena. As a second objective for our research, we will construct immersive worlds that enable learners to experience near light-speed travel or quantum events, thus attempting to inculcate an instinctive, qualitative appreciation for these situations. This provides a phenomenological foundation for scientific principles that have been very difficult to teach.

Over the next two years, we will extend our early designs of ScienceSpace to a variety of phenomena from the physical, life, and earth sciences. Controlled trials will be conducted to assess the leverage for learning that different characteristics of these artificial realities provide. We plan to compare some types of learner outcomes in these artificial realities to similar outcomes using small-screen, two-dimensional simulations. These contrasts will help to clarify the relative utility of physical immersion and may suggest design principles for optimizing the educational value of artificial reality interfaces.

Through distributed simulation approaches, we can support shared interaction in a distributed virtual reality—even across merely moderate-bandwidth networks, such as the Internet—thus enabling telepresence and collaboration among learners' avatars. Designing the visual appearance of these avatars and what communications modes they can use to maximize constructivist learning is an intriguing challenge. Issues of mimesis, fluidity of identity, and disinhibition are among the important themes to consider. If synthetic environments for constructivist learning are not eerily beautiful, magical places that arouse curiosity and empower shared fantasy, we will lose our potential audience of students to the mindless videogame worlds of Sonic, the SuperMario Brothers, and the "death patrols."

Conclusion

Alfred, Lord Tennyson's poem, "The Lady of Shalott," depicts the complexities of understanding the real world via vicariously experiencing its mirrored, magical reflections in a synthetic environment. His poem ends tragically; ultimately, its protagonist is unable to live either in the virtual or the real world. Nonetheless, fairyland continues to attract both children and adults as a magical alternate reality. With careful design, I believe that occasional immersion of the self in distributed simulations and virtual worlds can enhance learners' understanding of phenomena and culture in our shared physical/social reality.

Gelerntner (1992) is quite optimistic about how soon we will be able to utilize "mirror worlds" to understand and manipulate nature, artifacts, and society. However, creating distributed, constructivist learning environments is likely to be quite challenging, as avatars and immersion introduce new subtleties to the intercommunication that evolves shared cultural interpretations of reality. This chapter sketches the beginnings in a long journey of exploration on how to use the power of imagination wisely in creating collective universes that facilitate learning.

Despite these challenges, however, incorporating collaboratively evolved virtual worlds into many aspects of public education may empower more than mastery of material. As America's National Information Infrastructure evolves, Rheingold (1993) portrays a fundamental choice between a virtual forum that enables true democracy and open-ended learning ("Athens without slaves") or a pervasive surveillance medium for propaganda and escapism (virtual "bread and circuses"). Creating constructivist, collaborative educational experiences that encourage the former outcome is an important means for ensuring full public access to and control of this emerging meta-medium.

References

Bruckman, A. (1992). *Identity workshops: Emergent social and psychological phenomena in text-based virtual reality* (Master's thesis, MIT Media Laboratory). Cambridge, MA: Massachusetts Institute of Technology.

Dede, C. (1992). The future of multimedia: Bridging to virtual worlds. *Educational Technology*, 32(5), 54–60.

Feiner, S., & Beshars, C. (1990). Worlds within worlds: Metaphors for enclosing n-dimensional virtual worlds. *1990 Proceedings of the User Interface Software and Technology Conference*. New York: Academic Press.

Fosnot, C. (1992). Constructing constructivism. In T. M. Duffy & D. H. Jonassen (Eds.), *Constructivism and the technology of instruction: A conversation* (pp. 167–176). Hillsdale, NJ: Lawrence Erlbaum Associates.

Gelerntner, D. (1992). *Mirror worlds*. New York: Oxford University Press.

Goffman, E. (1959). *The presentation of the self in everyday life*. Garden City, New York: Doubleday.

Laurel, B. (1991). *Computers as theater*. Menlo Park, CA: Addison-Wesley.

Morningstar, C., & Farmer, F. R. (1991). The lessons of Lucasfilm's *Habitat*. In M. Benedikt (Ed.), *Cyberspace: First steps* (pp. 273–302). Cambridge, MA: MIT Press.

Orlansky, J., & Thorp, J. (1991). SIMNET — an engagement training system for tactical warfare. *Journal of Defense Research*, 20(2), 774–783.

Papert, S. (1988). The conservation of Piaget: The computer as grist for the constructivist mill. In G. Foreman & P.B. Pufall (Eds.), *Constructivism in the computer age* (pp. 3–13). Hillsdale, NJ: Lawrence Erlbaum Associates.

Perkins, D. (1991). Technology meets constructivism: Do they make a marriage? *Educational Technology*, 31(5), 18–23.

Reid, E. (1991). *Electropolis: Communications and community on Internet Relay Chat* (Honors thesis, Department of History). Melbourne, Australia: University of Melbourne.

Reif, F., & Larkin, J. (1991). Cognition in scientific and everyday domains: Comparison and learning implications. *Journal of Research in Science Teaching*, 28, 743–760.

Rheingold, H. (1993). *The virtual community: Homesteading on the electronic frontier*. Reading, MA: Addison-Wesley.

Sachter, J. E. (1991). Different styles of exploration and construction of 3-D spatial knowledge in a 3-D computer graphics microworld. In I. Harel & S. Papert (Eds.), *Constructionism* (pp. 335–364). Norwood, NJ: Ablex.

Sherin, B., diSessa, A. A., & Hammer, D. M. (1993). Dynaturtle revisited: Learning physics through collaborative design of a computer model. *Interactive Learning Environments*, 3(2), 91–118.

Smith, M. (1992). *Voices from the WELL: The logic of the virtual commons* (Master's thesis, Department of Sociology). Los Angeles, CA: University of California at Los Angeles.

Sproull, S., & Kiesler, S. (1991). *Connections: New ways of working in the networked world.* Cambridge, MA: MIT Press.

Stevens, S. (1989). Intelligent interactive video simulation of a code inspection. *Communications of the ACM, 32*(7), 832–843.

Turkle, S. (1984). *The second self: Computers and the human spirit.* New York: Simon & Schuster.

Walker, J. (1990). Through the looking glass. In B. Laurel (Ed.), *The art of computer-human interface design* (pp. 213–245). Menlo Park, CA: Addison-Wesley.

White, B. (1993). *ThinkerTools*: Causal models, conceptual change, and science education. *Cognition and Instruction, 10*, 1–100.

Yoshida, A., & Kakuta, J. (1993). *People who live in an on-line virtual world.* Kyoto, Japan: Department of Information Technology, Kyoto Institute of Technology.

The National Science Foundation's Program in Advanced Applications of Technology is sponsoring the author's research in artificial realities for science education.

Chris Dede is a Professor at George Mason University in Fairfax, Virginia, where he has a joint appointment in the Schools of Information Technology & Engineering and of Education. He is Director of Federal Relations and Strategic Alliances for the university and is on the core advisory faculty of GMU's Institute for Public Policy.

Part Four

Reflections on the Effectiveness of Constructivist Learning Environments

14

Mapping More Authentic Multimedia Learning Environments

Brockenbrough S. Allen
Robin T. Chiero
Robert P. Hoffman

One of the more important problems facing the multimedia industry is how to adapt past ideas about systematic development of educational products to new technologies of design and production. Consider the remarkably robust and powerful "desktop" editing systems that are dramatically increasing the ease with which videographers can gather and manipulate moving images. Fast, flexible, low-cost, quality video challenges several assumptions that are embedded in traditional instructional development models about the need to pre-define subject matter and about the utility of elaborate specifications of message detail (flowcharts, scripts, storyboards). The complexity and cost of early, more cumbersome, multimedia technology encouraged prudent designers and developers to adopt postures that were in some respects defensive; the hope was that pre-specifying content as early as possible would make it easier and less expensive to identify and correct design flaws. However, such "top-down" design models can drive authenticity out of media products by omitting representations of "undocumented" or implicit knowledge and by eliminating information that might support multiple interpretations (Allen, 1992). Among the potential benefits of the technical revolutions in video and multimedia is that they may enable designers to work closer to phenomena of interest and make greater use of strategies such as rapid prototyping and user-centered design (Mack, 1992; Shneiderman, 1992; Tognazzini, 1992) by permitting a controlled melding of subject-matter analysis, documentation, and design.

This case study summarizes our efforts to test in the crucible of quasi-commercial product development a "bottom-up" model for developing multimedia software. To accomplish this, we deliberately sought opportunities to design instruction in the context of fluid, unstructured events that contained informal educational opportunities related to language and culture. The resulting product, a multimedia visit to a "Chicano" party, was successful by several standards: it was produced at low cost (less than $30,000); has been favorably reviewed by faculty and students (Cuevas, 1993); won a Cindy Award from the Association of Visual Communicators; and is headed for commercial publication.

Authenticity in Cinema and Multimedia

The concept of *authenticity* was at the core of our interest in this project. To be authentic implies that a thing conforms to or agrees with known facts and experiences—for example, that its origins and history have been traced. Issues of authenticity are obviously important to many curatorial, journalistic, forensic, and scientific endeavors, and they are central to the work of ethnographers and case-study researchers. Such investigators attempt to establish authenticity by employing rich, thick detail in written descriptions and by offering direct quotations of subjects and excerpts from documents. Ethnographers attend to patterns and themes in order to develop ideas about what is fundamental or central to the situation under study, and they use multiple sources in attempts to verify their hypotheses. Case study research involves constructing logical and historical chains of evidence to tie conclusions directly to observable, verifiable facts.

An authentic report represents all available perspectives in an effort to describe the typical (Merriam, 1988). Multimedia appears to offer potential for representing such multiple perspectives and for ameliorating the loss of information that may result when artifacts or realia are isolated from their natural context (Allen & Sterman, 1990).

Two factors influence the perception of and verification of authenticity: indexical and historical bonds. Indexical bonds (Nichols, 1991) are points of correspondence between a depiction or portrayal and its referent. For example, since photochemical or electronic images are formed by objective processes and mediated by a lens similar to that of the human eye, "photos" can be presumed to have strong indexical bonds with the subjects they represent. Yet such presumptions must be weighed against the possibility that lighting, camera position, lens characteristics, photochemical reactions—and, more recently digital image processing techniques—might be deliberately employed to emphasize, mislead, or confuse.

While indexical bonds offer a basis for presumptions about the *occurrence* of an event, the *historical* authenticity of such an event depends on the availability of information that may not be part of the portrayal—information about the subjects as well as information about recording, editing, and preservation processes. Therefore, historical authenticity depends on the integrity and reliability of systems for documenting and identifying portrayals.

Documentary filmmakers have long struggled with issues of authenticity; their perspectives are relevant to the challenges facing multimedia designers.

Nichols (1991) defines documentary film as *evidence from* and *discourse about* the real world. Multimedia technology offers possibilities for organizing such evidence and discourse from multiple perspectives and somewhat separate layers. A principal difference between conventional "linear" cinematographic programs and multimedia programs is that users of multimedia presumably share with authors some responsibility for editing the layers of evidence and discourse.

Nichols (1991) identifies four basic modes of representation in documentary filmmaking: the expository, or "voice of God," mode; the observational mode, in which the filmmaker's own presence is minimized; the interactive mode, which explicitly makes the filmmaker part of the film; and the reflexive mode, in which the filmmaker draws the viewer's attention to the form of the work itself.

We propose a similar classification system for multimedia documentaries. In the *interpretive mode*, end-users access images and sounds that illustrate or otherwise support the multimedia author's exposition. The *database mode* affords users access to an organized collection of recorded images and sounds of events and voices of authentication and interpretation. The *interactive mode* allows users to act on the database and alter the multimedia environment itself. The *auto-reflexive mode* continually adjusts the level and mode of representations in response to user choices.

Toward Models for Development of More Authentic Multimedia

Figure 15.1 illustrates our team's model for mapping the structure of actual events into multimedia environments. It assumes that no representation of events is unbiased or omniscient. Yet it also assumes that enterprises will develop more authentic multimedia products when design and production activities are organized as a framework of transformations that progress from some preliminary understanding of anticipated events to some representation of the events in a multimedia computing environment. The purpose of the model is to support the development of learning environments that represent actual events and related information in ways that afford opportunities for exploration and reflection in the context of individual or group study. The model could support implementation of any of the four multimedia modes described earlier, and with appropriate safeguards such a model could support the development and maintenance of indexical and historical bonds so crucial to curatorial and forensic applications.

Actual Events and Event Maps

The model does not assume any specific set of conventions for analyzing events. However, it does assume that useful knowledge about a forthcoming event can be mapped as a network of nodes and links, as in semantic networks (Fisher, 1990) and concept maps (Novak & Gowin, 1989). Moreover, it assumes that such maps can be easily updated and that records of successive modifications can be archived. The *event map* functions as a kind of "anticipatory schemata" (Neisser, 1976) for the multimedia designers and producers—an "updatable" document that represents evolving understanding about the

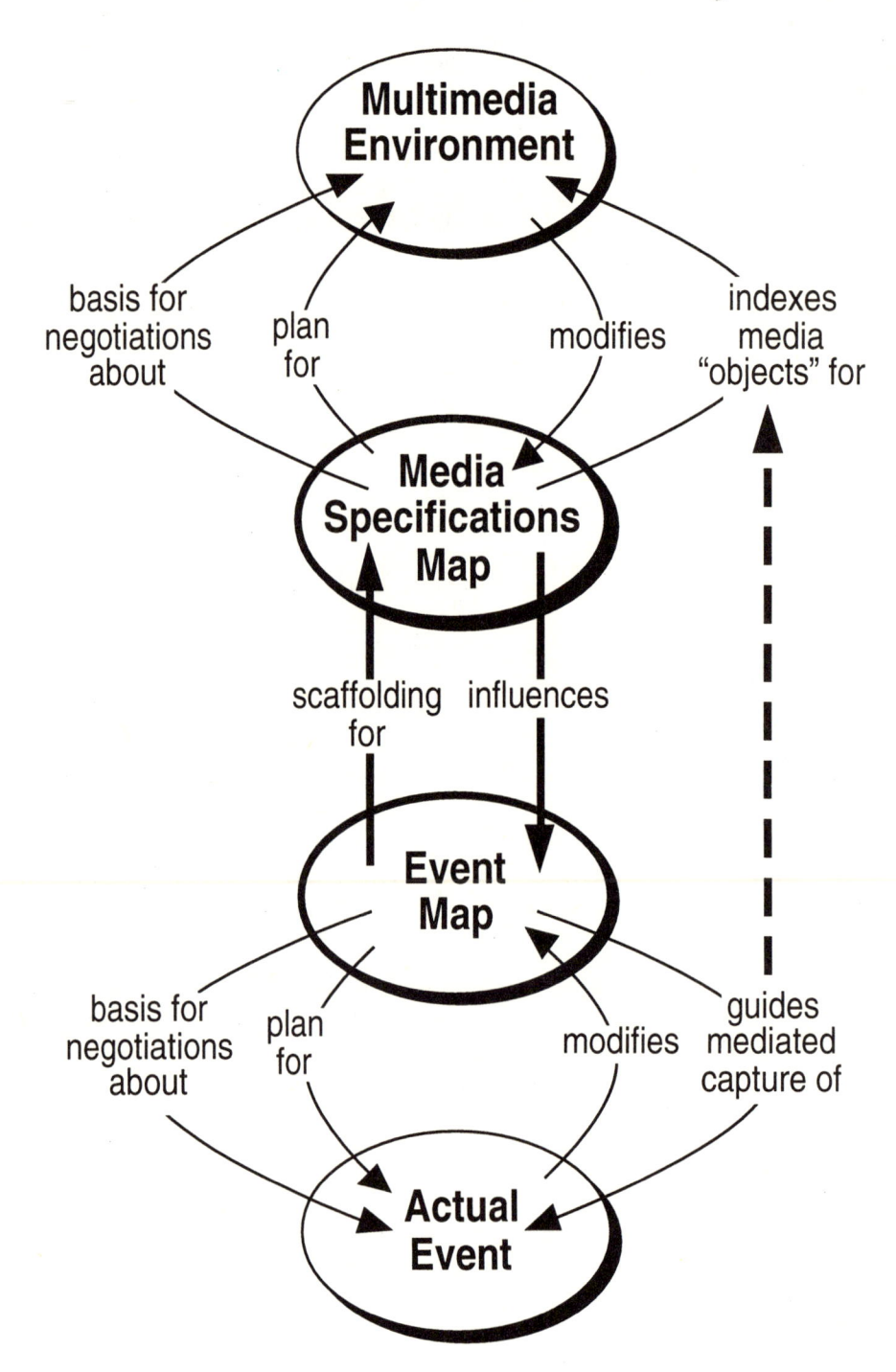

Figure 15.1. Model for Developing More Authentic Multimedia Learning Environments. © 1993, B. S. Allen, R. Chiero, & R. P. Hoffman. Used with permission.

forthcoming event as a network of nodes (objects, events, and ideas) and links (relationships). Our thinking about event maps and our decision to test the design model in the context of a party was influenced by the work of Mandler (1984), who examined event and scene schemas in the context of "scripts" for "going to a party."

The team used *SemNet®* (Faletti et al., 1993), a computer-based semantic networking program for creating event maps, although other software could probably be adapted for this purpose (see, for example, Jonassen, in press). Since the model assumes that understanding of the event structure will change as a result of negotiations between clients, producers, designers, and subjects or "talent," it will be advantageous if the software can accommodate frequent changes, represent multiple viewpoints or perspectives, and archive various "editions" of the event map. The event map can be "updated" following the actual event and can be further modified to include analytical or interpretive content.

Media Specifications Map

Prior to the actual event, the event map provides a framework for organizing and scheduling both the activities of those who will participate as subjects or "talent" and those who will participate by orchestrating and operating the media systems that will gather or create audio, video, photographic, textual, and diagrammatic representations. Maps in *SemNet®*, which can be thought of as *n*-dimensional networks (or alternatively as visual relational data bases), allowed us to develop separate maps for (1) the events and (2) the mediated *representations* of these events. The designer/developers could isolate or integrate information from either map as necessary (Figure 15.2).

As the model in Figure 15.1 implies, the event map serves as a scaffolding for additional clusters of nodes and links that specify (1) how the representation of events, objects, and ideas will be allocated to different modalities and (2) how end-users will navigate or activate such representations. We refer to these clusters collectively as a *media specifications map* and view it as a flexible alternative to flowcharting and storyboarding. While the event map might show how a particular occurrence, such as a dance, was related chronologically, spatially, and conceptually to other events, the specifications map is concerned with how the dance will be represented as "media objects" (for example, as a still photo, as motion pictures with audio, as a text description, or as a combination of all three modalities) and under what conditions end-users will access the media objects—whether, for example the objects will be activated automatically by the system ("system control") or by the user ("learner-control"). The scaffolding metaphor may be misleading; as implied by the directional arrows connecting the event map with the media specifications map—influence can flow in both directions.

Contemporary multimedia developers organize their software around media databases that store representations as "media objects," for example, sound, picture, text, and graphics documents that can be retrieved and activated by software programs. Object oriented programming encourages developers to use "object-oriented thinking" (Martin, 1993) as a means for reducing the complexity

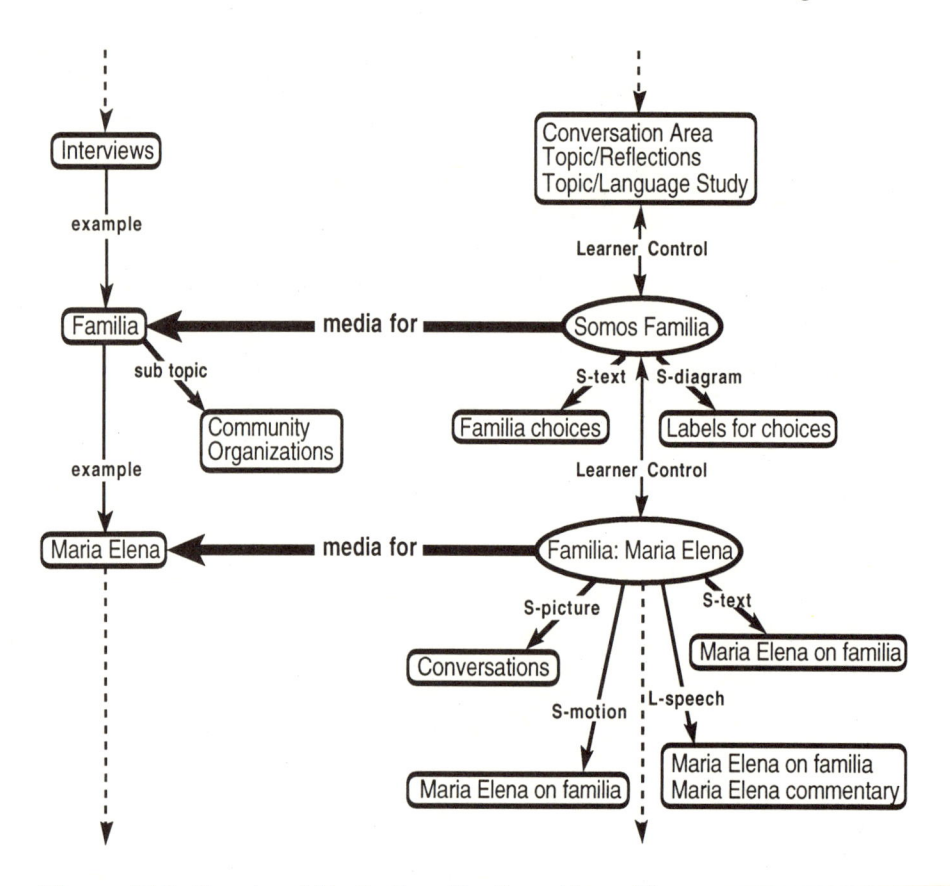

Figure 15.2. Event and Media Specifications Maps. The event represented in the maps is a conversation with María Elena on family. Representation in the multimedia environment consists of audio and video of the conversation; a second audio track with a commentary on the conversation; the text of the conversation; and graphics. The letter "L" specifies that the learner (end-user) will control access to the multimediated representations. The letter "S" indicates that the system will control access.

of projects and as a means for managing resource allocation. In our test implementation of the model, a fairly straightforward way to reduce this complexity was (after a preliminary analysis of anticipated events) to specify a finite number of media formats in advance of capture activities and to assign maximum file sizes for types of media objects. However, such constraints can work against authenticity by interfering with decision making by capture specialists who are responding to local or unanticipated contingencies.

Implementation of the Model

The model was tested by graduate students in the Department of Educational Technology at San Diego State University enrolled in Interactive Multimedia Instruction (EDTEC 653) in collaboration with the SDSU Upward Bound Alumni

Club (UBAC); Movimiento Estudiantil Chicano de Aztlán (MEChA); the SDSU Language Acquisition Resource Center (LARC); and the Multicultural Infusion Initiative in SDSU's College of Education.

MEChA and UBAC determined the agenda and content of the afternoon fiesta which can be considered a Chicano event in the sense that it was planned by students who identify themselves as *Chicanos*. This term generally implies an interest in improving civil rights for Mexicans and Mexican-Americans and a concern for advancement of the indigenous peoples of northern Mexico.

Somos (We Are) is not intended as a source of generalized interpretations of Chicano culture or even as a source of recordings of authentic Chicano cultural events. Rather it offers a set of opportunities for understanding the concerns and interests of Chicano college students in the context of an event they have planned and orchestrated. *Somos* also provides end-users with opportunities for practicing their comprehension of spoken Spanish—especially "border Spanish." Actually a widely-spoken collection of informal variants, "border Spanish" is distinct from "standard international Spanish" taught in high schools and colleges. Border Spanish includes many colloquialisms and sometimes combines English and Spanish in a form frequently referred to as "Spanglish."

Developing the Event Map

A simple and somewhat naive event map developed by several educational technology students established the initial conceptual framework for the MEChA/UBAC "fiesta" by anticipating activities that typically occur at parties. Nodes in this map were labeled with phrases such as "meet new people," "eat food," "dance," and "talk to friends." These nodes were linked in multiple ways to describe the kind of party environment in which individuals can determine the order in which they pursue their interests (see Figure 15.3 for a sample frame).

On the actual day of the fiesta, production activities were guided by video shot sheets created from activities represented in the event map. The educational technology students recorded all video shots on log sheets; black and white photographs provided additional documentation of the event. Because this was an authentic rather than a scripted event, activities that actually took place on the day of the party were slightly different than originally represented by the event map. Following the fiesta, the event map was updated to represent events as they actually transpired.

The educational technology students and UBAC and MEChA planners were particularly concerned about means by which the Chicano students would express feelings about their identity, their university experience, and their interactions with other cultural groups. To facilitate the gathering of these expressions by multimedia technology, Professor Gail Robinson, Director of Research at SDSU Language Acquisition Resource Center, and her assistant, Honorine Nocon, trained selected educational technology students in ethnographic interviewing techniques. According to Dr. Robinson, few foreign language programs describe cultures from the natives' point of view. "By doing ethnographies of the cultures relevant to local societies and providing authentic accounts, ethnography can contribute an essential first step in culture teaching: namely, what to teach" (Robinson, 1985, p. 75).

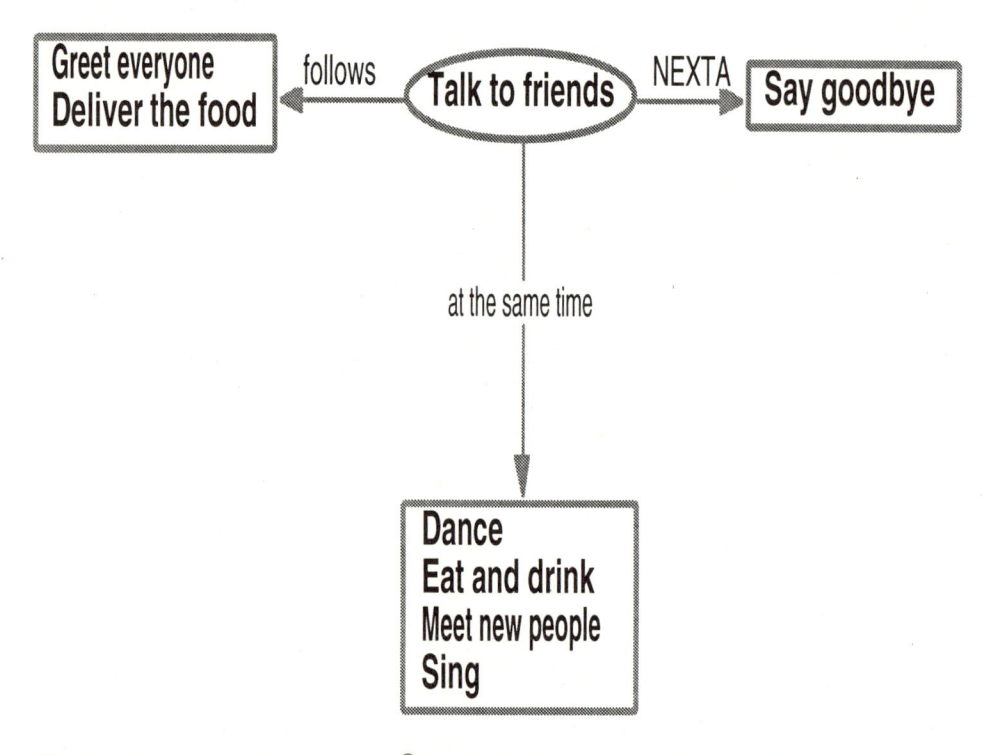

```
┌──────────────────┐  follows   ╱‾‾‾‾‾‾‾‾‾‾╲  NEXTA  ┌──────────────┐
│ Greet everyone   │◄──────────│Talk to friends│────►│ Say goodbye  │
│ Deliver the food │            ╲_____╱         └──────────────┘
└──────────────────┘                  │
                                      │ at the same time
                                      ▼
                            ┌──────────────────┐
                            │ Dance            │
                            │ Eat and drink    │
                            │ Meet new people  │
                            │ Sing             │
                            └──────────────────┘
```

Figure 15.3. Portion of SemNet® from the original event map. The map served as the basis for negotiations between the educational technology graduate student steering committee and UBAC and MEChA. When decisions affected the activities, the map was updated. For example, the UBAC and MEChA students elected to hire a "disc jockey" as well as stage traditional folklorico dances and a piñata event.

Ethnographic interviews require active listening. Unlike journalists who are often guided by predetermined agendas or "ideas for stories," the aim of ethnographic interviewers is to inquire about issues important to the person being interviewed. Ethnographic interviewers use open-ended questions and use responses to these questions to construct additional probes and follow-ups.

Multimedia Environment

Figure 15.2 shows the relationship (expressed in two dimensions) between a portion of the fiesta event map and corresponding clusters on the media specifications map. The central node in each cluster represents an event, idea, or object, anchoring surrounding nodes that specify the modalities that will represent the event, idea, or object in the multimedia environment (for example motion, speech, sound, picture, text, or a diagram). A variety of modalities is particularly advantageous for language learning and presenting cultural content.

Links between the clusters map the navigation planned for the multimedia environment. Navigation in *Somos* can be spatial ("Mapa") or topical ("Temas"). Spatial navigation is by (motion video) "hypertrails" that approximate physical walking from place to place in the environment. Figure 15.4 represents the interface for spatial navigation, map of the party site with trails to four different locations. Navigation by topic ("Temas") affords access to a particular topic of interest through hierarchical "concept maps" (Figure 15.5).

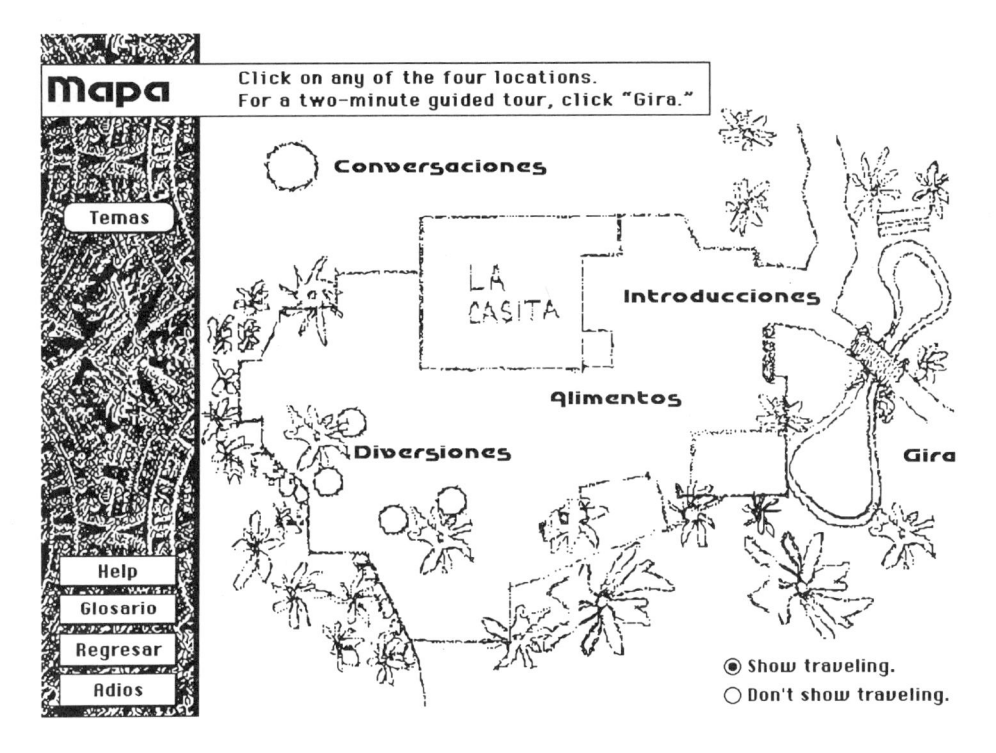

Figure 15.4. Hypertrail interface (Mapa). The user can choose from four destinations: the introduction area, the conversation area, the entertainment area, and the food area. When the user clicks on a destination button, the program plays a video path simulating a walk to that destination.

All computer controls are in Spanish; instructions on how to run the program and on-line help are available in both Spanish and English. After receiving a brief, optional tutorial on the interface, users enter the multimedia environment and can select or bypass a two-minute walking tour by a guide who speaks in an authoritative Mexico City accent about opportunities for learning more at the party. Following this advice from the "guira," the user can use the "mapa" and "temas" interfaces to access the four major components of the multimedia environment. *Introducciones* presents the user with four students from the fiesta who offer greetings in simple Spanish. *Diversiones* enables viewing of Mexican folklorico dances, "disco" dancing by revelers, and the breaking of a piñata. *Alimentos* takes the user to pictures and recipes of Mexican dishes served at the fiesta. *Conversaciones* presents options for listening in Spanish to the Chicano students as they discuss various topics including Nuestro Idioma (Our

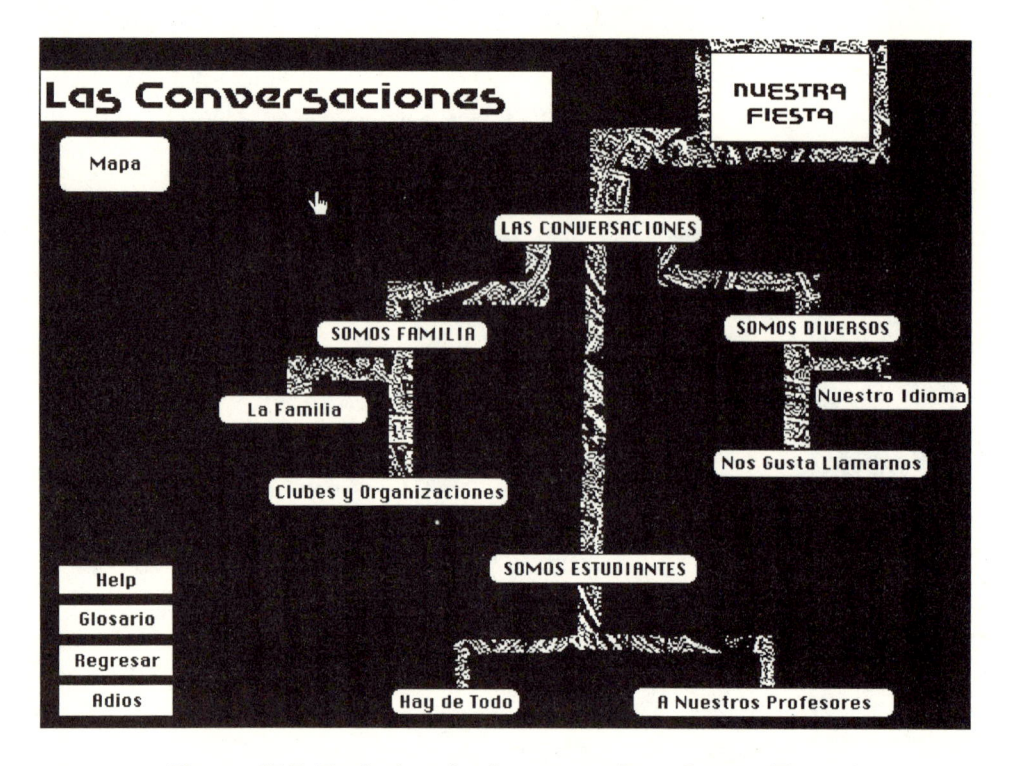

Figure 15.5. Topical navigation screen from *Somos* (Temas).

Language), Nos Gusta Llamarnos (We Like to be Called), La Familia (The Family), Clubs y Organizaciones (Clubs and Organizations), Hay de Todo (A Little of Everything), and A Nuestros Profesores (To Our Professors). The program provides access to over two dozen interview segments.

A parser control system allows users to break these segments into smaller chunks for systematic review or study (Figure 15.6). Scrolling text fields provide word-by-word transcriptions with hypertext links to a glossary, and the user can select a second audio channel to hear a commentary (spoken in the third person by a speaker of standard international Spanish) on the original speaker's remarks.

References

Allen, B. S. (1992). Constructive criticisms. In T. M. Duffy & D. Jonassen (Eds.), *Constructivism and the technology of instruction: A conversation*. Hillsdale, NJ: Lawrence Erlbaum Associates.

Allen, B. S., & Hoffman, R. P. (1993). Varied levels of support for constructive activity in hypermedia-based learning environments. In T. M. Duffy, J. Lowyck, & D. H. Jonassen (Eds.), *Designing environments for constructivist learning*. Berlin: Springer-Verlag.

Allen, B. S., & Sterman, N. T. (1990). The mediated museum: Computer-based technology and museum infrastructure. *Journal of Educational Technology Systems, 19*(1), 21-31.

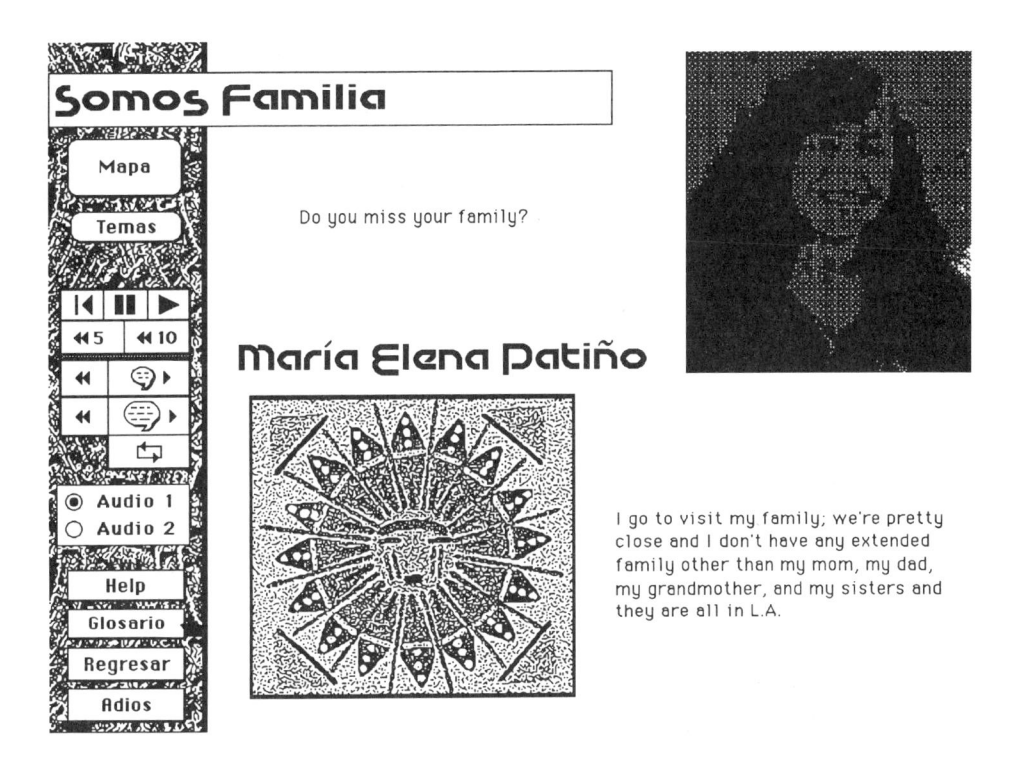

Figure 15.6. A sample screen from *Somos*. The text field is a transcription of the conversation. The user can click on the smaller speech bubble to review the conversation one phrase at a time or on the larger speech bubble to hear one sentence at a time.

Cuevas, G. L. (1993, May). *Evaluation report for the multimedia computer program "Somos."* Unpublished manuscript. San Diego: Department of Educational Technology, San Diego State University.

Faletti, J., Fisher, K. M., Patterson, H., Lipson, J. I., Allen, B. S., Logan, J. D., & Thornton, R. M. (1993). *SemNet®* [Computer Program]. San Diego: SemNet Research Group.

Fisher, K. M. (1990). Semantic networking: The new kid on the block. *Journal of Research in Science Teaching, 27,* 1001-1018.

Jonassen, D. (in press). *Mind tools.*

Mack, R. (1992). Questioning design: Toward methods for supporting user-centered software engineering. In T.W. Lauer, E. Peacock, & A. C. Graesser (Eds.), *Questions and information systems.* Hillsdale, NJ: Lawrence Erlbaum Associates.

Mandler, J. M. (1984). *Stories, scripts, and scenes: Aspects of schema theory.* Hillsdale, NJ: Lawrence Erlbaum Associates.

Martin, J. (1993). *Principles of object-oriented analysis and design.* Englewood Cliffs, NJ: Prentice-Hall.

Merriam, S. (1988). *Case study research in education: A qualitative approach.* San Francisco: Jossey-Bass Publishers.

Neisser, U. (1976). *Cognition and reality.* San Francisco: W. H. Freeman.

Nichols, B. (1991). *Representing reality: Issues and concepts in documentary.* Bloomington, IN: Indiana University Press.

Novak, J. D., & Gowin, D. B. (1989). *Learning how to learn.* New York: Cambridge University Press.
Robinson, G. L. (1985). *Crosscultural understanding: Processes and approaches for foreign language: English as a second language and bilingual educators.* New York: Pergamon Press.
Shneiderman, B. (1992). *Designing the user interface: Strategies for effective human-computer interaction.* Reading, MA: Addison-Wesley.
Tognazzini, B. (1992). *Tog on interface.* Reading, MA: Addison-Wesley.

Brockenbrough S. Allen is Professor of Educational Technology at San Diego State University where he teaches graduate courses on educational product design, interactive multimedia, and the psychology of technology-based learning. **Robin Chiero** is a doctoral student in multicultural education and educational technology. **Robert P. Hoffman** is Assistant Professor of Educational Technology at SDSU and a consultant on multimedia design.

15

Alternative Assessment for Constructivist Learning Environments

Thomas C. Reeves
James R. Okey

Introduction

Perkins (1991) identified three basic goals for education: retention, deep understanding, and active use of knowledge. Assessment in education, defined as the process of determining whether students have attained curricular goals (Choppin, 1990), has traditionally focused on retention of knowledge and its application in severely limited contexts as measured by standardized tests (Wiggins, 1993). Although traditional assessment has long been a target of criticism within the context of U.S. education (*cf.* Houts, 1977; Owens, 1985; Strenio, 1981), it has proven to be remarkably resilient. Major corporations as well as federal, state, and local educational agencies continue to spend millions of dollars to develop, administer, and process traditional testing programs. Nonetheless, the current popularity of alternative assessment reflects deep-rooted frustration with traditional approaches to assessment as well as the desire to expand its power to determine the attainment of higher order educational goals that involve deep understanding and active use of knowledge in complex, realistic contexts (Herman, Aschbacher, & Winters, 1992).

The increasing interest in alternative assessment (Mitchell, 1992) is reflected in the proliferation of terms such as (1) authentic assessment (Puckett & Black, 1994), (2) performance assessment (Wiggins, 1993), and (3) portfolio assessment (Knight, 1994). We distinguish among these three approaches to alternative assessment below and attempt to answer some important questions about them such as: What are the implications of different forms of alternative assessment for constructivist learning environments? How can these different approaches be implemented within the context of the "open," "classroom," and "virtual" constructivist learning environments? What is the role of technology in the shift from traditional assessment to alternative assessment? And most importantly, what challenges must be met before alternative assessment can be effectively and efficiently incorporated into constructivist learning environments?

Where We Stand

To even discuss assessment within the context of constructivist learning environments may appear inappropriate to some constructivist educators. Therefore, we must preface our perspectives about assessment with an orientation to our views of the value and future of constructivist learning environments. Perkins (1991) distinguished between BIG (Beyond the Information Given) and WIG (Without the Information Given) constructivism wherein the former involves the integration of direct instruction with opportunities to explore, experiment, and problem-solve and the latter involves discovery learning with minimal scaffolding by teachers and virtually no direct instruction. If advocates of WIG constructivist learning environments might be characterized as "radical constructivists," we view ourselves as proponents of BIG constructivism, i.e., "moderate constructivists."

We also recognize that traditional educational enterprises such as schools and colleges have a long way to go before the dominance of teacher talk and text is replaced by an appropriate blend of instructivist and constructivist learning opportunities. In fact, we agree with Perelman (1992), who might be characterized as a radical constructivist, in his conclusion that research conducted on "out-of-context teaching and testing confirms what many of us suspected all along: The 'best and the brightest' aren't really so smart. And the 'least and the dullest' aren't really so dumb" (p. 149).

Regardless of where one might be on the issue of how much constructivism is appropriate in education, it seems obvious to us that alternative assessment is absolutely required by constructivist learning environments, whether these environments are established in real world, classroom, or virtual contexts. Traditional assessment has been a major force in retarding educational reform, and it could have the same deleterious effect on the development and implementation of constructivist learning environments. Previous educational reforms have been prematurely held accountable for their effects using inappropriate outcome measures such as achievement tests that are poorly matched to the goals of innovative programs (Fullan, 1993). The innovation adoption process itself is sometimes stymied by teachers fearful of straying from established curriculum and methods lest their students falter on standardized tests. In addition, traditional assessment is often used to label individuals unfairly and force them into restrictive learning environments with limited goals. Constructivism demands new approaches to assessment.

Authentic Assessment

The very best teachers have used authentic constructivist learning assignments for decades, and now similar tasks are increasingly being used for assessment in schools. Consider the mathematics teacher who assigns students to poll other students about their favorite foods, rock bands, or movie stars to collect data which the students can use to learn how to tabulate data and draw graphs. The same teacher might initiate an authentic assessment by asking students to survey their peers concerning school dress code policies and report the data back to the class using appropriate graphs and figures. Allowing students to decide upon the content of a survey will likely increase student motivation and acceptance of the assessment even more, especially if they perceive that there is a real audience hungry for the results of their survey. The "ownership" of the task is a major factor in strengthening the authenticity of an assessment.

The fidelity of an assessment is paramount for those concerned with authentic assessment. Supporters of authentic assessment stress replicating as faithfully as possible the conditions under which ultimate performance will occur. Another important aspect of authenticity is the students' attitudes toward the assessment. It is not sufficient for a task to look realistic for an assessment to be authentic. It is also important that learners perceive value in the assessment, and that their motivation to participate in the assessment is genuine (Baker & O'Neil, 1994).

Critics of authentic assessment complain that the knowledge and skills measured via this approach do not permit easy comparisons among students and that these assessments lack generalizability to other contexts. The first criticism has some merit, and it is one of the primary issues that must be resolved before authentic assessment becomes widely accepted (see "Assessment Challenges" section below). The issue of generalizability, on the other hand, may not be as problematic as it first seems to be. Contemporary cognitive psychologists have revealed that knowledge is heavily contextualized and that its generalizability is severely limited (*cf.* Brown, Collins, & Duguid, 1989). Traditional psychometricians over-emphasize the measurement of decontextualized knowledge, assuming that the less contextualized their instruments are, the more likely they are to assess generalizable knowledge and skills. Proponents of authentic assessment, on the other hand, seek to estimate learning within specific contexts that approximate the ill-defined, uncontrollable aspects of the real world, a world in which the much vaunted generalizability of standardized tests may have little relevance.

Performance Assessment

Performance assessment requires learners "to demonstrate their capabilities directly, by creating some product or engaging in some activity" (Haertel, 1992). Wiggins (1993) and others promote performance assessment over traditional assessment because performance assessment is focused on students' ability to apply knowledge in ill-defined, ambiguous contexts that demand judgment. Proponents of performance assessment assert that traditional testing largely measures inert knowledge that may or may not be cued by a few artificial stimuli. Linn, Baker, and Dunbar (1991) list the following key attributes for performance assessment: (1) it focuses on complex learning, (2) engages higher order thinking and problem-solving skills, (3) stimulates a wide range of active responses, (4) involves challenging tasks that require multiple steps, and (5) requires significant commitments of student time and effort.

Validity with reference to a specific purpose such as diagnosis or certification is the primary concern of developers of performance assessments whereas traditional test developers emphasize the reliability or consistency of their instruments (Baker & O'Neil, 1994). Performance assessment is not as strictly concerned with fidelity as is "authentic assessment," and it does not focus as much on the interim drafts that learners produce during performance as does "portfolio assessment." Although performance assessment is somewhat novel in classroom contexts, it has long been a highly valued assessment strategy in the performing arts, especially music.

Finch (1991) provides guidance to developing, implementing, scoring, and reporting performance assessments. Performance tests take many forms, ranging from simple written tests to complex face plate simulators. In the former case, asking a student to write a brief essay in reaction to a poem would be considered a performance test by some in that it would be an improvement over a multiple-choice quiz about the meaning of the poem. In the latter case, airlines regularly certify the flying skills of their pilots using expensive, technically sophisticated flight simulators. Performance tests have been heavily used in the military since World War II (Finch, 1991). (For example, to graduate from the U. S. Army's Audiovisual School at Ft. Hamilton, New York, in 1969, the first author had to thread a 16mm projector in six and half seconds while blind-folded!)

Portfolio Assessment

A portfolio, per se, is merely a receptacle or storage mechanism for a learner's work (Herman, Aschbacher, & Winters, 1992). The assessment doesn't occur until the assessment's purpose is specified, guidelines for assembling a portfolio are clarified, and criteria and procedures for judging it are identified. Although the criteria for reliable, valid portfolio assessment are not as refined as those established for more traditional assessment instruments such as achievement tests, progress is being made. For example, Arter and Spandel (1992) spell out several questions that must be addressed in portfolio assessment, e.g., how representative is the work in a portfolio of what students can really do?

Portfolio assessment is focused on process as well as product. "Portfolios are collections of a student's work assembled over time" (Feuer & Fulton, 1993, p. 478). Whereas administrators of performance assessment often focus on students' solutions alone, judges of portfolios also consider the interim steps and draft products that are involved in completion of a task. Portfolios have an honored history of use in fields such as art, architecture, and engineering, and they are increasingly being used in education (Knight, 1994). A critical, often overlooked, aspect of portfolio assessment is that the student's evaluation of his/her own work is just as important as the evaluation rendered by others. Ideally, students will take great pride in their portfolios and eagerly share them with their peers, teachers, parents, and others.

Several countries (e.g., Australia and England) and states (e.g., Kentucky, Rhode Island, and Vermont) have invested considerable research and development funds in establishing portfolio assessment programs (Maeroff, 1991). Language arts teachers have led the way in using portfolios to collect and assess samples of student writing over time (*cf.* Johnston, 1992). A portfolio might include samples of student work across a variety of tasks (e.g., a letter, a poem, or a short story) or sequential drafts of work samples that are produced in completing a major task (e.g., a term paper). Portfolios can be amplified by logs or journals that students write and to which teachers react. These reflections aid learners in the process of evaluating their own work.

Connecting Alternative Assessment and Constructivism

Constructivist learning environments are concerned with both what and how one learns. The "what," or outcomes of learning, are principally focused on higher-order outcomes such as problem-solving or the ability to apply knowledge in ill-defined situations. The "how," or procedures of learning in the constructivist environment, are typically that of active involvement in learning by solving problems in a real or simulated setting. Constructivist learning environments may be designed for multiple levels of learning, including verbal information and discrete skills as well as higher-order problem solving, cognitive strategies, and attitudes, but the focus in learning activities is on application and active use of knowledge. For a physics student in a constructivist-oriented classroom, rather than recalling specific verbal knowledge (e.g., light rays bend when passing through convex lenses), the emphasis is more typically on using the knowledge in a way that demonstrates an active understanding of the verbal principle. In a middle school program focused on different approaches to inquiry, instead of describing or listing the steps in conducting a survey (establish the purpose, identify the audience, develop survey questions, etc.), students might carry out a survey as part of a serious effort to obtain views on an issue important to them.

The range of what and how learning takes place in constructivist learning environments is broad. Consider the BIG and WIG environments described by Perkins (1991). With respect to outcomes or objectives, learning might be focused on specific outcomes known to learners in advance all the way to learning where no objectives are set and learners pursue outcomes of their own interest. In terms of how learning is accomplished, the range may be from direct and guided learning activities that learners initiate themselves to placing learners in the vicinity of phenomena with only the most indirect advice about how to proceed.

Assessment in constructivist learning environments is (and needs to be) as varied and broad as the environments themselves. Thus an assessment task might have learners write an original sonnet if the goal of the learning environment is to help students develop such a talent. Or, the assessment might consist of self reports or journals if the learning was aimed at unique learning outcomes individually selected by the learners.

Put aside for a moment the often artificial distinction between learning and assessment. In most cases, the same or similar activities may legitimately be used for either purpose. In fact, constructivist learning environments and alternative assessment help blur the division between learning and assessment that is endemic in most instructional settings. Consider the following example. The U. S. Air Force Academy, in conjunction with the Smithsonian Institution, is developing a large-scale virtual learning environment called "Air Power" (Marlino, 1993). Air Force Academy cadets are afforded opportunities to explore the "Air Power" multimedia database in their rooms or anywhere on campus through a high speed digital network. Although the ability to explore this database is powerful, it actually becomes a virtual learning environment when faculty pose problems in it for the cadets to solve. For example, a professor may post a hypermedia description to the database about the design, mechanics, tactics, firepower, and costs of a German fighter plane developed during World War I and challenge students to design an Allied fighter capable of winning an air battle over the German machine. Cadets work in teams over a period of weeks to solve this problem, studying the historical contexts regarding design and production of Allied aircraft, integrating their engineering, mathematical, and scientific skills with their own creativity to arrive at a viable solution. Whether such a task is used for learning or assessment is really up to the faculty; it usually involves aspects of both.

In addition, time and resource constraints will often dictate that the same activity must serve both for learning and assessment. Almost by definition, assessments that are aimed at evaluating learning that is meant to be applied and actively used will take more time regardless of whether the setting is children learning geography or adults learning productivity procedures. In most work environments, we do not separate assessment from actual work performance, but instead we assess people based on their actual performance. Similarly, we should strive to eliminate the often artificial separation between performance and assessment in the school context unless safety or economic reasons justify the separation.

Although the primary function in assessment is to determine whether learners have achieved the goals and objectives of the instruction, assessment can be and is used for a variety of purposes by a variety of persons. For example, a manager may need to know if expert performance has been reached by a trainee before certifying him or her for a job. A fourth grader may need to know if her skill in pitching is adequate to make the team. A parent may wish to know how proficient his child is in reading books that are considered "age appropriate" for the child. A teacher may need to diagnose students' readiness to benefit from a certain type of virtual science experiment. The multiple uses to which assessment information is put do not dictate the fundamental nature of the assessment task—to determine if achievement of outcomes has occurred.

To be faithful to learning in constructivist environments where understanding and application of knowledge are promoted, assessment should look markedly different than the traditional testing that has been dominant in virtually all instructional settings whether for adults or children. Regrettably, it is more common in so called academic learning contexts that knowledge is fragmented and decontextualized both in terms of teaching and assessment. Learners may learn how to add algebraic expressions, form plurals of nouns, list the major rivers in North America, and describe three methods of heat transfer. While the learning may be important in some sense and the assessment may be aligned with what is learned, the knowledge is essentially inert and unconnected to its use or application. It is knowledge without power or purpose, and as such, it is knowledge that is unconnected to what Perkins (1991) labeled "deep understanding" and others might call wisdom.

Ironically, we don't have to look far and wide for good examples of exceptions to the predominance of traditional testing. Think about where learning is focused on contextualized performance in your educational setting. Consider students in music, vocational areas such as carpentry, or on-the-job training in equipment operation. In all these areas it would be ludicrous not to focus the assessment on the real world performance of the tasks. And so they are.

Another important aspect that connects alternative assessment to constructivism is "openness and transparency" (Sheingold & Frederiksen, 1994, p. 118) with respect to the procedures and standards for assessment. Whereas in many forms of traditional assessment, what's going to be "on the test" and how tests will be graded are closely guarded secrets, alternative assessment requires an on-going dialogue among teachers, students, parents, and the larger community about the purposes of assessments, how they should be done, and what standards are applied to them. Constructivism encourages a similar debate about the ultimate goals and methods of education.

Neimeyer (1993) provides guidance to a constructivist approach to assessment. Constructivist learning environments, whether open, structured, or virtual, place learners in positions where they explore, experiment, and actively solve problems. The appropriate assessment may be called authentic, performance, or portfolio, but the common theme in such activities is their similarity to or direct relationship with the learning tasks themselves. The appropriate assessment for such outcomes is manifest in the performances it enables and/or products it produces. Included in these are project reports, oral presentations, written essays, experiments, demonstrations, and portfolios of work (Office of Technology Assessment, 1992).

The Role of Technology

Haney and Madaus (1989) pointed out that technology has played a much bigger role in improving the power and efficiency of traditional testing than it has in enabling alternative assessments on a widespread basis. But perhaps this is changing. For example, computer-based portfolio tracking systems such as the *Grady Profile* (Aurbach & Associates, 1993) are being used by teachers and students to assemble, keep track of, and analyze the large amount of information and numerous artifacts that are involved in portfolio assessment. The sheer amount of paper documentation required for portfolio assessment has thwarted its adoption by many teachers (Maeroff, 1991), but technology promises to ease that burden.

In addition to commercial packages specifically developed for portfolio assessment, many teachers and students are experimenting with computer-based portfolio development using software construction programs such as *HyperCard* (Apple Computer, Inc.) or *ToolBook* (Asymetrix Corporation). In a project supported by the National Reading Research Center at the University of Georgia, elementary school students in Barrow County, Georgia have developed multimedia portfolios about the books they read during the school year. In addition, the children have combined their individual portfolios into a large database that can be used by other students seeking guidance to "good reading."

Computer-based simulations such as *Investigating Lake Iluka*, developed at the University of Wollongong in Australia (Hedberg & Harper, 1993), are not just virtual learning environments. They can also be used for assessment, especially if a library of such simulations is developed or the parameters of specific tasks can be modified for either learning or assessment. Virtual reality systems are already being used for both learning and assessment by trainers in military settings, and the time when these systems will be available for use in schools or at home is not far off.

Sheingold and Frederiksen (1994) describe both the potential and challenge involved in using technology to support alternative assessment. They maintain that alternative assessment won't be realized unless technology is employed in changing the forms of assessment, establishing procedures for judging performance, and sharing criteria and standards for assessment. They describe several functions of technology in alternative assessment, including:
- supporting extended, authentic learning activities,
- making work portable and accessible,
- making performances replayable,
- providing libraries of examples and interpretive tools,
- expanding the community of participants in assessment, and
- publishing and sharing student work.

Assessment Challenges

Despite the progress that has been made, the integration of assessment into constructivist learning environments is hardly what young people today call a "no brainer." Here are a few of the issues that must be resolved before assessment can progress in step with the movement toward the establishment of constructivist learning environments in mainstream educational contexts:

- The purposes of assessment must be understood and agreed upon in any given educational context. Traditional tests have been justly criticized when they have been used for purposes for which they were not designed. If alternative assessments are to be valid, their purposes must be clarified because whether a test is valid is determined by its intended use. In short, statements about the validity of an assessment cannot be separated from statements of purpose.

- There is a tension between reliability and validity in any form of assessment that must be dealt with in a straightforward manner. Traditional assessment in the context of education over-emphasizes reliability to the sacrifice of validity with respect to ultimate criteria such as performance in real life. Alternative assessments may be designed to have high degrees of face validity (Wiggins, 1993), but their ultimate validity depends upon their purpose. At the same time, some purposes will demand a certain degree of consistency and replicability across various instances of alternative assessment, and so reliability cannot be ignored.

- Assessment standards must be established if comparative uses of assessment data are to be continued. The challenge of establishing standards in virtually any educational context is extremely complex and controversial. The National Council of Teachers of Mathematics (NCTM) took six years to establish outcomes and standards for mathematics (Feuer, Fulton, & Morrison, 1993); similar efforts in other fields are likely to take much longer and reach lower levels of consensus. At the same time, standards should not mean that everyone must attain the same standards in every field. Constructivist educators stress that learning is personal, unique, and contextualized for each learner. Hence, which standards should be applied in which contexts is a process for negotiation in most situations. According to Sheingold and Frederiksen (1994), "The power of assessment as a reform agent derives as much from the standards of performance used in evaluating work as from the value of performance tasks themselves as learning activities" (p. 114).

- Just as not everyone accepts the notion of constructivist learning environments, not everyone will value or support alternative assessment. Segments of the population are already attacking outcomes-based education and alternative assessment. Why? Perhaps because authentic assessment will inevitably entail deliberation and judgment about values that may differ from the values prescribed by dogmatists on the right or the left. Ernest House (1973) made the point that evaluation is a political process. No less can be said about assessment.

- Student motivation is an issue too often ignored in traditional testing approaches. Alternative assessment affords us the ability to include motivation as an important factor in the assessment process, e.g., by encouraging student commentary on the nature and value of an assessment. This is especially relevant to constructivist learning environments which rely much more on intrinsic motivation than traditional learning environments that depend heavily on extrinsic motivation factors.

- Much more research on assessment is needed. Worthen (1993) describes twelve critical issues facing alternative assessment, including technical issues such as reliability, theoretical issues such as validity, and practical issues such as feasibility. Funding for educational research has steadily shrunk over the past decade, but significant resources must be invested before the potential of alternative assessment can be realized. Research is especially needed in what has been called "cognitive assessment." Cognitive assessment focuses on the higher order thinking skills possessed by learners as well as the metacognitive skills learners employ during learning (Merluzzi, Glass, & Genest, 1986). Metacognition refers to the mental processes we use to monitor and regulate our own learning (Flavell, 1976). What problem-solving and metacognitive skills mean in a virtual learning environment is still unknown. Some have predicted that humans and machines will evolve into a new interdependent organism (*cf.* Stock, 1993). The implications of such a development for assessment are profound to say the least.

Conclusion

The development of policies, methods, and technologies for alternative assessment must keep pace with the development of constructivist learning environments. Other chapters in this book describe the bright promise of open, school, and virtual learning environments. Technology is essential to the establishment and maintenance of these environments (Jonassen, in press; Papert, 1993). The full realization of alternative assessment approaches within constructivist learning environments is equally dependent upon technological innovations.

But all the technology in the world won't enable fundamental changes in the nature of assessment unless we free ourselves from the insidious effects of a testing dependent society. Whether intentional or not, the testing industry has been very successful in encouraging us to think of each other in terms of our test scores. Students leave classrooms asking each other, "What did you get on the test?" instead of "What did you learn?" Teachers judge students in terms of their tests scores, e.g., "I didn't think she was that smart, but you should see her SAT score." We often fail to see people in terms of what they actually do.

Another form of alternative assessment, responsive assessment, may help us free ourselves from these outmoded perceptions. Responsive assessment is not so much a methodology as it is a shift in the focus or purpose of assessment. According to Henning-Stout (1994), traditional academic assessment focuses on learners' deficiencies so that others (teachers, administrators, psychologists, etc.) can categorize, select, and track them. Responsive assessment, on the other hand, emphasizes learners' strengths and provides information directly to learners so that they are empowered to make their own decisions about learning goals and activities. The learners themselves are regarded as the major stakeholders in the assessment process. Anything less would be unfaithful to the constructivist philosophy of education that undergirds the innovative learning and assessment developments described in this volume.

References

Apple Computer. (1994). HyperCard 2.2 [program construction software]. Cupertino, CA: Apple Computer, Inc.

Arter, J., & Spandel, V. (1992). Using portfolios of student work in instruction and assessment. *Educational Measurement: Issues and Practice*, 11(1), 36–44.

Asymetrix. (1994). ToolBook 3.0 [program construction software]. Bellevue, WA: Asymetrix Corporation.

Aurbach & Associates. (1993). The Grady Profile 2.0. [portfolio assessment software]. Elgin, IL: Educational Resources.

Baker, E. L., & O'Neil, H. F. (1994). Performance assessment and equity: A view from the USA. *Assessment in Education*, 1(1), 11–26.

Brown, J. S., Collins, A., & Duguid, P. (1989). Situated cognition and the culture of learning. *Educational Researcher*, 18(1), 32–42.

Choppin, B. H. (1990). Evaluation, assessment, and measurement. In H. J. Walberg & G. D. Haertel (Eds.), *The international encyclopedia of educational evaluation* (pp. 7–8). New York: Pergamon.

Feuer, M. J., & Fulton, K. (1993). The many faces of performance assessment. *Phi Delta Kappan*, 74(6), 478.

Feuer, M. J., Fulton, K., & Morrison, P. (1993). Better tests and testing practices: Options for policy makers. *Phi Delta Kappan*, 74(7), 530–533.

Finch, F. L. (Ed.). (1991). *Educational performance assessment*. Chicago, IL: Riverside.

Flavell, J. (1976). Metacognitive aspects of problem solving. In L. Resnick (Ed.), *The nature of intelligence*. Hillsdale, NJ: Lawrence Erlbaum Associates.

Fullan, M. (1993). *Change forces: Probing the depth of educational reform*. New York: Falmer Press.

Haertel, E. (1992). Performance measurement. In M. C. Alkin (Ed.), *Encyclopedia of educational research* (pp. 984–989). New York: Macmillan.

Haney, W., & Madaus, G. (1989). Searching for alternatives to standardized tests: Whys, whats, and whithers. *Phi Delta Kappan*, 70(9), 683–687.

Hedberg, J., & Harper, B. (1993). Investigating Lake Iluka [CD-ROM simulation]. Canberra, ACT, Australia: Interactive Multimedia Pty Ltd.

Henning-Stout, M. (1994). *Responsive assessment: A new way of thinking about learning*. San Francisco, CA: Jossey-Bass.

Herman, J. L., Aschbacher, P. R., & Winters, L. (1992). *A practical guide to alternative assessment*. Alexandria, VA: Association for Supervision and Curriculum Development.

House, E. R. (Ed.). (1973). *School evaluation: The politics and process*. Berkeley, CA: McCutchan.

Houts, P. L. (Ed.). (1977). *The myth of measurability*. New York: Hart.

Johnston, P. H. (1992). *Constructive evaluation of literate activity*. New York: Longman.

Jonassen, D. H. (in press). *Mind tools*.

Knight, M. E. (1994). *Portfolio assessment: Application of portfolio analysis*. Lanham, MD: University Press of America.

Linn, R. L., Baker, E. L., & Dunbar, S. B. (1991). Complex, performance-based assessment: Expectations and validation criteria. *Educational Researcher*, 20(8), 15–21.

Maeroff, G. I. (1991). Assessing alternative assessment. *Phi Delta Kappan*, 73(4), 272–281.

Marlino, M. R. (1993, December). *Air power: A digital database with historical integrity*. Paper presented at the Instructional Technology for Education and Training Conference, Orlando, FL.

Merluzzi, T. V., Glass, C. R., & Genest, M. (Eds.). (1986). *Cognitive assessment*. New York: New York University Press.

Mitchell, R. (1992). *Testing for learning: How new approaches to evaluation can improve American schools*. New York: Free Press.

Neimeyer, G. J. (1993). *Constructivist assessment: A casebook*. Newbury Park, CA: Sage.

Office of Technology Assessment, Congress of the United States. (1992). *Testing in American schools: Asking the right questions*. Washington, DC: Government Printing Office. ED 340 770.

Owens, D. (1985). *None of the above: Beyond the myth of the SAT*. New York: Houghton Mifflin.

Papert, S. (1993). *The children's machine: Rethinking school in the age of the computer*. New York: Basic Books.

Perelman, L. J. (1992). *School's out: Hyperlearning, the new technology, and the end of education*. New York: William Morrow.

Perkins, D. N. (1991). Technology meets constructivism: Do they make a marriage? *Educational Technology*, 31(5), 18–23.

Puckett, M. B., & Black, J. K. (1994). *Authentic assessment of the young child*. New York: Macmillan.

Sheingold, K., & Frederiksen, J. (1994). Using technology to support innovative assessment. In B. Means (Ed.), *Technology and educational reform: The reality behind the promise* (pp. 111–132). San Francisco, CA: Jossey-Bass.

Stock, G. (1993). *Metaman: The merging of humans and machines into a global superorganism.* New York: Simon & Schuster.

Strenio, A. J. (1981). *The testing trap.* New York: Rawson, Wade.

Wiggins, G. P. (1993). *Assessing student performance: Exploring the purpose and limits of testing.* San Francisco, CA: Jossey-Bass.

Worthen, B. R. (1993). Critical issues that will determine the future of alternative assessment. *Phi Delta Kappan, 74*(6), 444–456.

Thomas C. Reeves and **James R. Okey** are Professors of Instructional Technology and Research Associates in the Learning and Performance Support Laboratory (LPSL) at the University of Georgia, Athens.

16

Instructional Design and Development of Learning Communities: An Invitation to a Dialogue

Xiaodong Lin, John D. Bransford, Cindy E. Hmelo, Ronald J. Kantor, Daniel T. Hickey, Teresa Secules, Anthony J. Petrosino, Susan R. Goldman, and The Cognition and Technology Group at Vanderbilt

Our goal in this chapter is to encourage discussion among members of the instructional design community and members of research groups who are attempting to transform typical classrooms into "learning communities." A strength of the instructional design community is its efforts to articulate, manage, and systematize the processes involved in designing effective learning environments. A strength of researchers attempting to create "learning communities" is their emphasis on new sets of principles that have important implications for the nature of teaching, learning, and assessment. By discussing insights from these two communities, we hope to begin a conversation that strengthens the communication and collaboration between the two.

The structure of this chapter is as follows:

(1) an overview of frameworks for instructional design;
(2) a brief discussion of some key principles of learning communities;
(3) an exploration of relationships between the concept of learning communities and instructional design frameworks; and
(4) further issues in designing and understanding learning communities.

An Overview of Frameworks for Instructional Design

Instructional design is a discipline that is concerned with understanding and improving the process of instruction. The purpose of design activities is to prescribe optimal methods of instruction that would induce desired changes in student knowledge, skills, and affect (Dick & Reiser, 1989; Reigeluth, 1983; Reigeluth, Bunderson, & Merrill, 1978). Reigeluth (1983) describes the result of instructional design as a professional "architect's blueprint" for what the instruction should be like. This "blueprint" is then used as a prescription for instructors as to what methods of instruction should be used, given the outcomes students are to achieve and the conditions under which they are to achieve them.

On the basis of these assumptions, numerous design models have been generated (e.g., Dick & Carey's Systems Approach Model, Landa's Algo-Heuristic Design Model, Reigeluth's Elaboration Model, Merrill's Component Display Model, and Keller's Motivation-Design Model) with the intention of yielding a list of fundamental steps for the instructional design process (Reigeluth, 1983). These steps represent the most commonly identified actions recommended for conducting instructional design. Andrews and Goodson's (1980) analysis of 60 instructional design models suggests that these models share a number of common basic components, although some models contain more complex and detailed steps than others. A typical instructional design process consists of the following steps:

(1) identify objectives (e.g., what do you want students to be able to do when they have completed the instruction?);
(2) assess students' prior knowledge and skills (e.g., determine whether the target students have the prerequisites to benefit from the instruction);
(3) specify the content to be taught (e.g., what content skills should be taught to students?);
(4) identify instructional strategies (e.g., what instructional methods should be used?);
(5) develop instruction (e.g., a learner's manual, instructional materials, tests, and an instructor's guide);
(6) test, evaluate, and revise (e.g., how should students be evaluated to determine the degree to which students have meet the performance objectives?).

Using such models to plan instruction, designers have to make instructional decisions based on their judgment about what learners should learn, how they should learn, what their learning contexts should be, what learning strategies they should employ, and how they should be assessed. Instructional design is thus concerned with prescriptive theory. Most of the prescriptive theory assumes that design can be carried out separately from the situation in which the instruction is implemented (Winn, 1993).

The systematic approach is valued in the instructional design community because it helps ensure that designers follow predefined steps in a model during the design process to guarantee that what is taught is needed for students to achieve predefined learning goals and that students are evaluated in terms of how closely they achieve the objectives (see Dick & Carey, 1990; Smith & Ragan,

1993). As Winn (1990) has pointed out, instructional design conducted this way assumes that if the designers have enough knowledge of the students and what it is the students have to learn, then they can bring about predictable changes in students' knowledge and skills. The only way to determine whether designers have succeeded in their selection of strategies for the learners and creation of instructional activities is by observing student performance. Such an approach makes a complete instructional package that is relatively easy to implement and evaluate. Overall, instructional design is seen as fundamentally context-free and plan-based.

A Brief Discussion of Some Key Principles of Learning Communities

Our goal in this section is to provide a brief description of the concept of learning communities. An emphasis on this concept focuses attention on the social contexts of learning—contexts that have pervasive cognitive and motivational effects. DeCorte, Greer, and Veschafel (in press) argue that social considerations are part of the second wave of the cognitive revolution. During the first wave, the primary focus was on individual thinkers and learners, with a de-emphasis on affect, context, culture, and history (Gardner, 1985). During the second wave, theorists have attempted to relocate cognitive functioning within its social, cultural, and historical contexts (e.g., J. S. Brown, Collins, & Duguid, 1989).

We argue elsewhere that social context is to individuals as water is to fish: The effects are pervasive and hence easy to overlook (Barron, Vye, Zech, Schwartz, Bransford, Goldman, Pellegrino, Morris, Garrison, & Kantor, in press). For example, it is easy to overlook the fact that the social structures necessary to conduct most psychological experiments are very special; they are based on agreements that participants will temporarily assume the role of "subjects" who allow experimenters to rule (Bransford, 1981).

The social structure of most classrooms involves students who adopt the role of passive receivers of the wisdom that is dispensed by teachers, textbooks, and other media (A. L. Brown, 1992). The role of the teacher is to deliver information and manage learning. Usually, everyone is taught the same thing at the same time. Assessments typically measure how much each student learned about what was taught. Most computer-based laboratories involve a similar model of knowledge transmission and testing. Learning is usually individualized in the sense that students are allowed to work at their own pace and at various levels of difficulty. Ideally, however, all students are expected to learn more or less the same things.

A number of theorists argue that the structure of typical classrooms is ill-suited to the goal of encouraging the kinds of learning necessary for the twenty-first century (e.g., Barron *et al.*, in press; A. L. Brown, Ash, Rutherford, Nakagawa, Gordon, & Campione, 1993; J. S. Brown *et al.*, 1989; Hmelo, 1993). The "basics" required for success in our increasingly changing society are no longer simply reading, writing, and arithmetic, but the ability to think critically and reason about important content, plus the ability and motivation to learn independently throughout one's life (e.g., Bransford, Goldman, & Vye, 1991;

A. L. Brown et al., 1993; Bruer, 1993; Resnick & Klopfer, 1989). Furthermore, these new basics are necessary for everyone rather than for only a select few (Resnick, 1987).

An emphasis on the goal of helping students become independent learners has prompted many researchers to focus on the development of classroom communities that foster continuous, independent learning. Much of the interest in learning communities stems from analyses of successful informal learning environments that exist outside of school (e.g., Barron et al., in press; Bransford & Heldmeyer, 1983; J. S. Brown et al.,1989; Lave & Wenger, 1991; Resnick 1987; Senge, 1990). For example, students who participate in successful informal learning environments typically do not spend most of their time simply memorizing what others teach them. In many settings (e.g., many apprenticeships), there is little formal teaching, yet a great deal of learning occurs (Holt, 1964; Lave & Wenger, 1991; Sternberg & Wagner, 1986).

In many learning communities, students are provided with opportunities to plan and organize their own research and problem solving, plus opportunities to work collaboratively to achieve important goals (e.g., A. L. Brown et al., 1993; The Cognition & Technology Group at Vanderbilt (CTGV), 1994, in press; Collins, Hawkins, & Carver, 1991; Lamon, 1994). In addition, learning communities usually emphasize the importance of distributed expertise (e.g., Barron et al., in press; A. L. Brown et al., 1993; Pea, 1993). Students are allowed to specialize in particular areas so that the community can capitalize on diversity . An emphasis on distributed expertise is distinctively different from environments where all students are asked to learn the same things at the same points in time.

An Exploration of Relationships Between the Concept of Learning Community and Instructional Design Frameworks

Our goal in this section is to further explore the concept of learning communities by discussing them from the perspective of the generic instructional design framework discussed in the first section. The design framework provides a useful context for highlighting some of the key features of the concept of learning communities that differentiate them from the classroom environments typically found in schools.

Our discussion will focus primarily on our experiences with learning communities in two different projects: (1) Our SMART challenges that link together different classrooms and teachers (Barron et al., in press; CTGV, 1994), and (2) our participation in the Schools for Thought Collaborative that involves collaboration with A. L. Brown & Campione (1994), Scardamalia, Bereiter, & Lamon (1994), and the St. Louis Science Center. An overview of the Schools for Thought project is available in Lamon (1994).

Identify Objectives in Learning Communities (e.g., what do you want students to be able to do when they have completed the instruction?).

The focus on independent, lifelong learning that is characteristic of learning communities is very different from a focus on tests that assess students' mastery of specific factual and procedural objectives. For example, students can learn particular sets of skills and strategies yet fail to spontaneously use them to solve problems (e.g., Bransford, Franks, Vye, & Sherwood, 1989; Dominowski, 1990; Lin, 1993; Simon, 1980). In Whitehead's (1929) terms, their knowledge remains "inert."

Even studies that provide evidence of transfer from a set of learning experiences to a set of transfer tasks do not guarantee that students are being prepared to be lifelong, independent learners (CTGV, 1993c). Most studies of transfer are static tests; people learn something and then receive a set of transfer problems (e.g., Gick & Holyoak, 1980, 1983). Scores on such problems can be increased by "teaching to the test," which includes explicitly "teaching for transfer." However, high scores on a specific, static transfer test do not guarantee that students have learned to learn on their own.

Static transfer should be differentiated from dynamic transfer. Dynamic transfer refers to those skills that efficient learners bring to a learning opportunity that facilitate learning in a new domain, whereas static transfer refers to the transfer of facts or very specific, fixed procedures (A. L. Brown, Bransford, Ferrara, & Campione, 1983). Learning to learn can be accessed by using tests of dynamic transfer. A. L. Brown et al. (1983) discuss a situation in which a learner did very poorly on tests of static transfer yet was able to demonstrate a rich variety of learning to learn skills when given a dynamic test. The dynamic test provided the opportunity to access resources that could help him learn to solve problems that he needed to solve.

Differences between "learning to solve a particular set of problem types" and "learning to learn" are illustrated in Figure 16.1. Points A and B represent two different people who are being considered for a job. In both cases, there is a lot for the individuals to learn. On static tests taken during the initial interviews, Person B scores better than person A. However, when observed after several months with the company, Person A demonstrates that she is much better than B at learning on her own.

When learning to learn is one's primary objective, many approaches to instruction become questionable. As noted above, it is quite possible to provide practice at solving a fixed set of problem types in some area such as mathematics or science. These experiences can help students do well on static tests of transfer (to similar problem types). However, these experiences may be very poor for helping students learn to learn on their own.

An emphasis on learning to learn does not mean that one focuses exclusively on general skills of learning. Evidence for the importance of domain specific knowledge in directing thinking is ubiquitous (e.g., Bransford, Kinzer, Risko, Rowe, & Vye, 1989; Bransford & Stein, 1993; A. L. Brown, Campione, Reeve, Ferrara, & Palincsar, 1991; Resnick & Klopfer, 1989). As discussed later, learning to learn can be enhanced by focusing on the "big ideas" or "deep principles" that underlie specific content areas such as history, science, or math (e.g., A. L. Brown et al., 1993). An emphasis on deep principles is different from but complementary to an emphasis on general skills of learning and problem solving. General skills such as "define at least two different goals for your problem" become important when one confronts non-routine problems that require the acquisition of new concepts and strategies (Bransford & Stein, 1993). Deep principles involve concepts and theories that help one organize thinking and see analogies. For example, as illustrated in Figure 16.2, the principle of interdependence of systems

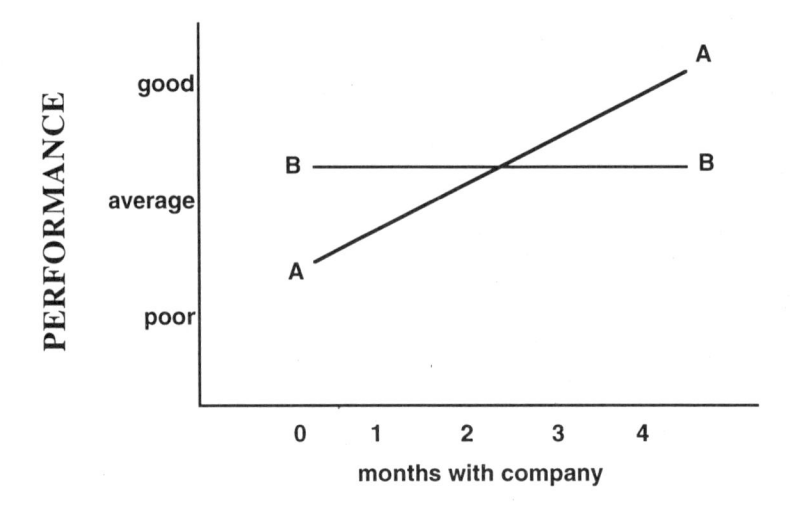

Figure 16.1. Effects of learning to learn. Worker A, who performed poorly on an early test, outperforms Worker B after several months with the company.

can be applied to many different domains, such as economics, endangered species, human circulation and respiration, etc. By learning the principle in several domains, more productive learning and flexible transfer should be promoted (A. L. Brown & Campione, 1992).

Assess the Prior Knowledge and Skills of Students in Learning Communities (e.g., determine whether the target students have the prerequisites to benefit from the instruction).

The design of learning communities has important implications for assessing students' existing skills and knowledge. First, effective communities involve multiple opportunities to "make the thinking of students visible" (e.g., Collins et al., 1991; Minstrell, 1989). Therefore, there are frequent opportunities to assess what students understand. The goal is always to build on students' current understanding rather than simply provide instruction designed to help them reach pre-set objectives by particular points in time. Following Bruner (1990), there is also a strong assumption that everyone can learn something relevant to the particular topic of the learning community no matter what their entry skill levels are.

A second implication of the concept of learning communities for assessing student knowledge stems from the notion of distributed expertise. The expectation in learning communities is that everyone is not ready to learn the same things at the same time. Allowing students to "major" (A. L. Brown et al., 1991) in different areas provides flexibility with respect to individual student development.

In many ways, the idea of distributed expertise makes the process of assessing students skills and knowledge more difficult than in standard classrooms. However, in our experience, communities based on distributed expertise are extremely beneficial; they have powerful effects on how students think about

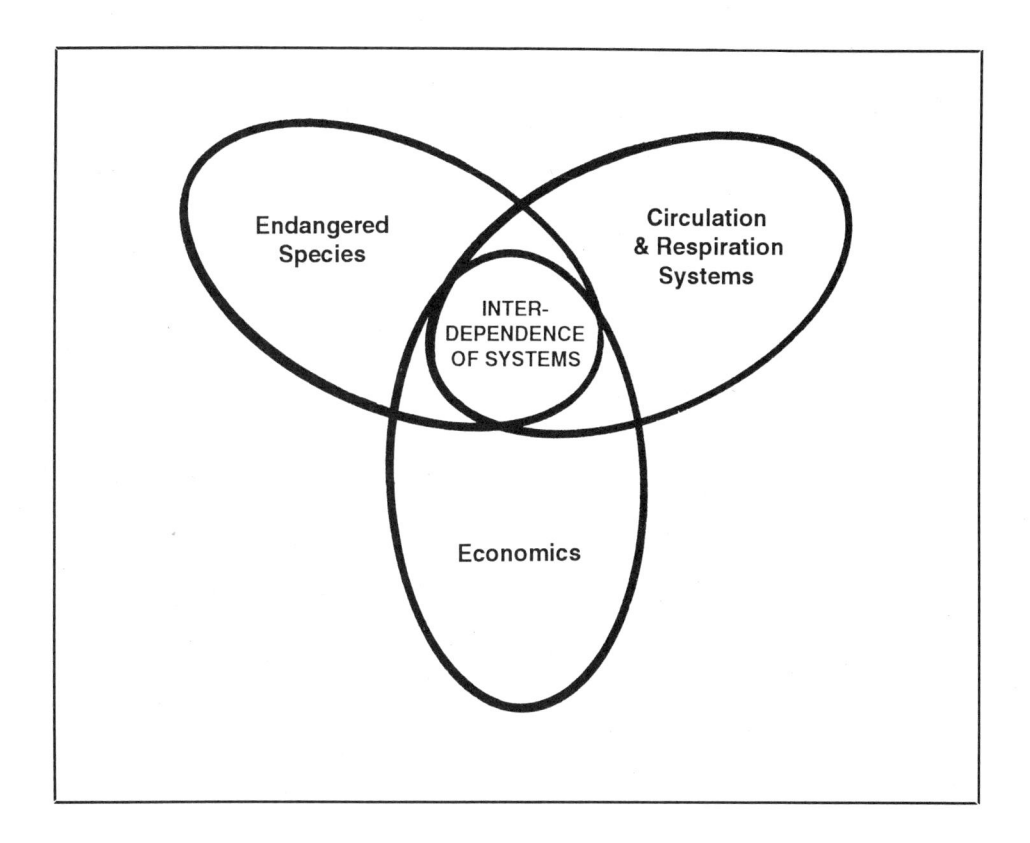

Figure 16.2. The deep principle "Interdependence of Systems" helps students to understand a number of different subjects.

themselves and about one another. Instead of talking about "the smart ones versus the other ones," students refer to the fact that different students know different things. And when the community is designed to capitalize on a diversity of skills and knowledge, students develop mutual respect because they realize that they need one another to accomplish important goals.

For example, in our Schools for Thought project in 1994, a significant amount of time was devoted to a "Mission to Mars" curriculum (Hickey, Petrosino, Pellegrino, Goldman, Bransford, Sherwood, & CTGV, in press). One of the components of the curriculum was a project which required actual building of model rockets. The major purpose of the project was to provide opportunities and contexts by which students would investigate such phenomena as thrust, acceleration, force, and gravity. Additionally, multiple expertise was needed in designing and implementing the project. As the activity progressed, each group took ownership over their specific area of expertise which they had been studying for the past five weeks. They deferred when it was clear that the problem was not in their domain and took leadership when the problem was within their area of focus. As the project progressed, students took on more and more of a leadership role and actually began to assist each other within and across groups. This collaboration around distributed expertise was particularly appreciated during the difficult technical activities, such as triangulating launch altitude. It was rewarding to witness individuals spontaneously supervising aspects of the shared field activity that corresponded to their expertise domain during the classroom "Mars Mission" planning.

Specify the Content to Be Taught in Learning Communities (e.g., what content skills should be taught to students?).

Effective learning communities involve sustained thinking and discussion about authentic, complex topics. Because of this, materials that attempt to provide a breadth of factual coverage need to be replaced with ones that involve opportunities for in-depth exploration. In our work on learning communities, we have tended to use problem-based and project-based activities that sustain students' interests for 4 to 16 weeks (e.g., Barron et al., in press; CTGV, 1993a). We prefer to begin with problem-based anchors prior to moving to projects because the former provide models of effective thinking and problem solving that allow students to begin their subsequent projects from a more informed perspective.

The anchors that we and our colleagues use for instruction are organized around sets of "big ideas," such as sampling in the domain of statistics, measurement in the domain of geometry, and interdependence in the domain of biology (A. L. Brown & Campione, 1994; CTGV, 1991, 1993b, 1994). The use of anchors permits a great deal of flexibility; the exact content to be explored emerges as a function of community interests and interactions. Students are encouraged to identify and define their own issues that are related to the anchors and to then seek relevant resources. This is very different from always being told when, where, and what to study and read.

Identify Instructional Strategies in Learning Communities (e.g., what instructional methods should be used?).

The instructional strategies most frequently used in learning communities involve strategies for organizing the activities of students rather than strategies for delivering information. The overall goal is to help students learn to interact with one another as well as with teachers and other experts, and to interact in a way that involves a reciprocal interchange of ideas, data, and opinions.

Several organizational strategies proposed by researchers such as A. L. Brown and Campione (1994) involve activities such as reciprocal teaching (e.g., Palincsar & A. L. Brown, 1984) and jigsaw teaching (e.g., Aronson, 1978). Reciprocal teaching is a process in which student-led groups master use of strategies to comprehend difficult material. Students learn to ask teacher-type questions (and in the process find important information) as well as learning to summarize, predict, and pinpoint confusing portions of the text and ask for clarification. Comprehending difficult text is vital for students in learning communities because they use authentic materials in their research. Jigsaw groups are a structure for sharing the distributed expertise students gain in their in-depth research. After the initial large problem is presented, students break it into manageable subproblems, each researched by a small group. At certain points in the course of the unit, students regroup so that each person from a subproblem group gets together with one person from each other subgroup. Each individual is responsible for teaching what they have found out to everyone else in the jigsaw group. This structure makes each student responsible for the whole group's learning and solution of the larger problem.

Technology-based tools such as Scardamalia and Bereiter's CSILE (Computer Supported Intentional Learning Environments) also provide strategies for organization that can greatly facilitate student thinking (e.g., Bruer, 1993; Lamon, 1994; Scardamalia, Bereiter, & Lamon, 1994). In CSILE's collaborative database, students can share ideas asynchronously. They can retrieve current and previous thoughts by their classmates by accessing a variety of categories, such as "topic," "author," "comments on my notes," etc. CSILE was designed to be used in the context of a community that stresses "knowledge building" rather than "knowledge telling." In knowledge building, students continually struggle to identify what they don't know and, as a group, attempt to collaboratively extend their understanding. The emphasis on knowledge building is extremely important for lifelong learning, and it is very different from typical classrooms where the emphasis is on restating the facts that have been presented by a teacher or a text.

It is important to note that effective learning communities are not simply "discovery" environments. A great deal of structure is necessary in order to make them work optimally. For example, teachers and other community experts focus on deep principles of the domains being studied (e.g., science, mathematics). They constantly work to help reframe student-generated questions from the perspective of these principles (e.g., A. L. Brown et al., 1993). Nevertheless, within a domain such as science or mathematics, the exact issues defined by the students in the community may vary from year to year. This provides an advantage of ownership and distributed expertise while also ensuring that students learn the deep principles that experts in the domain use to organize their thoughts.

In our experiences with learning communities, there is also room for more traditional activities such as skill building. Students need to explicitly learn facts and skills that allow them to read, compute, and reason with fluency (e.g., Goldman & Pellegrino, 1987; Goldman, Pellegrino, & Mertz, 1988; Hasselbring, 1992). As an illustration, consider students who have to compute the dollar value of 4, 6, and 8 quarters rather than simply retrieve the answers from memory. This takes attentional resources away from thinking about other aspects of the problems to be solved (e.g., Bransford, Goin, Hasselbring, Kinzer, Sherwood, & Williams, 1988).

However, skill building is only a portion of the activities in effective learning communities. In contrast to the typical good classroom, in which the teacher is the one who identifies students' weaknesses, in a learning community students are encouraged to identify and choose the sets of skills on which they need to work. These processes of identifying areas where one needs help, and finding ways to work on them, are extremely important for lifelong learning (e.g., Bransford & Stein, 1993).

An important instructional strategy that enhances the sense of community within classrooms is to help students and teachers see themselves as part of a larger community that has similar interests and values. Technology that can help break the isolation of traditional classrooms provides a promising vehicle for creating these larger communities (Barron et al., in press; CTGV, 1994; Goldman, Pellegrino, & Bransford, 1994). There are also useful strategies for community building that are designed to integrate classrooms with the larger community. For example, teachers with whom we have worked came up with the idea of having adults attempt to solve various anchor problems and letting the students act as expert guides. This strategy has worked extremely well (CTGV, 1992b, in press).

Instructional strategies typically used in learning communities are also chosen to enhance motivation. Our most basic motivational assumption is that authentic problem solving and opportunities to conduct research on self-selected topics are inherently motivating to students (e.g., Blumenfeld, Soloway, Marx, Krajcik, Guzdial, & Palincsar, 1991; Hickey, Pellegrino, Goldman, Vye, Moore, & CTGV, 1993; Pintrich, Marx, & Boyle, 1993). Initial support for this belief is provided by both classroom observations and controlled studies (e.g., Hickey et al., 1993; Van Haneghan, Barron, Young, Williams, Vye, & Bransford, 1992).

Our efforts to design effective learning communities have also included the strategy of creating extrinsic challenges that students and teachers prepare for (e.g., Barron et al., in press; CTGV, 1994; Goldman et al., 1994; Kantor, Moore, Bransford, & CTGV, 1993). These challenges provide deadlines for meeting particular performance objectives, and this motivates teachers, students and often entire school systems to work to meet important goals.

Develop Instruction in Learning Communities (e.g., learner's manual, instructional materials, tests, instructor's guide).

Because of the need for flexibility, the instruction for learning communities cannot be designed by what Duffy (1992) calls "absentee curriculum developers." There are some general principles that guide instruction (e.g., the use of anchors that exemplify big ideas, student generated projects, reciprocal teaching and jigsaw teaching, motivating challenges, etc.), but most of the instructional details depend on content being taught and the interests and questions of the students in the class.

This emphasis on flexibility also means that the development of learning communities is not something that can or should be packaged as a finished curriculum. Instead, a curriculum framework must be developed based on deep principles of relevant content domains and pedagogy. As A. L. Brown and Campione (1994) note, effective learning communities must be re-invented from location to location rather than simply "transported" and then "implemented." These reinventions involve adaptations that take into account the particular interests and expertise of the students, teachers, and larger community involved.

A major challenge for people interested in learning communities is reinventing the idea for themselves without (a) losing the key ingredients necessary to make communities successful, and (b) simply repeating a scripted version of what worked someplace else. In our experience, there is a tradeoff between the flexibility required for successful re-invention of learning communities and the need by novices for some degree of initial structure so that they do not become overwhelmed by novelty. We are currently researching this issue and welcome any suggestions and help.

Further Issues in Designing and Understanding Learning Communities

As noted earlier, our goal in this chapter is to encourage discussion among members of the instructional design community and members of research groups who are attempting to transform typical classrooms into "learning communities." A strength of the research community is its theoretical expertise and investigation of a learner-centered approach. A strength of the instructional design community is its ability to articulate, manage, and systematize the processes involved in designing effective learning environments. Use of a generic instructional design framework has already proved useful to us in thinking through what a concept of learning communities entails.

Therefore, the design and development of learning communities can be based on a confluence of the strengths from both communities rather than shifting towards either one. There are many aspects of the design, development, and assessment of learning communities that need to be further articulated and explored jointly by both communities. The issues fall into two major categories. One set of issues focuses on approaches to designing classrooms, schools, and communities so that they function as efficient learning communities. A second set of issues involves a focus on the research and evaluation of learning communities.

Approaches to the Design and Development of Efficient Learning Communities

The nature of efficient learning communities can be summarized as providing students opportunities to : (1) plan, organize, monitor, and revise their own research and problem solving; (2) work collaboratively and take advantage of distributed expertise from the community to allow diversity, creativity, and flexibility in learning; (3) learn self-selected topics and identify their own issues that are related to the problem-based anchors and then identify relevant resources; (4) use various technologies to build their own knowledge rather than using the technologies as "knowledge tellers"; and (5) make students' thinking visible so that they can revise their own thoughts, assumptions, and arguments.

Given the nature of learning communities, we need to develop open-ended objectives and criteria for success. This needs to be done collaboratively so that teachers and students have opportunities to negotiate, revise, and construct their own goals for instruction and learning. Such objectives should be generated through extended interaction, observation, and research in the classrooms. The guidelines and procedures for actually developing such objectives, and continuing to refine and adjust them over time, are needed. This is an area in which the instructional design community can contribute a great deal of expertise.

To encourage collaborative learning, we also need to consider how we can help students plan and organize their collaborative learning activities. One approach is to develop a wide variety of anchors (e.g., videos, computer simulations, games, and hands-on activities, etc.) that can serve as common grounds for further exploration (CTGV, 1990, 1991). Especially useful are anchors that are designed to allow open-ended exploration of topics that are introduced by the teachers or experts or that are identified by the students. Within the anchored instruction model, we should also consider how much information should be embedded within the initial anchor story, how much within the auxiliary sources that accompany the anchor, and how much should be seeded by the teacher (CTGV, 1992a). The key idea is to have students contribute to the construction of knowledge and to demonstrate their learning in a variety of possible ways, such as software design or the creation of written and other products. As an illustration, Rieber (1994) helped students develop their own interactive learning environments that demonstrated their understanding of various scientific principles and blended several important attributes of different technologies (e.g., microworld, simulations, and games). His research suggests that learning and intrinsic motivation can be optimized by providing opportunities for personal discovery, exploration, ownership, and construction of knowledge.

To encourage distributed expertise in learning communities, we also need to develop user-friendly communication tools, such as the CSILE database for inter- and intra-classroom exchange of information and expertise. The research on hypertext interfaces and their effects on navigation can be of enormous value in this context. The results of the research can be used as formative evaluations to improve design and development of future effective networked learning environments. (See Hasselbring [1992] for an example of how the technological recording of the learner's interactions with the instructional materials and context can enhance design, development, and evaluation in a situated learning environment.)

Members of the instructional design community can also help design products that make students' thinking visible to themselves as well as others. Software shells, such as "Second Generation Instructional Design" (ID$_2$) created by Merrill and his colleagues (Merrill, Li, & Jones, 1990), would be especially exciting if they could be used to help students author their own programs designed to help them achieve particular learning goals. In addition, students could create programs that utilize knowledge gained from their own research projects. For example, if they want to share with younger students what they learned about endangered species, they could use shells to quickly develop a program that contains the information they have gathered in the course of their research. These kinds of experiences allow students to teach as well as to learn.

Another important issue for learning communities is the management of new kinds of classrooms. Organizational and managerial expertise in the instructional design community can be very helpful as teachers coordinate with outside content experts, technologists, parents, other teachers, and principals. For example, they can help teachers create a timeline for students to complete a project. They can also help teachers create resources by introducing new technology, allocate existing resources to different segments of the students' projects, and help teachers with some aspects of collaborative team design. Presently, the learning communities model leaves a number of particular instructional activities and procedures unspecified in terms of actual implementation. Developing a structure for organization and management could be of great benefit to those attempting to implement the idea of learning communities.

Overall, the design and development of efficient learning communities requires the combined wisdom and exploration of teachers, students, cognitive researchers, developmental psychologists, content experts, instructional designers, and technologists. Communication among the members in the community is the key to success in this joint venture. As a link between the scientific knowledge of human cognition and development and educational applications, the contributions from the instructional design community are crucial for the building of learning communities. By the same token, distributed expertise implies that everyone in the community needs to understand the purpose and value of their particular expertise as well as the expertise of others.

Research and Evaluation Issues for Learning Communities

There are several areas of research and evaluation that need contributions from members of both the instructional design and cognitive communities. One involves managing a large number of human resources and bringing them together to reach consensus on their goals. Just as people who implement have to coordinate inputs from teachers, students, parents, advisory board members, etc., members of research teams who design and study learning communities face similar challenges. Members of the instructional design community have a great deal of experience in this area. These experiences could be beneficial to the larger community of individuals attempting to bring about effective change in schools.

Another area in need of further development is the area of assessment. Just as the objectives for learning communities are more open ended than is true in typical classrooms, models for assessing and evaluating the degree to which the objectives have been met also need to be expanded. Performance-based and portfolio assessment are two ideas that are compatible with the goals of learning communities. These assessments need to be formative as well as summative so that they can be used for instructional decision making. Assessments of the processes of learning should include both teacher assessment and students' self-assessment (Collins, Greeno, & Resnick, in press). The development of self-assessment skills is particularly important for the goal of achieving lifelong learning. Technology-based strategies for enhancing assessment and the construction of portfolios are very much needed. This is another area in which instructional design science can contribute valuable ideas.

Ideally, formative evaluation and revision is a daily process within effective learning communities. By designing activities that make students' thinking visible to others, and by creating performance goals that are clear and motivating, students need to have frequent opportunities to "debug" their thoughts, assumptions, and arguments. There are a number of activities that can support students' development of these self-assessment skills; one is the jigsaw group activity discussed earlier. Many of these activities require that teachers step back from their roles as knowledge providers and take on the role of facilitators or coaches. This is not to diminish the role of the teachers in any way. Teachers can provide needed models of self-monitoring and an underlying sense of direction and purpose for learning. Teachers can also guide students' knowledge construction and evaluation processes toward specific domains.

Effective learning communities also involve outside evaluations that are summative as well as formative. These activities involve real deadlines, and they let students see how well they have accomplished particular goals. For example, we noted earlier that we have experimented with several interactive, video-based "public performance challenges" that have been extremely motivating for students and teachers and have provided them with real deadlines and with important sets of feedback about their learning (Barron *et al.*, in press; CTGV, 1994). These public performance arenas make available to the teacher many of the advantages available to coaches and music and art teachers-their students actually perform and get opportunities to reflect on their performances and decide whether and how they need to improve. Ideally, students also have opportunities to revise their ideas and try again (much like playing the same team a second time).

Learning communities also need to be accountable to larger constituencies, and hence need to be subjected to summative evaluations. How to generate such evaluations is a major issue. Traditional achievement tests assess the acquisition of basic skills and knowledge, but they do not assess more sophisticated levels of thinking, reasoning or communicating, and they do not assess learning to learn. Furthermore, traditional tests are based on the assumption that everyone has had a chance to learn the same things (an assumption that is diametrically opposed to the assumptions underlying the concept of distributed expertise). A number of research groups, including ours, are working on issues of assessment (e.g. Barron, 1994; Goldman *et al.*, 1994). Again, we welcome suggestions and help.

Summary

We see the nineties as the decade of collaboration among members from different disciplines to provide new learning experiences by building learning communities in schools. Toward that end, we have discussed the strengths of researchers attempting to create learning communities and the strengths of the instructional design community. By discussing the insights of these two communities, we hope to set the stage for further dialogue. For example, members of the cognitive community can receive a great deal of help from the expertise of the instructional design community. Similarly, members of the instructional design community can benefit from the opportunity to incorporate into their designs the latest advances in cognitive theory and educational philosophies. Such a collaboration can help members of both communities achieve their ultimate goal: To create learning environments for all students that are extraordinarily effective.

References

Andrews, D. H., & Goodson, L. A., (1980). A comparative analysis of models of instructional design. *Journal of Instructional Development*, 3(4), 2–16.
Aronson, E. (1978). *The jigsaw classroom*. Beverly Hills, CA: Sage.

Barron, B. J. S. (1994). *Building a learning community for mathematics: An interactive workshop illustrating implementation and outcomes.* Paper presented at the annual meeting of the American Educational Research Association, New Orleans.

Barron, B. J. S., Vye, N., Zech, L., Schwartz, D., Bransford, J., Goldman, S., Pellegrino, J., Morris, J., Garrison, S., & Kantor, R. (in press). Creating contexts for community based problem solving: The Jasper challenge series. In C. Hedley, P. Antonacci, & M. Rabinowitz (Eds.), *Thinking and literacy: The mind at work.* Hillsdale, NJ: Lawrence Erlbaum Associates.

Blumenfeld, P. C., Soloway, E., Marx, R. W., Krajcik, J. S., Guzdial, M., & Palincsar, A. (1991). Motivating project-based learning: Sustaining the doing, supporting the learning. *Educational Psychologist, 26*(3&4)369–398.

Bransford, J. D. (1981). Social-cultural prerequisites for cognitive research. In J. H. Harvey (Ed.), *Cognition, social behavior, and the environment* (pp. 557–569). Hillsdale, NJ: Lawrence Erlbaum Associates.

Bransford, J. D., Franks, J. J., Vye, N. J., & Sherwood, R. D. (1989). New approaches to instruction: Because wisdom can't be told. In S. Vosniadou & A. Ortony (Eds.), *Similarity and analogical reasoning* (pp. 470–497). New York: Cambridge University Press.

Bransford, J. D., Goin, L. I., Hasselbring, T. S., Kinzer, C. K., Sherwood, R. D., & Williams, S. M. (1988). Learning with technology: Theoretical and empirical perspectives. *Peabody Journal of Education, 64*(1) 5–26.

Bransford, J. D., Goldman, S. R., & Vye, N. J. (1991). Making a difference in peoples' abilities to think: Reflections on a decade of work and some hopes for the future. In L. Okagaki & R. J. Sternberg (Eds.), *Directors of development: Influences on children* (pp. 147–180). Hillsdale, NJ: Lawrence Erlbaum Associates.

Bransford, J. D., & Heldmeyer, K. (1983). Learning from children learning. In J. Bisanz, G. Bisanz, & R. Kail (Eds.), *Learning in children: Progress in cognitive development research* (pp. 171–190). New York: Springer-Verlag.

Bransford, J., Kinzer C., Risko, V., Rowe, D., & Vye, N. (1989). Designing invitations to thinking: Some initial thoughts. Cognitive and social perspectives for literacy research and instruction. In S. McCormick, J. Zutrell, P. Scharer, & P. O'Keefe (Eds.), *Cognitive and social perspectives for literacy research and instruction* (pp. 35–54). Chicago, IL: National Reading Conference.

Bransford, J. D., & Stein, B. S. (1993). *The IDEAL problem solver.* New York: Freeman.

Brown, A. L. (1992). Design experiments: Theoretical and methodological challenges in creating complex interventions in classroom settings. *The Journal of the Learning Sciences, 2*(2), 141–178.

Brown, A. L., Ash, D., Rutherford, M., Nakagawa, K., Gordon, A., & Campione, J. C. (1993). Distributed expertise in the classroom. In G. Salomon (Ed.), *Distributed cognition* (pp. 188–228). New York: Cambridge University Press.

Brown, A. L., Bransford, J. D., Ferrara, R., & Campione, J. (1983). Learning, remembering, and understanding. In J. Flavell & E. Markman (Eds.), *Mussen handbook of child psychology* Vol. 1, 2nd ed. (pp. 77–166). Somerset, NJ: John Wiley & Sons.

Brown, A. L., & Campione, J. C. (1992). *Fostering a community of learners.* Progress Report to the Andrew W. Mellon Foundation. Berkeley: University of California.

Brown, A. L., & Campione, J. C. (1994). Guided discovery in a community of learners. In K. McGilly (Ed.), *Classroom lessons: Integrating cognitive theory and classroom practice* (pp. 229–270). Cambridge, MA: MIT Press/Bradford Books.

Brown, A. L., Campione, J. C., Reeve, R. A., Ferrara, R. A., & Palincsar, A. S. (1991). Interactive learning and individual understanding: The case of reading and mathematics. In L. T. Landsmann (Ed.), *Culture, schooling, and psychological development.* Hillsdale, NJ: Lawrence Erlbaum Associates.

Brown, J. S., Collins, A., & Duguid, P. (1989). Situated cognition and the culture of learning. *Educational Researcher, 18*(1), 32–42.

Bruer, J. (1993). *Schools for thought*. Cambridge, MA: MIT Press.

Bruner, J. S. (1990). *Acts of meaning*. Cambridge, MA: Harvard.

Cognition & Technology Group at Vanderbilt. (1990). Anchored instruction and its relationship to situated cognition. *Educational Researcher, 19*(6), 2–10.

Cognition & Technology Group at Vanderbilt. (1991). Technology and the design of generative learning environments. *Educational Technology, 31*(5), 34–40.

Cognition & Technology Group at Vanderbilt. (1992a). Anchored instruction in science and mathematics: Theoretical basis, developmental projects, and initial research findings. In R. A. Duschl & R. J. Hamilton (Eds.), *Philosophy of science, cognitive psychology, and educational theory and practice* (pp. 244–273). Albany, NY: SUNY Press.

Cognition & Technology Group at Vanderbilt. (1992b). The Jasper series: A generative approach to mathematical thinking. In K. Sheingold, L. G. Roberts, & S. M. Malcolm (Eds.), *This year in science series 1991: Technology for teaching and learning* (pp. 108–140). Washington, DC: American Association for the Advancement of Science.

Cognition & Technology Group at Vanderbilt. (1993a). Anchored instruction and situated cognition revisited. *Educational Technology, 33*(3), 52–70.

Cognition & Technology Group at Vanderbilt. (1993b). Integrated media: Toward a theoretical framework for utilizing their potential. *Journal of Special Education Technology, 12,* 71–85.

Cognition & Technology Group at Vanderbilt. (1993c). The Jasper series: Theoretical foundations and data on problem solving and transfer. In L. A. Penner, G. M. Batsche, H. M. Knoff, & D.L. Nelson (Eds.), *The challenges in mathematics and science education: Psychology's response* (pp. 113–152). Washington, DC: American Psychological Association.

Cognition & Technology Group at Vanderbilt. (1994). From visual word problems to learning communities: Changing conceptions of cognitive research. In K. McGilly (Ed.), *Classroom lessons: Integrating cognitive theory and classroom practice* (pp. 157–200). Cambridge, MA: MIT Press/Bradford Books.

Cognition & Technology Group at Vanderbilt. (in press). The Jasper series: A design experiment in complex, mathematical problem-solving. In J. Hawkins & A. Collins (Eds.), *Design experiments: Integrating technologies into schools*. New York: Cambridge University Press.

Collins, A., Greeno, J. G., & Resnick, L. B. (in press). Learning environments. In T. Husen & T. N. Postlethwaite (Eds.), *International encyclopedia of education* (2nd Ed.). Oxford: Pergamon.

Collins, A., Hawkins, J., & Carver, S. M. (1991). A cognitive apprenticeship for disadvantaged students. In B. Means, C. Chelemer, & M. S. Knapp (Eds.), *Teaching advanced skills to at-risk students* (pp. 216–243). San Francico: Jossey-Bass Publishers.

DeCorte, E., Greer, B., & Verschaffel, L. (in press). Center for instructional psychology and technology. To appear in D. Berliner & R. Calfee (Eds.), *Handbook of educational psychology*. New York: Macmillan.

Dick, W., & Carey, L. (1990). *The systematic design of instruction* (3rd ed.). Glenview, IL: Scott, Foresman and Co.

Dick, W., & Reiser, R. A. (1989). *Planning effective instruction*. Englewood Cliffs, NJ: Prentice-Hall.

Dominowski, R. L. (1990). Problem solving and metacognition. In K. J. Gilhooly, M. T. G. Keane, R. H. Logie, & G. Erdos (Eds.), *Lines of thinking, Volume 2* (pp. 313–327). London: John Wiley & Sons Ltd.

Duffy, T. M. (1992, April). *Learning from the study of practice: Where we must go with strategy instruction*. Paper presented at the annual meeting of the American Educational Research Association, San Francico.

Gardner, H. (1985). *The mind's new science*. New York: Basic.

Gick, M. L., & Holyoak, K. J. (1980). Analogical problem solving. *Cognitive Psychology, 12*, 306–365.

Gick, M. L., & Holyoak, K. J. (1983). Schema induction and analogical transfer. *Cognitive Psychology, 15*, 1–38.

Goldman, S. R., & Pellegrino, J. W. (1987). Information processing and educational microcomputer technology: Where do we go from here? *Journal of Learning Disabilities, 20*(3), 144–154.

Goldman, S. R., Pellegrino, J. W., & Bransford, J. D. (1994). Assessing programs that invite thinking. In E. Baker & H. O'Neil (Eds.), *Technology assessment in education and training*. Hillsdale, NJ: Lawrence Erlbaum Associates.

Goldman, S. R., Pellegrino, J. W., & Mertz, D. L. (1988). Extended practice of basic addition facts: Strategy changes in learning disabled students. *Cognition & Instruction, 5*, 223–265.

Hasselbring, T. S. (1992). *Interactive multimedia applications for special education*. Paper presented at the National Educational Computing Conference (NECC), Dallas.

Hickey, D. T., Pellegrino, J. W., Goldman, S. R., Vye, N.J., Moore, A. L., & CTGV (1993). *Interests, attitudes, and anchored instruction: The impact of one interactive learning environment*. Paper presented at the American Educational Research Association annual meeting, Atlanta.

Hickey, D. T., Petrosino, A., Pellegrino, J. W., Goldman, S. R., Bransford, J. D., Sherwood, R., & the Cognition & Technology Group at Vanderbilt (in press). The MARS mission challenge: A generative, problem-solving, school science environment. In S. Vosniadou, E. De Corte, R. Glaser, & H. Mandl (Eds.), *Psychological and educational foundations of technology-based learning environments*. Berlin: Springer-Verlag.

Hmelo, C. E. (1993) *Learning in school and learning in life: An exploration of issues* (Tech. Rep. No. 93-1). Nashville, TN: Vanderbilt University Learning Technology Center.

Holt, J. (1964). *How children fail*. New York: Dell, 1964.

Kantor, R.J., Moore, A.L., & Bransford, J.D. with the Cognition & Technology Group at Vanderbilt. (1993). *Extending the impact of classroom-bassed technology: The satellite challenge series*. Presented at the American Educational Research Association, New Orleans.

Lamon, M. (1994). *Cognitive studies for restructuring middle school education*. Prepublication manuscript. St. Louis Science Center, St. Louis, MO.

Lave, J., & Wenger, E. (1991). *Situated learning: Legitimate peripheral participation*. Cambridge: Cambridge University Press.

Lin, X. D. (1993). *Far transfer problem-solving in a non-linear computer environment: The role of self-regulated learning processes*. Unpublished dissertation, Purdue University.

Merrill, M.D., Li, Z., & Jones, M. K. (1990). Second generation instructional design (ID$_2$) *Educational Technology, 30*(2), 7–14.

Minstrell, J. A. (1989). Teaching science for understanding. In L. B. Resnick & L. E. Klopfer (Eds.), *Toward the thinking curriculum: Current cognitive research* (pp. 129–149). Alexandria, VA: ASCD.

Palincsar, A. S., & Brown, A. L. (1984). Reciprocal teaching of comprehension-fostering and comprehension-monitoring activities. *Cognition and Instruction, 1*, 117–175.

Pea, R. D. (1993). Practices of distributed intelligence and designs for education. In G. Salomon (Eds.), *Distributed cognition* (pp. 47–87). New York: Cambridge University Press.

Pintrich, P. R., Marx, R. W., & Boyle, R. A. (1993). Beyond cold conceptual change: The role of motivational beliefs and classroom contextual factors in the process of conceptual change. *Review of Educational Research, 63*, 167–199.

Reigeluth, C. M. (1983). Instructional design: What is it and why is it? In C. M. Reigeluth (Ed.), *Instructional-design theories and models: An overview of their current status* (pp. 3–37). Hillsdale, NJ: Lawrence Erlbaum Associates.

Reigeluth, C. M., Bunderson, C. V., & Merrill, M. D. (1978). What is the design science of instruction? *Journal of Instructional Development, 6*(2), 11–16.

Resnick, L. (1987). *Education and learning to think.* Washington, DC: National Academy Press.

Resnick, L. B., & Klopfer, L. E. (Eds.) (1989). *Toward the thinking curriculum: Current cognitive research.* Alexandria, VA: ASCD.

Rieber, L. P. (1994). *An instructional design philosophy of interaction based on a blending of microworlds, simulations, and games.* Paper presented at the annual meeting of the Association for Educational Communications and Technology, Nashville.

Scardamalia, M., Bereiter, C., & Lamon, M. (1994). The CSILE Project: Trying to bring the classroom into world 3. In K. McGilly (Ed.), *Classroom lessons: Integrating cognitive theory and classroom practice* (pp. 201–228). Cambridge, MA: MIT Press/Bradford Books.

Senge, P. M. (1990). *The fifth discipline: The art and practice of the learning organization.* New York: Doubleday.

Simon, H. A. (1980). Problem solving and education. In D. T. Tuma & R. Reif (Eds.), *Problem solving and education: Issues in teaching and research* (pp. 81–96). Hillsdale, NJ: Lawrence Erlbaum Associates.

Smith, P. L., & Ragan, T. J. (1993). *Instructional design.* New York: Macmillan Publishing Company.

Sternberg, R. J., & Wagner, R. K. (1986). *Practical intelligence.* Cambridge, MA: Cambridge University Press.

Whitehead, A. N. (1929). *The aims of education.* New York: Macmillan.

Winn, W. (1990). Some implications of cognitive theory for instructional design. *Instructional Science, 19*, 53–69.

Winn, W. (1993). Instructional design and situated learning: Paradox or partnership? *Educational Technology, 33*(3), 16–22.

Van Haneghan, J. P., Barron, L., Young, M. F., Williams, S. M., Vye, N. J., & Bransford, J. D. (1992). The Jasper series: An experiment with new ways to enhance mathematical thinking. In D. F. Halpern (Ed.) *Enhancing thinking skills in the sciences and mathematics* (pp. 15–38). Hillsdale, NJ: Lawrence Erlbaum Associates.

Acknowledgment

Special thanks to Jim Hood and Mitch Nathan for their comments on this chapter.

The Cognition and Technology Group at Vanderbilt (CTGV) is a collaborative, multidisciplinary group made up of approximately 70 individuals from a variety of disciplines. All CTGV projects are based on social and cognitive theories of learning and development, and refined through extensive testing in real-world settings. Students in CTGV projects range from kindergarten age to adults.

A Constructivist Sampler

May Lowry, Victoria L. Wood, R. Scott Grabinger, Robert W. Davis, Maggie Trigg, Richard Morse, and Karen M. Myers
University of Colorado at Denver

As interest in constructivism has mushroomed in the past decade, so has the professional literature. The following is a sampler of published work on both the theory and practice of constructivism in education. These selections are meant to provide the reader with a cross-section of ideas from a variety of sources, rather than an exhaustive list. Besides the inspiring ideas and instructive applications contained in these writings, each one of the articles and chapters includes a rich and extensive reference list, linking to further sources on constructivism and related topics.

Ballard, R. (1992, October). The JASON project: Hi-tech exploration promotes students' interest in science. *T.H.E. Journal*, pp. 70–74.

JASON is an underwater remote control robot. The JASON Project is an interactive distance learning experience for students in grades 7–10, in which they view, interact with, and study the robot and its scientific experiments. For several weeks, students follow a curriculum from the National Science Teachers Association. Then they can visit an interactive site containing a full-scale replica of JASON's control room, with two-way audio and video feed. Students discuss discoveries with scientists, and are allowed to remotely control JASON themselves. The authors describe the project and its applications, and provide an address and phone number for further information.

Berliner, D. C. (1992, October). Redesigning classroom activities for the future. *Educational Technology,* pp. 7–13.

Berliner sees the middle school, fifth through ninth grade, as the center of educational change in the next decade. Change within middle schools is motivated by advances in technology, as well as the theory of constructivism. Multidimensional learning environments, authentic portfolios and projects, and modified curriculum are all dimensions of this discussion on change.

Blakey, E., & Spence, S. (1990). Developing metacognition. *ERIC Digests.* **Syracuse, NY: ERIC Clearinghouse on Information Resources.**

Metacognition is the act of thinking about and evaluating mental processes. The authors describe six strategies for developing metacognitive skills in the area of problem solving: (1) identifying what is known and what is not known; (2) talking about thinking; (3) writing a thinking journal; (4) planning; (5) debriefing the thinking process; (6) self-evaluation. The authors emphasize the importance of establishing learning environments which support and encourage learners in developing these metacognitive skills.

Chi, M., & Bassok, M. (1989). Learning from examples via self-explanations. In L. Resnick (Ed.), *Knowing, learning, and instruction: Essays in honor of Robert Glaser (pp. 251–282).* **Hillsdale, NJ: Lawrence Erlbaum Associates.**

This chapter is devoted to three fundamental issues of instruction and design, namely "...how one learns, what one learns, and how one uses what one has learned." The authors describe a research study in which they conclude that successful learners combine the strategy of providing themselves with their own explanations of the problem and solution (self-explanations), with the strategy of monitoring their own level of comprehension. These two techniques together seem to result not only in successful problem-solving, but also in the ability to generalize problem-solving skills.

Clancey, W. (1993). Guidon-manage revisited: A socio-technical systems approach. *Journal of Artificial Intelligence in Education,* 4(1), pp. 5–34.

Clancey reflects on his past dozen years of research and development of products designed to support critical thinking in a variety of educational settings. In the light of situated cognition theories, he criticizes these products as being limited because they do not take into account the everyday context in which the learners operate. Clancey describes his evolution to a socio-technical design approach which begins with the users and their social and physical environment, and still retains the best of expert systems instructional design. This issue of the journal also includes four articles in response to Clancey.

Cognition & Technology Group at Vanderbilt. (1991, May). Technology and the design of generative learning environments. *Educational Technology,* **pp. 34–40.**

The Jasper adventures are a series of engaging videodisc-based instructional tools. They are developed to encourage problem-solving and generation of active knowledge. One "walk-through" episode provides a flavor of the finished product. The authors describe the seven key instructional design principles behind the Jasper series: (1) video format; (2) narrative; (3) generative learning; (4) embedded data design; (5) problem complexity; (6) pairs of related adventures; (7) links across curriculum. Teachers are encouraged to use the Jasper series to create environments that emphasize complex problem-solving, communication, and reasoning.

Collins, A., Brown, J. S., & Holum, A. (1991, Winter). Cognitive apprenticeship: Making thinking visible. *American Educator,* **pp. 6–11, 38–46.**

The authors define cognitive apprenticeship as the process which "makes thinking visible," and argue that apprenticeship is the most natural way to learn. As a model of instruction, cognitive apprenticeship begins with the traditional apprenticeship strategies of demonstration, practice, and coaching. It then adds the element of making the teacher's thinking visible to the student, and the student's thinking visible to the teacher. The core components of cognitive apprenticeship (modeling, scaffolding, fading, and coaching) are illustrated through classroom examples of teaching reading, writing, and math. The article discusses principles for designing cognitive apprenticeships.

Cunningham, D. J., Duffy, T. M., & Knuth, R. A. (1993). The textbook of the future. In C. McKnight (Ed.), *Hypertext* **(pp. 19–49). Chichester, England: Ellis Horwood Limited.**

New technologies, as well as the development of the theory of constructivism, prompt educators to re-examine the function and design of the traditional textbook. The authors suggest that the role of the traditional textbook, a well-designed presentation of information on paper, needs to shift from being the deliverer of all knowledge to being a resource which provides one perspective on a particular subject. Technology becomes the vehicle for providing multiple perspectives, a key concept in knowledge construction. Intermedia, a hypertext computer database, provides an example of the textbook of the future.

Dreyfus, H. L., & Dreyfus, S. E. (1986). Five steps from novice to expert. In *Mind over machine: The power of human intuition and expertise in the era of the computer* (pp. 16–51). New York: The Free Press.

The authors discuss the five stages that a person passes through in the process of skill acquisition: novice, advanced beginner, competent, proficient, and expert. As a novice, a person learns to recognize facts, features, and rules of the subject matter. An advanced beginner moves beyond the rules to recognize meaningful elements. In stage three, competence, the person distinguishes between relevant and irrelevant information. In the proficiency stage, the person intuitively understands and organizes the task, but continues to analyze and assess the performance. In the final stage, an expert is engaged in the performance, and the skills and necessary decisions are automatic.

Duffy, T., Lowyck, J., & Jonassen, D. (1993). *Designing environments for constructivist learning.* **Berlin: Springer-Verlag.**

This book grew out of an international conference on constructivist learning environments. The dozens of contributing authors explore the implications of constructivism for both theory and practice. Several chapters describe constructivist learning environments for adult learners. Other chapters discuss technological support for constructivist learning environments, analyze design issues, and provide case studies of constructivism in practice.

Educational Technology. **(1991, May). Special issue on constructivism.**

This issue features papers by some of the leading contemporary authors in the area of constructivism— Perkins, Bransford, Cunningham, and Spiro. It also contains a reaction to the ideas of these authors by a number of instructional design theorists, including M. David Merrill and Walter Dick. A second special issue followed (September, 1991) carrying further responses and commentary.

Fishman, B. J., & Duffy, T. M. (1992). Classroom restructuring: What do teachers really need? *ETR&D, 40,* **pp. 221–239.**

This article details a needs assessment conducted to identify the requirements of teachers who desire to restructure their classes. Results of this assessment include tools and resources necessary to facilitate change in the classroom. Among these tools is the Strategic Teaching Framework (STF), a hypermedia computer system.

Grabowski, B., & Curtis, R. (1991). Information, instruction, and learning: A hypermedia perspective. *Performance Improvement Quarterly, 4*(3), pp. 2–12.

The article discusses the relationship between teaching (a process external to the learner) and learning (a process internal to the learner). The authors argue that an important factor in encouraging learning is proving the learner with control over the learning process. Hypermedia technology provides self-directed, independent, individualized environments designed to support learner control.

Gelman, R., & Greeno, J. G. (1989). On the nature of competence: Principles for understanding in a domain. In L. B. Resnick (Ed.), *Knowing, learning, and instruction: Essays in honor of Robert Glaser* (pp. 125–186). Hillsdale, NJ: Lawrence Erlbaum Associates.

Gelman and Greeno posit that children have implicit knowledge of counting principles. This knowledge provides a foundation for formal mathematics instruction, leading to an explicit understanding of counting. Three types of competence allow children to count without formal instruction; they are procedural, interpretative, and conceptual. The authors suggest that analysis of implicit competence has implications for the design of curriculum and instruction in mathematics and other subjects.

Griest, G. (1993, April). You say you want a revolution: Constructivism, technology, and language arts. *The Computing Teacher*, pp. 8–11.

Constructivism has prepared a path for the revolutionary use of computers in the language arts. Constructivism itself is revolutionary, emphasizing learner self-direction, and demanding new educational strategies. Revolution in the language arts argues for returning control of the writing process to the writer. Technology has fueled this revolution with the introduction into the classroom of word processing and multimedia capability, which helps learners explore complex symbolic relationships. The author stresses the role of the change agent in encouraging transition from didacticism to a computer-mediated, constructivist language arts classroom.

Hannafin, M. J. (1992). Emerging technologies, ISD, and learning environments: Critical perspectives. *ETR&D, 40*(1), pp. 49–63.

Hannafin defines learning environments as "multifaceted, integrated systems that promote learning through student-centered activities." He examines the role of Instructional Systems Design (ISD) in response to new learning technologies and increasing understanding of student knowledge construction. He argues that traditional ISD is too narrow a model to accommodate strategies like anchored instruction and situated cognition, and that new design models are needed to support advances in research and technology.

Hawkins, J., Frederiksen, J., Collins, A. W., Bennett, B., & Collins, E. (1993). Assessment and technology. *Communications of the ACM, 36,* **(5), pp. 74–76.**

Authentic assessment is a way to assess student learning based on actual performance and products, rather than by inferring learning from indirect measures like standardized tests. Students are told what proficiencies are expected of them, and then complete tasks and create projects that demonstrate their ability. The article offers examples of student products using a variety of media, including text, graphics, video, and multimedia. There is a discussion of four components helpful in implementing authentic assessment in the classroom: (1) selection of tasks which are appropriate to the subject; (2) a criteria of what constitutes good work; (3) a library of samples; and (4) proper training in scoring projects for students and teachers.

Jones, B. F., Knuth, R., & Duffy, T. (1993). Components of constructivist learning environments for professional development. In T. Duffy, J. Lowyck, & D. Jonassen (Eds.), *Designing environments for constructivist learning.* **Berlin: Springer-Verlag.**

The authors describe the "Strategic Teaching Framework" (STF), which is a conceptual model for designing and evaluating learning environments. This model was developed for the teaching of teachers and educational administrators. Examples for the use of the STF are drawn from two projects, one designed around a hypermedia library and the other from a nine program video conference and guidebook series. The goal of the projects was to help teachers and administrators become strategic thinkers in seven key areas: (1) goals and metaphors that drive learning and instruction; (2) learner characteristics, responsibilities, and values; (3) teacher characteristics, responsibilities, and values; (4) tasks that define the nature and level of achievement; (5) school characteristics that support teaching and learning; (6) principles of sequencing; and (7) principles of assessment.

Kennedy, M., Fisher, M., & Ennis, R. (1991). Critical thinking: Literature review and needed research. In L. Idol & B. F. Jones (Eds.), *Educational values and cognitive instruction: Implications for reform.* **Hillsdale, NJ: Lawrence Erlbaum Associates.**

This chapter provides an historical overview of the topic of critical thinking, from John Dewey through the mid-1980's report, *A Nation at Risk*. It discusses a variety of definitions of the term critical thinking. The authors also cover topics relevant to the teaching of critical thinking (subject matter specificity, transfer, classroom atmosphere, assessment), and to the learning of critical thinking (developmental readiness, prior knowledge, and student characteristics). They include a detailed outline of behavioral goals for a critical thinking curriculum, as well as a list of specific instruments designed to assess critical thinking.

Knox-Quinn, C. (1988, November). A simple application and a powerful idea: Using expert systems shells in the classroom. *The Computing Teacher,* **pp. 12–15.**

This is an easily understood explanation of expert systems and shells. Shells are software that provide a structure for students to capture information. Students enter their information and essentially create an expert system based on their own understanding of how the information fits together. Using shells encourages students to create a "problem-solving microworld" that fosters higher order cognitive skills.

Larkin, J. H. (1989). On the nature of competence: Principles for understanding in a domain. In L. B. Resnick (Ed.), *Knowing, learning, and instruction: Essays in honor of Robert Glaser* **(pp. 125–186). Hillsdale, NJ: Lawrence Erlbaum Associates.**

Larkin defines transfer as the ability to apply old knowledge to facilitate the acquisition of new knowledge. Her research found that teaching people general problem-solving skills results in very little transfer of those skills to other subject matter. Using the computer problem-solving program FERMI, she identifies management and learning skills that are transferable and helpful in learning general problem-solving skills. Larkin suggests that more direct attention to instruction of these skills may promote transfer.

Levine, D., & Cooper, E. (1991). The change process and its implications in teaching thinking. In L. Idol & B. F. Jones (Eds.), *Educational values and cognitive instruction: Implications for reform* **(pp. 387–409). Hillsdale, NJ: Lawrence Erlbaum Associates.**

The authors describe the teaching of critical thinking as an innovation in schools. They conclude that the teaching of critical thinking skills could represent "large, complex, and difficult changes" in a school, and they offer suggestions for supporting the innovation. Some of their suggestions are training and staff development for teachers, incentives for participation in the program, stable school leadership, clarity of objectives and procedures, and developing conflict resolution skills.

Lincoln, B., & Strommen, E. F. (1992, August). Constructivism, technology, and the future of classroom learning. *Education and Urban Society, 24(4),* pp. 466–476.

The authors believe that recent technological advances have escaped the educational system. This has created a large gap between the school experience for children and everyday life. This challenge results in children viewing school as uninteresting and sometimes alienating. The authors suggest constructivism as a foundation for a bridge between school activities and real-world experiences. They recommend an immediate change in educational practice by incorporating modern technology to a greater extent in the classroom.

Mayer, J. (1990). Uncommonsense learning. In J. Mayer (Ed.), *Uncommon sense: Theoretical practice in language education* **(pp. 75–105). Portsmith, NH: Boynton/Cook Publishers.**

Mayer's metaphor of learning is that of a story in which learners have the possibility of expressing the story line and changing the plot, and where others (parents, teachers, peers) have the power to influence the course of events. The emphasis in school, therefore, should be on active, intentional and self-directed learning. Learning is part of life, and we learn by "constructing our story of the way the world works" through experience, testing our ideas, and reflection. The book is dedicated to exploring how to design schools of "uncommon sense" that support effective learning.

McLellan, H. (1993, March). Evaluation in a situated learning environment. *Educational Technology, 33(3),* pp. 39–45.

McLellan uses the term evaluation to mean both assessing student performance and measuring instructional effectiveness. Collins' methods for assessment in a computer-based learning environment (portfolio, on-going diagnosis, and summary statistics) are discussed in depth. The author introduces the additional assessment methods of reflection and self-assessment, creating stories and scenarios, designing instruction for others, and diagnostic testing. These methods are described in enough detail to allow practitioners to adopt them in a classroom.

Palincsar, A. S. (1990, November/December). Providing the context for intentional learning. *Remedial and Special Education, 11(6),* pp. 36–39.

This article focuses on teaching strategies that encourage intentional learning in order to promote lifelong learning. Palincsar attempts to bridge the gap between theory and practice by suggesting application of a concrete example in teaching reading comprehension in a classroom setting. Understanding the learner's representation of the classroom activities, modeling the thinking process, and guided practice are the strategies addressed.

Perkins, D. N. (1991, May). Technology meets constructivism: Do they make a marriage? *Educational Technology, 31*(5), pp. 18–23.

Perkins describes three goals of education: retention, understanding and the active use of knowledge. Although other goals exist, the potential effectiveness of a learning environment depends on this trio. He argues that technology offers powerful tools for supporting these goals and constructing five key elements of an effective learning environment. These elements are information banks, symbol pads, construction kits, phenomenaria, and task managers. These elements can be used in a constructivist learning environment that is BIG (Beyond the Information Given), which is based on a strategy that gives direct instruction; and WIG (Without the Information Given), which is based on a strategy of starting with learner discovery before giving direct instruction.

Perkins, D. N. (1991, September). What constructivism demands of the learner. *Educational Technology, 31*(9), pp. 19–21.

The nature of a constructivist learning environment imposes increased demands on the learner when compared to traditional instruction. Among these demands are higher cognitive load, increased responsibilities for self-management of learning, and an imposed dual agenda requiring learners to learn both the subject matter and metacognitive processes associated with learning. Perkins suggests solutions that may reduce the demands of constructivism.

Perkins, D. N. (1992). *Smart schools.* **New York: The Free Press.**

This is a very readable explanation of the philosophy of constructivism and how it could be implemented in American classrooms. Perkins bases his ideas on both contemporary research and classic thinking in the field of education. At best, we can expect traditional teaching to result in students' having a limited grasp of a subject. Perkins envisions schools where students are encouraged to think and grapple with the subject. He calls the centerpiece of his work Theory One: "People learn much of what they have a reasonable opportunity and motivation to learn." He then builds his model of a smart school around what it would take to create schools which operate on Theory One.

Resnick, L. (1989) Introduction to knowledge construction. In L. Resnick (Ed.), *Knowing, learning, and instruction: Essays in honor of Robert Glaser* **(pp. 1–24). Hillsdale, NJ: Lawrence Erlbaum Associates.**

This introduction to the book provides an overview of constructivist ideas, including definitions of terms and references for further research. Resnick begins with a discussion of three widely accepted learning principles: learning is a process of knowledge construction, learning is based on prior knowledge, and learning is situation dependent. These basic principles give rise to a number of instructional issues that need to be addressed, including teaching metacognition, providing scaffolding, and transfer of knowledge. These topics are discussed in the remaining chapters of the book.

Roschelle, J. (1994). Designing for cognitive communication: Epistemic fidelity or mediating collaborative inquiry? *The Arachnet Electronic Journal on Virtual Culture,* **2(2).**

Roschelle contrasts two approaches to instruction: High Fidelity, which attempts to accurately representing an expert's mental model; and MCI (mediated collaborative inquiry), which begins with the learners and their mental model, and supports them in engaging the topic and communicating about it. He argues that the novice's mental models often get in the way of understanding the expert's mental models. Information is not something to be delivered, but something to be explored in collaboration with others. He supports the MCI design approach, and offers principles for MCI design.

Scardamalia, M., Bereiter, C., McLean, R., Swallow, J., & Woodruff, E. (1989). Computer-supported intentional learning environments. *Journal of Educational Computing Research,* **5(1), pp. 51–68.**

CSILE (Computer-Supported Intentional Learning Environment) is an educational media system designed to make knowledge construction overt, provide feedback, and give students a chance to see and respond to each others' work. CSILE allows students to enter their work in text, drawings, and graphs of different kinds. The authors suggest eleven principles for designing computer environments that support intentional learning: (1) make knowledge construction activities overt; (2) maintain attention to cognitive goals; (3) treat knowledge lacks in a positive way; (4) provide relevant feedback; (5) encourage learning strategies other than rehearsal; (6) encourage multiple passes through information; (7) support varied ways for students to organize their knowledge; (8) encourage maximum use and examination of existing knowledge; (9) provide opportunities for reflectivity and individual learning styles; (10) facilitate transfer of knowledge across contexts; and (11) give students more responsibility for contributing to each other's learning.

Spiro, R. J., & Jehng, J. (1992). Cognitive flexibility and hypertext: Theory and technology for the nonlinear and multidimentional traversal of complex subject matter. In D. Nix & R. Spiro (Eds.), *Cognition, education, and multimedia: Exploring ideas in high technology* **(pp. 163–205). Hillsdale, NJ: Lawrence Erlbaum Associates.**

This chapter discusses Spiro's Cognitive Flexibility Theory. Cognitive flexibility is "the ability to spontaneously restructure one's knowledge..." This is an important ability when facing complex and advanced subject matter. The authors wanted to understand how to make a complicated subject as easy to learn as possible without losing its complexity. They used computer technology to randomly access certain scenes from the film *Citizen Kane*. Each clip shows Kane from a different perspective and in a different context. As the information about Kane grows, it shows many new dimensions. The effect is to give the learner a way to build an understanding of the complexity of the character, and gives them a process for understanding other multidimensional subjects in the future.

Woodward, J., & Carnine, D. (1989). The Genisys program: Linking content area to problem-solving through technology-based instruction. *Journal of Special Education* **10(2), pp. 99–112.**

Genisys (General Science Instructional System) is a computer program designed to teach learners how to solve complex earth science problems. Through thirty-five lessons on videodisc, the earth science content knowledge (e.g., rain cycle, mass and density, etc.) is alternated with opportunities to apply the knowledge in problem-solving challenges. Details of the program's feedback, practice, and review functions are included.

Author Index

A

Abelson, R., 54
Allen, B. S., 8, 179, 180, 182
Alley, W. E., 34
Alport, J. M., 152
Anderson, R., 113
Anderson, R. C., 135
Andrews, D. H., 204
Aronson, E., 210
Arter, J., 194
Aschbacher, P. R., 191, 194
Ash, D., 205
Ashley, K. D., 51

B

Baker, E. L., 193, 194
Baker, L., 72
Ballard, R., 221
Barron, B. J. S., 205, 206, 210, 212, 216
Barron, L., 212
Barrows, H. S., 135, 140, 141, 142, 143, 145
Bartlett, F. C., 83
Bassock, M., 222
Battista, M. T., 122
Bearison, D. J., 122
Bednar, A. K., 74
Belenky, M., 108
Bennett, B., 226
Bereiter, C., 45, 107, 115, 138, 159, 206, 211, 230
Berliner, D. C., 222
Bielaczyc, K., 36

Bingham, A., 124
Black, J. B., 25
Black, J. K., 191
Black, J. R., 7
Blakey, E., 222
Bloom, B., 40
Blumenfeld, P. C., 138, 212
Boud, D., 141, 143
Boyle, R. A., 97, 212
Bransford, J. D., 67, 113, 205, 206, 207, 207, 208, 209, 211, 212
Braunhardt, L., 7, 125, 126, 130
Bredderman, T., 152
Brescia, W., 12
Bridges, E., 140, 143
Briggs, L., 66
Brooker, C., 122
Brooks, J. G., 140
Brooks, M. G., 140
Brown, A., 45, 72
Brown, A. L., 36, 83, 107, 113, 205, 206, 207, 208, 210, 211, 212
Brown, G., 113
Brown, J. S., 22, 26, 44, 45, 67, 74, 79, 83, 129, 139, 153, 193, 205, 206, 223
Brown, M. D., 154
Bruckman, A., 169
Bruer, J., 206, 211
Bruner, C., 152
Bruner, J., 75, 77, 94, 127, 208
Brunner, C., 159
Bunderson, C. V., 204
Bunzo, M., 34
Butterfield, E., 66

C

Calegher, J., 107
Campione, J. C., 83, 113, 205, 206, 207, 208, 210, 212
Carey, L., 204
Carnine, D., 231
Carver, S. M., 98, 103, 206
Chen, P., 12
Chi, M. T. H., 36, 152, 222
Chiero, R. T., 8, 182
Choppin, B. H., 191
Clancey, W., 222
Clements, D. H., 122, 124
Clift, R., 140
Clinchy, B., 108
Cole, M., 96, 114
Collins, A., 5, 22, 26, 44, 45, 58, 67, 74, 83, 109, 110, 111, 129, 139, 153, 193, 205, 206, 208, 215, 223
Collins, A. W., 226
Collins, E., 226
Confry, J., 83
Connell, T., 98
Cooper, D., 227
Coulson, R. J., 26
Crowder, E., 108, 109, 112
Cuban, L., 107
Cunningham, D. J., 11, 12, 83, 137, 140, 223
Curtis, R., 225

D

D'Amico, L., 152, 156
DeCorte, E., 205
Dede, C., 8, 166
DeFanti, T. A., 154
Derry, S., 7
Dewey, J., 84, 104, 136
Dibble, E., 34
Dick, W., 204
diSessa, A. A., 172
Doise, W., 122
Dominowski, R. L., 207
Dreyfus, H. L., 224
Dreyfus, S. E., 224
Duffy, T., 224, 226
Duffy, T. M., 7, 11, 12, 95, 122, 137, 138, 140, 145, 212, 223
Duguid, P., 26, 67, 74, 83, 129, 153, 193, 205

Dunbar, S. E., 193
Dunlap, J. C., 7

E

Edelson, D. C., 8, 107, 115, 140, 156, 159
Edwards, D., 107
Eggan, G., 34
Egido, C., 107
Elman, S., 66
Ennis, R., 226–227
Ericksen, J., 98

F

Faletti, J., 183
Fano, A., 51
Farmer, F. R., 166
Feletti, G., 141, 143
Feltovich, P. J., 26
Ferguson, W., 52, 109, 110, 111
Ferrara, R. A., 113, 207
Feuer, M. J., 194, 199
Filardo, E. K., 122
Finch, F. L., 194
Fisher, K. M., 181
Fisher, M., 226–227
Fishman, B. J., 12, 115, 138, 156, 224
Flavell, J., 71, 72, 199
Flores, F., 25
Forman, G., 67
Fosnot, C. T., 67, 139, 140, 165
Franks, J. J., 207
Frederiksen, J., 197, 198, 199, 226
Freire, P., 93
Fullan, M., 192
Fulton, K., 194, 199

G

Gadamer, H., 25
Gaffney, J. S., 135
Gagné, R., 66
Gardner, H., 205
Garrison, S., 205
Garrod, S., 113
Gelerntner, D., 173
Gelman, R., 225
Genest, M., 199
Gibson, J. J., 121, 129
Gick, M. L., 207
Glaser, R., 34, 76

Glass, C. R., 199
Globerson, T., 96
Godwin, D. B., 181
Goffman, E., 169
Goin, L. I., 211
Goldberger, N., 108
Goldman, S. R., 205, 206, 209, 211, 212, 215
Goldsmith, L. D., 154
Gomez, L., 8, 115, 152
Goodlad, J. I., 95, 104
Goodman, N., 67
Goodson, L. A., 204
Gordin, D. N., 115, 154, 156
Gordin, M., 34
Gordon, A., 205
Gorry, A. G., 159
Gott, S. P., 7, 34, 36, 37, 42
Grabinger, R. S., 7, 94
Grabowski, B., 225
Greenburg, L., 34
Greeno, J. G., 129, 215, 225
Greer, B., 205
Griest, G., 225
Griffin, P., 96, 114
Grosslight, L., 154
Guzdial, M., 97, 138, 212

H

Haertel, E., 193
Hall, E. P., 34, 36
Hallinger, P., 140, 143
Hammer, D., 113
Hammer, D. M., 172
Hammond, K. J., 51
Hancock, C., 154
Haney, W., 197
Hannafin, M. J., 225–226
Harel, I., 7, 154
Harper, B., 198
Hasselbring, T. S., 211, 215
Hawkins, J., 159, 206, 226
Hays, K. E., 97
Hedberg, J., 198
Heidegger, M., 25
Heldmeyer, K., 206
Herman, J. L., 191, 194
Hickey, D. T., 209, 212
Hickman, P., 115, 116
Hmelo, C. E., 205
Hoffman, R. P., 8, 182

Holt, J., 206
Holubec, E., 26
Holum, A., 223
Holyoak, K. J., 207
Honebein, P. C., 7, 12, 69, 138, 145
Horwitz, P., 115, 116
House, E. R., 199
Houston, W., 140
Houts, P. L., 191
Hughes, E., 34
Hultman, D., 122

J

Jackson, S., 97
Jacob, E., 125
Jacobson, M. J., 26
Jehng, J., 76, 77, 231
Johnson, D., 26, 72
Johnson, D. W., 122
Johnson, R., 26, 72
Johnson, R. T., 122
Johnston, P. H., 194
Jona, M. Y., 58, 77, 93
Jonassen, D. H., 7, 29, 55, 94, 95, 122, 140, 183, 200
Jonassen, J., 224
Jones, B. F., 226
Jones, G., 34
Jones, M. K., 215
Jones, R. M., 36

K

Kahneman, D., 84
Kakos-Kraft, S., 145
Kakuta, J., 167
Kane, R. S., 7, 34, 39
Kantor, R. J., 205, 212
Kaput, J. J., 154
Kass, A., 54
Katz, S., 34
Keegan, M., 20
Kennedy, M., 226–227
Kiesler, S., 168
King, A., 107, 113
Kinzer, C. K., 207, 211
Klopfer, L. E., 66, 206, 207
Knight, M. E., 191, 194
Knox-Quinn, C., 227
Knuth, R. A., 11, 137, 140, 223, 226
Kolodner, J. L., 51

Konold, C., 85
Krajcik, J. S., 138, 212
Kraut, R., 107
Kuhn, D., 84, 86, 113
Kyle, D., 69
Kyle, W. C., 152

L

Lajoie, S., 34
Lamon, M., 206, 211
Larkin, J. H., 172, 227
Laurel, B., 169
Lave, J., 83, 84, 107, 122, 152, 206
Lebow, D., 67, 68, 69, 137
Lederberg, J., 153, 158
Lehrer, R., 97, 98
Lemke, J. L., 107
Lesgold, A., 7, 34
Levin, J. R., 7, 89
Levine, D., 227
Lewis, E. L., 154
Li, Z., 215
Lin, X. D., 8, 207
Lincoln, B., 228
Linn, M. C., 154
Linn, R. L., 193
Long, P., 88
Lowyck, J., 140, 224
Lynton, E., 65, 66
Lyons, V., 122

M

Macedo, D., 93
Mack, R., 179
Madaus, G., 197
Maeroff, G. I., 194, 197
Magzamen, S., 122
Mandler, J. M., 183
Margiano-Lyons, S., 125, 126, 130
Marlino, M. R., 195
Marrero, D. G., 145
Martin, J., 183
Marx, R. W., 138, 212
Mayer, J., 228
McClintock, R. O., 7, 25
McCormick, B. H., 154
McKillop, A. M., 7
McLean, R., 230
McLellan, H., 228
McNeese, M. D., 122
Mercer, N., 107
Merluzzi, T. V., 199
Merriam, S., 180
Merrill, M. D., 204, 215
Mertz, D. L., 211
Milter, R. G., 140, 141, 143
Minner, S., 108
Minsky, M., 113
Minstrell, J. A., 208
Mitchell, R., 191
Moore, A. L., 212
Morningstar, C., 166
Morris, J., 205
Morrison, D., 5, 108, 109, 112
Morrison, P., 199
Mugny, G., 122
Myers, A. C., 141, 142, 143
Myers, J., 106
Myers, J. M., 7

N

Nakagawa, K., 205
Nastasi, B. K., 7, 122, 124, 125, 126, 130, 131
Neimeyer, G. J., 197
Neisser, U., 181
Nelson, G., 66
Newman, D., 96, 114
Newman, S. E., 22, 26, 44, 45, 67, 129, 139
Nichols, B., 180, 181
Nichols, P., 34
Nisbett, R., 84
Nocon, H., 185
Novak, J. D., 181

O

Ocko, S., 154
Okey, J. R., 8
O'Neil, H. F., 193, 194
O'Neill, D. K., 107, 115, 140, 159
Orlansky, J., 166
Osana, H. P., 7
Osgood, R., 159
Owens, D., 191

P

Palincsar, A. S., 45, 72, 138, 207, 210, 212, 228–229
Palmer, R. E., 25
Papert, S., 7, 58, 93, 154, 165, 200
Partridge, W. L., 125

Author Index

Pea, R. D., 8, 96, 107, 113, 152, 154, 156, 159, 206
Pellegrino, J. W., 209, 211, 212
Pellegrino, S., 205
Perelman, L. J., 192
Perkins, D. N., 6, 28, 43, 53, 66, 94, 96, 97, 107, 115, 151, 165, 191, 192, 195, 196, 229
Perry, W., 108
Petrosino, A., 209
Piaget, J., 136
Pierson, W. T., 122
Pintrich, P. R., 212
Pirolli, P., 36
Pokorny, R. A., 34, 36
Polman, J., 115, 156
Puckett, M. B., 191
Pufall, P., 67
Pugach, M., 140

R

Ragan, T. J., 204
Rao, G., 34
Reeves, T. C., 8
Reid, E., 168
Reif, F., 172
Reigeluth, C. M., 6, 204
Reiser, R. A., 204
Resnick, L. B., 66, 84, 137, 206, 207, 215, 230
Resnick, M., 154
Rheingold, H., 167, 168, 174
Rieber, L. P., 58, 215
Riesbeck, C. K., 51
Risko, V., 207
Rissland, E. L., 51
Robinson, G. L., 185
Rogoff, B., 122
Rorty, R., 135, 136
Roschelle, J., 136, 154, 230
Ross, L., 84
Rowe, D., 207
Roy, P., 26
Ruopp, R., 140, 153
Rutherford, M., 205

S

Sachter, J. E., 172
Salomon, G., 66, 96
Sanford, A., 113
Savery, J. R., 7
Scardamalia, M., 45, 67, 107, 115, 138, 140, 159, 206, 211, 230

Schank, R. C., 51, 52, 54, 55, 58, 77, 93, 110, 159
Schensul, J. J., 125
Schensul, S. L., 125
Schneiderman, B., 179
Schoenfeld, A. H., 18
Schön, D. A., 75, 140
Schwartz, D., 205
Senge, P. M., 206
Shapiro, A., 99
Shaughnessy, J. M., 85
Sheingold, K., 197, 198, 199
Sherin, B., 172
Sherwood, R. D., 207, 209, 211
Shymansky, J. A., 152
Simon, H. A., 207
Simpson, R. L., 51
Smith, C., 154
Smith, J. P., 57
Smith, M., 168
Smith, P. L., 204
Snir, J., 154
Soloway, E., 97, 138, 212
Spandel, V., 194
Spence, S., 222
Spiro, R., 67, 76, 77
Spiro, R. J., 26, 139, 231
Spoehr, K. T., 99, 100
Sproull, S., 168
Stein, B. S., 207, 208, 212
Stein, R., 6
Steinbach, R., 107
Sterman, N. T., 180
Stern, J. L., 154
Sternberg, R. J., 206
Stevens, A., 57
Stevens, J. P., 58
Stevens, S., 166
Stewart, J., 154
Stinson, J. E., 140, 141, 143
Stitzman, J., 122
Stock, G., 199
Strenio, A. J., 191
Strommen, E. F., 228
Swallow, J., 230

T

Tarule, J., 108
Taylor, E. F., 115, 116
Theberge, C., 108, 109, 112
Thorp, J., 166
Tognazzini, B., 179

Turkle, S., 169
Tversky, A., 84

U

Uncapher, K., 153, 158

V

van Dijk, T., 113
Van Haneghan, J., 212
Van Lehn, K., 36
Verschaffel, L., 205
von Glasersfeld, E., 83, 136
von Wright, J., 72
Vye, N. J., 205, 206, 207, 212
Vygotsky, L., 79, 107, 114, 139

W

Wager, W., 66
Wagner, R. K., 206
Walker, J., 165
Wang, S., 94
Weingard, P., 97
Wellman, H., 72
Wenger, E., 83, 84, 107, 152, 206

White, B., 115, 172
White, B. Y., 154
Whitehead, A. N., 33, 84, 207
Wiggins, G. P., 191, 193, 198
Williams, S. M., 146, 211, 212
Wilson, B., 12
Wilson, B. G., 94
Winn, W., 66, 204, 205
Winograd, T., 25
Winters, L., 191, 194
Wittrock, M., 67, 114
Wolcott, H. F., 125
Woodruff, E., 230
Woodward, J., 231
Worthen, B. R., 199

Y

Yoshida, A., 167
Young, M., 125, 126
Young, M. F., 7, 122, 130, 212
Yule, G., 113

Z

Zech, L., 205

Subject Index

A

ACCESS Project (American Culture in Context: Enrichment for Secondary Schools), 99–100
Alternative assessment
   See also Assessment
   connecting with constructivism, 195–197
   as exceptions to traditional testing, 197
   increasing interest in, 191–192
   requiring on-going dialogue, 197
   technology supporting, 197–198
Anchored instruction
   contrasted with traditional instruction, 67–68
   defined, 74
   role of instructor, 75
Apprenticeship
   See also Sherlock
   intelligent coached apprenticeship, 34–36
   pedagogical advantages of, 58
   practical advantages for case-based teaching systems, 58
   vs. exploration, 58
Archaeotype program, 26–27, 28–29
Articulation, promoting, 77–78
Artificial realities. *See* Immersion in artificial realities; Jasper immersion
Assessment
   activities also useful for learning, 195–196
   alternative assessment, 191–192, 195–198
   authentic assessment, 192–193
   challenges, 198–199
   differing from traditional testing, 196
   establishing standards, 198–199
   guide to constructivist approach to, 197
   implications for, in design of learning communities, 208
   including student motivation, 199
   made more difficult by idea of distributed expertise, 209
   more research needed, 199
   not separated from work performance, 196
   performance assessment, 193–194
   as political process, 199
   portfolio assessment, 194–195
   primary function of, 196
   traditional assessment, 191, 192
   understanding purposes of, 198
   validity and reliability questions, 198
Authentic activity
   aim of, 20
   cultural aspects of, 19–20
   inherently motivating, 212
Authentic assessment, 192–193. *See also* Assessment
   criticism of, 193
   important aspects of, 193
   strengthened by ownership of task, 193
Authenticity
   in cinema and multimedia, 180–181
   historical bonds influencing perception and verification of, 180
   importance of, 180

Authenticity *(continued)*
  indexical bonds influencing perception and verification of, 180
  issues of, for documentary filmmakers, 180–181
  lacking in top-down media products, 179
Authentic learning environments, designing, 138–139
Auto-reflexive mode, in multimedia documentaries, 181
Avatars, learners as, 166

C

Carpenters vs. tool kits, in constructivism and case-based reasoning, 59
Case-based learning, 50–51
  strategies contrasted with Problem Based Learning, 146
Case-based learning environments, 52–55
  and goal-based scenarios (GBS), 52–55
  primary characteristics of, 52
Case-based reasoning (CBR)
  apprenticeship vs. exploration in, 58
  basic processes in, 49–50
  carpenters vs. tool kits in, 59
  compared with constructivism, 55–59
  compared with rule-based model, 50
  direct vs. indirect instruction in, 58
  examples in everyday life, 50
  implications of, 50
  indexing a problem in, 50–51
  knowledge construction in, 57
  knowledge deletion in, 57
  knowledge representation in, 56–57
  learning by doing in, 50
  learning by failure in, 51
CBR. *See* Case-based reasoning
Cinema
  authenticity issues for documentary filmmakers, 180–181
  documentary film defined, 181
  modes of representation in documentary filmmaking, 181
Classroom-based learning environments, 7
  SOCRATES an example of, 12, 17–18. *See also* SOCRATES
Classrooms
  new basic subjects needed in, 205–206
  new kinds needed, 215
  social structure of, 205–206
  structure ill-suited to encouraging learning, 205–206
Climate Visualizer, 157
Coached learning by doing, in Sherlock, 35
Cognition, situated nature of, 136
Cognitive apprenticeship
  altering role of teacher, 153
  in Interpretation Construction (ICON) Design Model, 26
  Problem Based Learning as, 143
Cognitive processing, distributing, 96–97
Collaboration, 21
  in achieving learning community, 140
  around distributed expertise, 210
  Collaboratory Notebook, 159–161
  computers supporting, 152
  in constructivist learning environments, 151–158. *See also* Constructivist learning environments
  critical to situated cognition, 122–123
  encouraging in learning communities, 214–215
  importance of, 79
  importance of, in testing understanding, 136
  important in Jasper immersion, 130–131
  in Interpretation Construction (ICON) Design Model, 26
  mediating, 21
  need for, 84
  promoted by Rich Environments for Active Learning, 78
  required in Rich Environments for Active Learning, 78–79
  in SOCRATES and Lab Design Project (LDP), 21
  technologies developed for industrial and research settings used for, 158–161
  technology increasing possibilities, 152
  using CoVis visualizers for, 158–161
Collaboratory Notebook, 159–161
  described, 159
  examples of use of, 159–161
  supporting social process of knowledge construction, 160
Communication
  computers supporting, 152
  in constructivist learning environments, 151–158. *See also* Constructivist learning environments

Communication *(continued)*
  enhancing quality of learning, 152–153
  transformative nature of, 152–153
  using CoVis visualizers for, 158–161
Communication and collaboration in constructivist learning environments, 151–158
Communication environments, supporting knowledge construction, 115
Community building, important in learning communities, 212
Community of practice
  connecting learning environment to, 34
  scientific community as, 152–153
Computer-based learning environments, open and closed environments contrasted, 8
Computer microworlds, as learning environments, 7
Computer Supported intentional Learning Environments (CSILE), 211
Conceptual changes, from Jasper immersion, 126–129
Constructionism
  distinguished from constructivism, 93–94
  distinguished from instructionism, 93
Construction kits, 115
  in learning environments, 6
Constructivism
  apprenticeship vs. exploration in, 58
  assumptions about, 95
  carpenters vs. tool kits in, 59
  compared with case-based reasoning, 55–59
  connecting alternative assessment with, 195–197
  core concept of, 136
  direct vs. indirect instruction in, 58
  distinguished from constructionism, 93–94
  distinguished from situated cognition, 122
  as educational philosophy, 83–84
  expecting interaction of theory and practice to alter both, 121
  guide to constructivist approach to assessment, 197
  instructional principles derived from, 137–140
  knowledge construction in, 57
  knowledge deletion in, 57
  knowledge representation in, 56–57
  outlined, 135–137
  primary propositions of, 136–137
  roots of, 84
Constructivism to constructionism, 93–94
Constructivist approach
  to assessment, 197
  growth of, 33
  necessity of, 34
  views of, 33–34
Constructivist/constructionist activities, producing hypermedia and multimedia as, 94
Constructivist instructional principles, 137–140
  anchor all learning activities to larger task or problem, 137–138
  design authentic tasks, 138–139
  design environment to support and challenge learner's thinking, 139–140
  design to reflect complexity faced at end of learning, 139
  encourage testing ideas against alternatives, 140
  give learner ownership of process to develop a solution, 139
  provide opportunity and support for reflection, 140
  support learner in developing ownership, 138
  used in Problem Based Learning, 140–145. *See also* Problem Based Learning
Constructivist learning, virtual cultures as lever for, 167–170
Constructivist learning environments
  See also Learning communities; Learning environments
  alternative assessment essential in context of, 192
  anchored instruction characteristic of, 67–68
  assessment difficulties, 124–125
  assumptions of, 67
  BIG (Beyond the Information Given) and WIG (Without the Information Given), 192, 195
  characteristics of, 67–68
  communication and collaboration in, 151–158. *See also* Collaboration; Communication

Constructivist learning environments *(continued)*
  concerned with both what and how of learning, 195
  cooperative learning characteristic of, 68
  CoVis Collaboratory, 153–158
  definition of, 5
  embedding learning in realistic and relevant contexts, 7–8
  embedding learning in social experience, 8
  encouraging ownership and voice in the learning process, 8
  encouraging self-awareness of the knowledge construction process, 8
  encouraging use of multiple modes of representation, 8
  epistemic-game theory as framework for design, 116–117
  generative learning characteristic of, 67
  immersing learners in synthetic worlds, 166–167
  Interpretation Construction (ICON) Design Model, 26
  introducing epistemic fluency into, 108
  Lab Design Project (LDP) an example of, 12–23
  objectives of, 69
  outlined, 5
  pedagogical goals of, 11–12
  principles of, 68
  providing experience in and appreciation for multiple perspectives, 11
  providing experience with the knowledge construction process, 11
  technology used to enhance, 165
Constructivist models of instruction, 95–96
Constructivist values, contrasted with traditional educational technology values, 137
Constructivist worlds, immersing learners in, 166–167
Contextualization, in Interpretation Construction (ICON) Design Model, 26
Cooperative instruction, in constructivist learning environments, 68
CoVis Collaboratory, 153–154

CoVis Project, 153–158
  aims of, 153
  outlined, 153–154
  providing collaboratory environment, 153–154
  visualization tools for open-ended inquiry, 154–158
CSILE (Computer Supported Intentional Learning Environments), 211
Cultural representations, creating, 99–100, 101
Culture of practice, simulating in school, 84

D

Dalton Technology Plan, Study Support Environment for, 26–30
Database mode, in multimedia documentaries, 181
Deterministic thinking, 85
Direct vs. indirect instruction, in case-based reasoning and constructivism, 58
Distance education, 152
Distributed expertise, 206, 208, 209
  collaboration around, 210
  encouraging in learning communities, 215
  making assessment more difficult, 209
Distributed simulation, 166
Distributed worlds, immersing learners in, 166–167
Dynamic transfer, 207

E

Education
  assessment in, 191
  basic goals for, 191
  changing views of, 107
  higher education, 65–66. *See also* Rich Environments for Active Learning
  most successful reform efforts, 152
  reform needed, 83
  reform retarded by traditional assessment, 192
Educational technology. *See* Technology
Epistemic complexity
  causing communications gaps, 108–109
  when epistemic fluency is lacking, 108–109

Epistemic fluency
  defined, 109, 114
  developing in context of social interactions, 114
  lack of, causing communication gaps, 108–109
  participation essential to development of, 114
  role of technology in development of, 114–116
Epistemic forms, defined, 109
Epistemic forms and games, 109–112
  language-based nature of, 114
Epistemic games
  characteristics of, 110–111
  in the classroom, 112–113
  constraints as list-constructing strategies, 110
  constraints as prompts, 115
  constraints as rules, 109–110
  defined, 109
  examples of, 111
  idea as framework for analysis, 111–112
  list game, 109–110
  not played in isolation, 111
Epistemic game theory
  and design of constructivist learning environments, 116–117
  linguistic and sociocultural basis of, 114
  and other paradigms, 113
Event maps
  developing, 185–186
  functioning as anticipatory schemata, 181
  for multimedia documentaries, 181–183
  SemNet used for, 183
  serving as scaffolding, 183
Existing knowledge, maximizing use of, 74
Experience, anchoring knowledge in, 34
Exploration, vs. apprenticeship, 58

F

Facilitators
  instructors as, 21
  roles in Problem Based Learning, 145
Filmmaking. *See* Cinema

G

Galileo program, 27, 29
Generative learning, 67, 114

requiring shift in student and teacher roles, 67
Goal-based scenarios (GBS)
  architecture of, 53
  outcome-driven, 54–55
  role-driven, 54
  tutor and expert roles separated in, 52
  types of, 53–55
  working prototypes of, 59
Greenhouse Effect Visualizer, 158

H

Habitat, 168
  centralized top-down planning failing in, 167
  empowering users to construct artificial cultures, 166–167
  opening up learning, 167
Hermeneutics, 25
Higher education
  See also Education; Rich Environments for Active Learning
  and employment requirements, 66
  problems in, 65–66
High-level thinking
  activities promoting, 76–77
  exploratory learning and experimentation, 76–77
  helping students with, 77
  making predictions, interpretations, and hypotheses, 76
Historical bonds, and authenticity, 180
HyperAuthor, 97–98
HyperComposition, 97–99
  motivating students, 98–99
Hypermedia/multimedia
  See also Technology
  authoring multimedia with Mediatext, 97
  constructing cultural representations, 99–100, 101
  creating with HyperComposition, 97–99
  distributing cognitive processing, 96–97
  encouraging knowledge construction, 95–96
  examples of, 97–103
  goal in using, 96–97
  learning with, not from, 96
  multimedia construction as a whole language experience, 100, 102–103

Hypermedia/multimedia *(continued)*
  not to be used like classic textbook approach, 104–105
  potential to change classroom learning activity, 104–105
  rationale for construction of, 94–97
  skills developed by creating, 102–103
  student reactions to, 102–103
  students benefiting from, 97, 98, 99, 100
  thinking skills needed by learner designers, 103–104
  using HyperAuthor, 97–99

I

ICON, 26
Immersion in artificial realities
  See also Jasper immersion
  enhancing learning, 171
  evolving mental models via, 170–171
  Habitat an example of, 166–167
  learners as avatars in, 166
  and learning, 167–170
  potential for learning-by-doing, 170
  ScienceSpace under development, 171–173
  SimNet an example of, 166, 170
Indexical bonds, and authenticity, 180
Information banks, in learning environments, 6
Instruction
  anchored, 67–68, 74, 75
  anchoring in realistic situations, 74–75
  anchors used in, 210
  constructivist models of, 95–96
  cooperative, 68
  direct vs. indirect instruction, 58
  flexibility of, characteristic of learning communities, 212–213
  jigsaw teaching, 210–211
  as learning environment, 3–4. *See also* Learning environments
  metaphors for, 3–4
  for out-of-school functioning, 84
  philosophical conceptions influencing, 3–4
  reciprocal teaching, 210
  traditional, 67–68, 69, 151–152
  views of knowledge influencing views of, 4
Instructional design
  frameworks for, 204–205
  frameworks' relationship with concept of learning communities, 206–213
  models sharing basic components, 204
  seen as context-free and plan-based, 205
  steps in the process, 204
  value of systematic approach, 204–205
Instructional events, sequencing, 43
Instructional goals, making learner goals consistent with, 138
Instructional principles
  derived from constructivism, 137–140
  used in Problem based Learning
Instructional strategies, in learning communities, 210–212
Instructionism
  defined, 93
  distinguished from constructionism, 93
Instructors. *See* teachers
Intelligence, patterns of study varying with, 36
Intelligent coached apprenticeship
  See also Apprenticeship
  differing from traditional instructional design, 36
  experience and reflection in, 34–36
  Sherlock as example of, 34–44. *See also* Sherlock
Intelligent hyperdisplay, in Sherlock, 36–37
Intentional transfer, 37–38
Interactive mode, in multimedia documentaries, 181
Internet Relay Chat, 167, 168
Interpretation Construction (ICON) Design Model, 26
  evaluation of, 28–30
  impact on students, 29
  interpretation in, 26
  wide applicability of, 28
Interpretative mode, in multimedia documentaries, 181

J

Jasper immersion
  See also Immersion in artificial realities
  analysis of videotapes of, 124
  assessment difficulties, 124–125
  collaboration important to, 130–131
  conceptual changes occurring, 126–129

Jasper immersion *(continued)*
   continuous collection and interpretation of data a feature of, 125–126
   findings summarized, 129–130
   implementation method for, 123–124
   quantitative and qualitative approach to analysis of, 124–126
   research and instructional focus changing during implementation, 126–129
Jigsaw teaching, 210–211

K

Knowledge
   acquisition of, seen as a process of design, 94–95
   anchoring in experience, 34
   assessing prior knowledge, 208–210
   contribution of social environment to, 136–137
   maximizing use of existing knowledge, 74
   socially negotiated, 140
Knowledge construction
   activities promoting high-level thinking, 76–77
   Collaboratory Notebook supporting, 160
   in constructivism and case-based reasoning, 57
   engaging students in dynamic, high-level knowledge construction, 75–78
   epistemic forms and games for studying, 109–112
   facilitating, 77–78
   game-like qualities of, 113
   higher-level structures involved in, 113
   important for lifelong learning, 211
   more effective than knowledge reproduction, 95–96
   order in, 57
   with simulations or phenomenaria, 115–116
   supported by communication environments, 115
Knowledge construction process
   encouraging self-awareness of, 21, 22–23
   experience with, in Lab Design Project and SOCRATES, 18–19
   in goals of constructivist learning environments, 11–12
   self-directed learning at heart of, 18–19
   studying as, 25
Knowledge deletion, in case-based reasoning and constructivism, 57
Knowledge representation, in case-based reasoning and constructivism, 56–57

L

Lab Design Project (LDP)
   analysis of, 18–23
   data included in, 12–13
   experience in and appreciation for multiple perspectives provided by, 19
   experience with knowledge construction process in, 18–19
   learning in social experience provided by, 21
   linking a feature of, 15–16
   ownership and voice in learning process provided by, 20–21
   purpose of, 12
   realistic and relevant activity provided by, 19–20
Learner goals, making consistent with instructional goals, 138
Learners
   See also Students
   activity analyzed, 36
   as authors, 95
   as avatars, 166
   becoming acculturated members of communities of practice, 153
   becoming designers, 94
   helping independence of, 206
   immersing in distributed, synthetic, constructivist worlds, 166–167
   interaction with variety of resources needed by, 151
   motivating. *See* Student motivation
   other learners needed by, 151
   outcome achievement skills needed by, 54
   ownership of learning process needed by, 12, 20–21, 69–73, 138, 139
   patterns of study varying with intelligence, 36
   process skills needed by, 53
   resources used by, 179–180

Learners *(continued)*
  supporting in complex environments, 139
  support needs varying, 7
Learning
  by designing, 94–95
  designing authentic tasks for, 138–139
  fostered by reflective activities, 36, 44, 72–73, 80, 140
  function of content, context, and learner activity and goals in, 136
  learner's goal central to what is learned, 136
  stimuli needed for, 136
  virtual cultures as lever for constructivist learning, 167–170
Learning activities
  also useful for assessment, 195–196
  anchoring to larger task or problem, 137–138
  making nonthreatening, 79–80
  making purpose clear to learner, 137–138
  using learner problems, 138
  using problems learners will adopt, 138
Learning by doing
  in case-based reasoning, 50
  potential for, in artificial realities, 170
  in Sherlock, 35, 43
Learning by failure, in case-based reasoning, 51
Learning by reflection, value of, 44
Learning communities
  See also Constructivist learning environments
  accountable to larger constituencies, 213
  anchors for instruction, 210
  approaches to design and development of efficient learning communities, 214–216
  assessing prior knowledge and skills of students in, 208–210
  assessment needs for, 216
  authentic activities inherently motivating, 212
  communities involved in creating, 203
  critical to design of learning environment, 208–210
  developing instruction for, 212–213
  emphasizing distributed expertise, 206
  flexibility of instruction characteristic of, 212–213
  focusing on independent lifelong learning, 207
  formative and summative evaluations needed, 213
  further issues in designing and understanding, 213–216
  gaining from research and instructional design communities, 213–214
  helping students become independent learners, 206
  identifying instructional strategies in, 210–212
  identifying objectives in, 206–207
  implications for assessment in design of, 208
  instructional strategies enhancing motivation, 212
  instructional strategies enhancing sense of community, 212
  instructional strategies used in, 210–212
  jigsaw teaching used in, 210–211
  key principles of, 205–206
  learning to learn as primary objective, 207–208
  management of new kinds of classrooms for, 215
  nature summarized, 214
  need for open-ended objectives and criteria for success, 214
  not simply discovery environments, 211
  outside evaluations motivating for students, 213
  overall goal of, 210
  product design for, 215
  reciprocal teaching used in, 210
  relationship between concept of and instructional design frameworks, 206–213
  requiring combined wisdom of many experts, 215–216
  research and evaluation issues for, 216
  skill building in, 211–212
  specifying content to be taught, 210
  technology-based tools useful for, 211
  testing, evaluation, and revision in, 213
  ways to encourage collaborative learning in, 214–215
  ways to encourage distributed expertise in, 215

Learning environments
  See also Constructivist learning environments
  classroom-based, 7
  computer microworlds as, 7
  and connotation of environment, 5
  contrasted with instructional environment, 3
  design and assessment of, 8
  designing authentic environments, 138–139
  designing to support and challenge learner's thinking, 139–140
  different degrees of instruction and guidance in, 7
  hard to prepackage or define, 4–5
  key components analyzed, 6–8
  and learner need for support, 7
  learning community critical to design of, 140
  minimalist, 6
  open, virtual environments, 8
  as place or space for instruction, 3–5
  planning student support in, 7
  providing access to resources and tools, 3
  reflecting complexity of environments students will work in, 139
  reflecting constructivist instructional principles, 140
  richer, 6–7
Learning in the social experience
  as goal of constructivist learning environments, 12
  provided by SOCRATES and Lab Design Project (LDP), 12
Learning process, ownership and voice in provided by SOCRATES and Lab Design Project (LDP), 20–21
Learning to learn, 207–208
Lifelong learning, knowledge construction important for, 211
Linking, featured in Lab Design Project (LDP), 15–16

M

Meaningful contexts, situating learning in, 73–78
Media. *See* Hypermedia/multimedia; Multimedia; Multimedia documentaries; Technology
Mediatext
  authoring multimedia with, 97
  success of, 97
Mental models, evolving via immersion in artificial realities, 170–171
Mentors, teachers as, 21, 83
Metacognitive skills, helping students develop, 71–72
Microworlds, as learning environments, 7
Minimalist learning environments, 6
Motivation. *See* Student motivation
Multimedia
  See also Hypermedia/multimedia; Multimedia documentaries; Technology
  authenticity in, 180–181
  constructing with mediatext, 97
  environments, illustrated, 186–188
  model for mapping structure of actual events into environments, 181–184
  selection of, 22
  testing bottom-up software model for, 180
  top-down design models driving authenticity out of products, 179
  types used in constructivist learning environments, 21–22
Multimedia documentaries
  actual events and event maps, 181, 183
  auto-reflexive mode, 181
  database mode, 181
  event maps, developing, 185–186
  ethnographic interviews for event maps, 185–186
  implementation of the model, 184–185
  interactive mode, 181
  interpretative mode, 181
  mapping model for, 181–184
  media specifications map, 183–184
  modes of representation in, 181
Multimedia industry, adapting past ideas to new technologies, 179
Multiple interpretations and manifestations, in Interpretation Construction (ICON) Design Model, 26
Multiple perspectives
  experience in and appreciation for as a goal of constructivist learning environments, 11

Multiple perspectives *(continued)*
  experience in and appreciation for in SOCRATES and Lab Design Project (LDP), 19
  supporting, 19
Multiple representations
  enhancing learning, 75
  use of encouraged by constructivist learning environments, 12

O

Observation, in Interpretation Construction (ICON) Design Model, 26
Open-ended inquiry, visualization tools for, 154–158
Open learning environments, design challenges of, 8
Organization skills, needed by learners as designers, 103
Outcome achievement skills, 54
Outcome-driven goal-based scenarios, 54–55
Ownership, strengthening authentic assessment, 193
Ownership and voice in learning process
  extended by Rich Environments for Active Learning, 69–73
  as goal of constructivist learning environments, 12
  in SOCRATES and Lab Design Project (LDP), 20–21
  supported by constructivist instructional principles, 138, 139

P

Performance assessment, 193–194
  See also Assessment
  guidance for, 194
  key attributes of, 193
  useful in performing arts, 194
Phenomenaria, 115–116
  in learning environments, 6
Playbill program, 27–28
Portfolio assessment, 194–195
  See also Assessment
  focusing on both process and product, 194
  questions to be addressed, 194
  self-assessment important, 194
Post-problem reflection, roles for, 36

Presentation skills, needed by learners as designers, 103
Probabilistic thinking, 85
Problem Based Learning
  as a cognitive apprenticeship environment, 143
  assessment in, 141, 143
  contrasted with other case based approaches, 146
  as detailed instructional model, 145–146
  development of, 140–141
  facilitator roles in, 145
  learner engagement with problems necessary, 144
  learning goals in, 143
  problem generation in, 143–144
  problem presentation in, 144–145
  problems addressing real issues, 143–144
  strategies for implementing, 141–143
Problem-solving skills
  essential for today's workforce, 65
  Jasper immersion providing opportunities to develop, 123–124
Process skills, 53
Product delivery metaphor for instruction, 3
Project management skills, needed by learners as designers, 103

R

Realistic activity. *See* Authentic activity
Realistic and relevant activity
  as goal off constructivist learning environments, 11–12
  in SOCRATES and Lab Design Project (LDP), 19–20
Reality, in the mind of each knower, 95
Reciprocal teaching, 210
Reflection
  constructivist instructional principles providing for and supporting, 140
  intelligent coached apprenticeship providing for, 34–36
  Rich Environments for Active Learning encouraging, 72–73, 80
  tools for, in Sherlock, 35–36, 44
  value of, 44
Reflection skills, needed by learners as designers, 103
Relevance of instruction, essential to students, 44

Subject Index

Relevant activity. *See* Authentic activity
RelLab, 115–116
Representation skills, needed by learners as designers, 103
Research skills, needed by learners as designers, 103
Rich Environments for Active Learning (REALs), 66–80
 anchored instruction in, 67–68
 anchoring instruction in realistic situations, 74–75
 based on constructivist values, 66–67
 characteristics of, 66
 cooperative learning in, 68
 enabling students to determine what they need to learn, 70
 enabling students to manage their own learning activities, 70–71
 encouraging students to reflect on learning processes used, 72–73, 80
 encouraging students to revisit content and problems from different perspectives, 77
 engaging students in dynamic, high-level knowledge construction, 75–78
 extending students' responsibility and ownership, 69–73
 generative learning in, 67
 helping students develop metacognitive skills, 71–72
 maximizing use of existing knowledge, 74
 nonthreatening atmosphere needed, 79–80
 promoting student articulation, 77–78
 providing appropriate scaffolding, 78
 providing multiple ways to learn content, 75
 reflecting current thinking in constructivist learning environments, 68–69
 requiring student collaboration, 78–79
 situating learning in meaningful contexts, 73–75
 supportive strategies for implementing, 78–80
 using activities promoting high-level thinking, 76–77
Role-driven goal-based scenarios, 54
Rule-based model of reasoning, compared with case-based reasoning (CBR), 50

S

Scaffolding
 developed to aid school use of scientific visualizations, 155–156
 needed, to learn to be independent learners, 71
 provided by Rich Environments for Active Learning, 76, 78
School curricula, deficiencies in, 95
ScienceSpace, 171–173
Scientific visualizations
 See also Visualization tools for open-ended inquiry
 alternative route to scientific understanding, 155
 challenge of use in educational settings, 155–156
 characteristics important to constructivist learning, 155
 reducing distances between scientists and students, 155
 scaffolding developed to aid school use of, 155–156
 similarity to digital photographs, 154
 traits of, 154
 use of color and motion in, 154
Self-awareness
 encouraging and examining, 22–23
 of the knowledge construction process, encouraged by constructivist learning environments, 12
Self-directed learning, heart of knowledge construction process, 18–19
Sherlock
 See also Intelligent coached apprenticeship
 effectiveness in socializing apprentices, 44
 as example of intelligent coached apprenticeship, 34–44
 holistic work as primary activity, 35
 input from multicomponent cognitive models, 42–43
 intelligent hyperdisplay an advantage of, 36–37
 providing simulation of work environment, 35
 sequencing instructional events in, 43
 as situated learning, 43–44
 success of, 35

Sherlock *(continued)*
   tools for post-performance reflection in, 35–36
   transfer effectiveness of, 37–38
   tutor evaluation study, 38–39
   tutor evaluation study results, 39–42
SimNet, 166
Simulated work environment, in Sherlock, 35
Simulations, 6, 115–116
Situated cognition
   collaboration a critical component for, 122–123
   distinguished from constructivism, 122
   duality of definition of, 122
   implementation method for Jasper immersion, 123–124
   perspectives of, 121–123
   teacher requirements for using videodisc technology, 122
   theoretical basis for, 121–122
   using videodisc problems to establish environments, 122, 123
Situated learning
   assessment difficulties, 124–125
   concept supported by findings from Jasper immersion, 129
   Sherlock as, 43–44
Skill acquisition, occurring incrementally, 43
Skill building, learned in learning communities, 211
Skills
   outcome achievement skills, 54
   process skills, 53
Social environment
   importance of, 136–137
   providing alternative views, 137
   role in developing understanding, 136
   role in development of knowledge, 136–137
Social structure of typical classrooms, 205–206
Sociology of the learning environment, 44
SOCRATES
   analysis of, 18–23
   as classroom-based learning environment, 12
   curriculum outlined, 17–18
   DiaSim activity, 17
   experience in and appreciation for multiple perspectives provided by, 19
   experience with knowledge construction process in, 18–19
   learning in the social experience provided by, 21
   ownership and voice in learning process provided by, 20–21
   Patient Case Analysis and Plan activity, 17–18
   realistic and relevant activity provided by, 19–20
   Stump the Specialist activity, 18
Static transfer, 207
Statistical concepts, teaching, 85–86
Statistical reasoning project
   general goals of, 85–86
   goals for students, 85–86
   goals for teachers, 86
   need for, 84
   procedure, 86–88
   results, 88–89
Statistical thinking, importance of, 84
Student articulation, promoting, 77–78
Student goals, in statistical reasoning project, 85–86
Student motivation
   authentic activity inherently motivating, 22
   in use of HyperComposition, 98–99
   including in assessment, 199
   instructional strategies enhancing, 212
   outside evaluations providing, 213
Student-Oriented Curriculum: Reflection and Technology as Educational Strategies. *See* SOCRATES
Student presentations, importance of, 77
Student roles
   changing in generative learning, 67
   changing when students manage their learning, 70–71
Students
   See also Learners
   developing metacognitive skills, 71–72
   managing their learning activities, 70–71
   maximizing use of existing knowledge, 74
   needing scaffolding to learn to be independent learners, 71, 78
   questioning and goal setting to determine learning, 70
   teaching and learning, 215

Subject Index

Study Support Environments (SSEs)
  Archaeotype program, 26–27, 28–29
  in Dalton Technology Plan, 26–30
  designing, 25
  elements of Interpretation Construction (ICON) Design Model in, 27–28
  examples of, 26–30
  Galileo program, 27, 29
  Playbill program, 27–28
Symbol pads, in learning environments, 6
Synthetic worlds, immersing learners in, 166–167
Systems and process definition of instruction, 3

T

Task managers, in learning environments, 6
Teacher goals, in statistical reasoning project, 86
Teacher roles
  altered by cognitive apprenticeship learning, 153
  to challenge learners thinking, 139
  changing in generative learning, 67
  changing when students manage their learning, 70–71
  in constructive learning environments, 20–21
  in traditional classroom, 205
Teachers
  challenging learners' thinking, 139
  as consultants and coaches, 139
  establishing culture of communication, 153
  as facilitators, 21, 153
  as mentors, 21, 83
  not to take over learner's thinking, 139
  as participants, 153
Technology
  See also Hypermedia/multimedia; Media; Multimedia
  challenging assumptions of traditional instructional developments, 179
  in communication environments, 115
  constructivist applications of, 96–97
  in distance education, 152
  early use based on transmission model of education, 151–152
  improving power and efficiency of traditional testing, 197
  increasing collaboration possibilities, 152
  new roles possible with computers, 152
  potential benefits of, 179
  role in assessment, 197–198
  role in development of epistemic fluency, 114–116
  seen as conveyor of information, 96
  simulations or phenomenaria, 115–116
  technology-based tools in learning communities, 211
  as tool for learners, 96–97
  tools or construction kits, 115
Textbook Toolbox, 100
Thinking, deterministic and probabilistic, 85
Time and place definition of instruction, 3
Tool kits vs. carpenters, 59
Tools, 115
Tools for post-performance reflection, in Sherlock, 35–36
Traditional assessment, 191
  See also Traditional testing
  labeling individuals unfairly, 192
  retarding educational reform, 192
Traditional educational technology values, contrasted with constructivist values, 137
Traditional instruction
  contrasted with anchored instruction, 67–68
  students performing only low level activities, 69
  transmission model of still in use, 151–152
Traditional testing
  See also Traditional assessment
  alternative assessment differing from, 196
  exceptions to predominance of, 197
  technology improving power and efficiency of, 197
Transfer
  instructional design decisions to improve, 38
  intentional, 37–38
  research on teaching for, 66
  static differentiated from dynamic, 207
  tutoring for, in Sherlock, 37–38
Tutor roles in Problem Based Learning, 145

U

Understanding
 development of, 136–137
 involving making inferences, 25

V

Videodisc problems, to establish and enrich learning environments, 122, 123
Virtual cultures
 behavior shifts in, 168
 collaboration valued in, 168
 collective goods of, 168
 fluidity of users' identity in, 168
 inducing communications addiction, 169
 as lever for constructivist learning, 167–170
 mastery offered by, 169
 Multi-User Dungeons (MUDs) an example of, 168–169
 Multi-User Simulation Environments (MUSEs), 169–170
 personality characteristics of users, 167–168
 users experiencing disinhibition in, 168
Virtual environments, 8
 Lab Design Project (LDP) an example of, 12–16. *See also* Lab Design project (LDP)
Visualization tools for open-ended inquiry, 154–158
 See also Scientific visualizations
 Climate Visualizer, 157
 Greenhouse Effect Visualizer, 158
 using for communication and collaboration, 158–161
 Weather Graphics Tool, 156–157
 Weather Visualizer, 156–157

W

Weather Graphics Tool, 156–157
Weather Visualizer, 156–157